ETHICS FOR THE JUNIOR OFFICER

The Officer's Code of Ethics

1.   We will put our country, organization, seniors, and subordinates before ourselves.

2.   We will never forget that all of our efforts are directed at making us successful in both peace and war and reflecting positively on the military and the United States of America.

3.   We will work for efficiency, timeliness, and economy in performing our duties.

4.   We will treat all equipment and material entrusted to us as if it were our own most prized possession.

5.   We will set the example and require its meeting by our juniors; and take action against those who do not meet our profession's standards.

6.   We will relentlessly pursue the welfare of our subordinates.

7.   We will encourage both seniors and subordinates to provide us with inputs that will improve unit performance.

8.   We will constantly strive for professional and personal improvement, on both the part of ourselves and our subordinates.

9.   Seniors will ensure that all hands recognize the senior's commitment to ethical behavior.

10.   Subordinates will make sure that they advise their seniors when the senior is contemplating acting on an unethical recommendation.

11.   We will not allow others to be misled by incorrect or unspoken information.

12.   We will ensure our seniors know our faults as well as our accomplishments.

13.   We will only take that action which we're prepared to have reported to our seniors and those whose opinion of us we respect.

14.   We will remember, while performing our military duties, that our families depend on us and deserve special consideration.

15.   In case of doubt about whether an action is ethical or not, we will seek counsel with our chain-of-command, ombudsman, a Legal Officer, and/or the Command Chaplain.

ETHICS FOR THE JUNIOR OFFICER

A Gift from the USNA Class of 1964 to the USNA Class of 1996

Managing Editor and Case-Compiling Author

Professor of Leadership Karel Montor, Ph.D.
United States Naval Academy

Editorial and Technical Evaluative Reviews by

Captain Gordon H. Clow, USNR (USNA '64, Project Manager)
Captain Harry A. Seymour, Jr., USN
Commander Richard A. Cataldi, USN
Major Christopher Breslin, USMC
Lieutenant Commander Michael C. Cosenza, USCG
Lieutenant Glenn M. Sulmasy, USCG

NAVAL INSTITUTE PRESS   ANNAPOLIS, MARYLAND

Portions of this book have been reprinted from *Leadership: Quotations
from the Military Tradition,* editor Robert A. Fitton, 1990, by
permission of Westview Press, Boulder, Colorado.

Library of Congress Cataloging-in-Publication Data

Ethics for the junior officer : a gift from the USNA Class of 1964 to
  the USNA Class of 1996 / managing editor and case-compiling
  author Karel Montor.
       p.   cm.
    Includes bibliographical references and index.
    ISBN 1-55750-591-8
    1. Military ethics--Case studies. I. Montor, Karel.
  U22.E834   1994
  172'.42--dc20   93-42085

Printed in the United States of America on acid-free paper

TO THE CLASS OF 1996

DEDICATION

As you join the active forces, the Naval Academy Class of 1964 provides this volume prepared especially for you. It is intended to guide you in the years ahead, that you may uphold the ethical traditions of our military profession. Reading the foreword by Vice Admiral James Stockdale will explain the importance of military ethics and how best you may use this book.

We, the Class of 1964, dedicate this volume to our own beloved Superintendent Rear Admiral Charles Cochran Kirkpatrick, USN, who inspired us as midshipmen and throughout our careers by his devotion to duty and the way he met ethical challenges during his long and distinguished career.

Admiral Kirkpatrick, a submariner, USNA '31, served as Commander in Chief of the U.S. Pacific Fleet. As commander of the submarine *Triton,* he conducted three successful war patrols during 1942-43 and was credited with sinking 22,949 tons of enemy shipping. For extraordinary heroism and outstanding courage during enemy action he was awarded three Navy Crosses, the Distinguished Service Cross (Army), the Silver Star Medal, the Legion of Merit with Combat "V," and Purple Heart.

As you start your career, we share with you the knowledge that during our careers we have been privileged to serve with honorable officers from all our armed forces. These officers have contributed to the esteem, respect, and confidence the American public has in our military profession.

This places great responsibility on you to maintain this fine tradition so that our nation may continue to have the greatest confidence in our word and be assured that we shall always act responsibly, with integrity, and be accountable for our actions.

The more you read this book the greater will be your understanding of the part ethics plays in the daily life of an officer and the greater your ability to be an ethical impact player in your unit. The volume will provide a rationale for thinking through ethical dilemmas. You are encouraged to make use of the indices at the back of the book to identify particular issues with which you may be wrestling.

We know you are prepared to give your life for your country. We also ask you to be prepared to give your career, if need be, to ensure ethical actions are taken. The good deeds and heroics of a million service personnel will be overshadowed when one individual puts his or her self-interest before that of their ship and shipmates. Our job is to be prepared to defend our nation. We need to be ready. It is we who set the moral and ethical standard for our service, there can be no weak link in the integrity chain.

T. C. LYNCH, RADM, USN
Superintendent, U.S. Naval Academy
15 September 1993

Contents

Foreword... viii
Preface and Acknowledgments xiii
Military Ethics - A Concept xv
Letter from the Class of 1964 xvii

Rationale for Acting Ethically 1
Secretary of the Navy's Letter 10
      Issues 1 - 24 .... 11 to 41

Treat Your Shipmate as Yourself 43
    by Captain Arnold E. Resnicoff, CHC, USN
      Issues 25 - 46.. 47 to 73

Team Spirit or Lack of Courage 75
    by Commander Richard Cataldi, USN
      Issues 47 - 65.. 76 to 97

Personal Integrity 99
    by Commander Randy Large, USN
      Issues 66 - 82.. 102 to 118

Trust: The Cornerstone of Ethical Leadership 119
    by Captain Gary E. Brown, USMC
      Issues 83 - 98.. 123 to 139

Thoughts On Ethics in Military Leadership 141
    by Admiral Leon A. Edney, USN
      Issues 99 - 110... 146 to 161

Integrity and the Nuclear Officer 163
    by Commander William P. McBride, USN
      Issues 111 - 121 .... 167 to 179

Solutions . ... 181 to 270
Appendix A - Integrity, by Admiral Arleigh Burke, USN 271
Appendix B - Cases, by Dr. John Johns 281
Appendix C - Bedrock Standards of Conduct............................ 285
Bibliography 287
Index 292
    Key Words 298

Foreword

This is a book of actual leadership dilemmas faced in modern times by junior officers of the armed services of the United States. It was commissioned by the U.S. Naval Academy, Class of 1964, to be bequeathed annually to upcoming graduates of their alma mater. It is designed for reflection and reference throughout a person's first few years as a commissioned officer. Periodically, the case studies of the volume will be reviewed for timeliness and applicability, with an eye toward keeping the book up-to-date and on the mark.

Underlying all these cases are ethical considerations that go a long way in the final determination of whether the young officer's real-life solution to the dilemma served our country ill or well. In fact, the focus of the whole book is to dramatize for Navy ensigns and Marine second lieutenants and their junior officer counterparts in other services just exactly what constitutes ethical behavior and what does not. Each case appears in two areas of the book. The fact situation is laid out first, in sufficient detail to allow the reader to take on the problem as a personal challenge and form a tentative solution of how one thinks it should have been handled. Then a section bearing on the ethical considerations of the case follows. This part at least makes sure the reader is aware of "what was out there" on the ethical side of things in case the reader may want to reconsider a tentative personal way of handling it. And lastly—sometimes with surprise! surprise!—is the section where the real-life results are delineated. Cases are picked with an eye toward their stimulating discussion in the junior officer quarters and, on occasion, independent queries of willing seniors, JAG corps officers, and chaplains—when appropriate—in the interest of our readers' *self education* and their speedy assimilation of the "feel" for what is expected of them in their new profession.

These real-life case studies were solicited from the Navy Inspector General, the Naval Safety Center, and senior officer sources of the Army, Air Force, Marine Corps, and Coast Guard, as well as the Navy. Their presentation and organization have gone through an extensive editorial review process under the direction of Karel Montor, Ph.D., Professor of Leadership at the Naval Academy.

What I hope this book serves to do is to create in each of your hearts a *happy* understanding of the down-to-earth "rules of the game" of this life of American military officership on which you are embarking. It is fitting that the focus of the whole book is on the military ethic, because that is *the core value* of every operational specialty of every service. Whether you go forth from the Naval Academy to fly or submerge or fight on the surface or go ashore with the Marines or the SEALs, you have to be worthy of the trust of both your seniors and juniors, or all is lost for you.

I've sat on many selection boards for officer promotion, read the candidates' jackets, heard the briefs and board discussion on many people of high operational qualification, advanced engineering degrees, and other intellectual badges of distinction. You should know that once the board agrees that a history of indirectness or deviousness is in the record of an aspirant, the probability of that person's promotion all but vanishes. All considerations fall before that of personal integrity. It is *the core value* expected of an American military officer. If it does not come naturally to you, be honest with yourself and choose some other line of work.

You might question my use of the word "happy" as a descriptive adjective in understanding all of this. I use it because if you develop the right "hang" of things, you will be happy as you realize that the military ethic in most units—certainly in all good ones—is not the nagging, nitpicking, hairsplitting bother that we hear complaints about in other professions. The military ethic comes naturally to people of many personality "cuts," many "cuts of their jib." The idea is not to hammer everybody into one mold; the services are rich in the *diversity* of leadership styles of their better officers. It's just that the people under them are our most precious asset, and how they are treated must be above board. We insist that they deserve trustworthy leaders of integrity.

There's that word again. It's not just a good-sounding term. The original meaning of integrity was "whole," a unity, as opposed to a broken thing, or something in parts only. The readers of Plato and Aristotle will relate it to those ancients' distinction between "living" and "living well." It refers to the possibility of living according to a strong and coherent sense of oneself as a person whose life, considered as a whole, reflects a definite and thoughtful set of preferences and aspirations. If well composed, the person who possesses it knows he or she is whole; not riding the crest of continual anxiety, but riding the crest of *delight!*

And this ethic is natural to, not artificially grafted to, the profession of arms, the profession of warfighting, where friendships are consumed by the more powerful and generous force of comradeship.

This was an idea propounded by philosopher Jesse Glenn Gray, who spent all of World War II as a ground soldier in Europe. He noted how men in battle would lay down their lives for unit companions they were known to not even like. People of integrity under a common danger coalesce into a unity that surpasses friendship. It is not a willful change of heart; it happens as a function of human nature. And I've seen it happen. Gray, in his book *The Warriors: Reflections on Men in Battle* (Harcourt Brace and Company, 1959) writes: "Loyalty to the group is the essence of fighting morale. Friendship is not just a more intense form of comradeship but its very opposite: While comradeship wants to break down the walls of self, friendship seeks to expand these walls and keep them intact." So whereas an "ethics program" may seem unnecessary or foreign to some professions (we read of businessmen who think it is foreign to those engaged in free enterprise), the profession of arms is at home with it. Our major product, you might say, is comradeship in the heart of battle. And in our business, how we lavish our skills of leadership on comrades is "bottom-line stuff."

Am I old-fashioned, in this post-Cold War period, to use the heart of battle as the control point for a personal strategy of how to live? The United States has never been far from wars, and now as the world's only superpower, we're the natural choice to resolve knotty problems in the world. Geoffrey Perret recently wrote a book about America and wars past, published by Random House and entitled *A Country Made by War*. In the 217 years between 1775 and 1992, we were involved in ten major wars. In over twenty percent of the years of our existence, we have engaged in major wars. (Indian wars, the Philippine Insurrection, the Mexican War of 1916, etc., excluded.) Between 1945 and 1993, the proportion of years we've engaged in major wars has been considerably higher than twenty percent. So keep your powder dry.

In tight spots in this service life of ours, the higher the pressure gets, the greater is our need for mutual trust and confidence among us. And the more trust and confidence among us, the more power we draw from each other. Oliver Wendell Holmes, Jr., for nearly thirty years one of America's favorite Supreme Court Justices, was famous for his tales of life as a young officer in our Civil War. In *The Mind and Faith of Justice Holmes* (Little Brown and Company, 1943), he says "Perhaps it is not vain for us to tell the new generation what we learned in our day, and what we still believe."

The essence of what I learned and what I still believe came about not in some grand office, but over 25 years ago, face down in a prison cell, leg irons attached, signaling under the door to my comrades across the courtyard during those few early morning minutes when the guards were too busy to watch us. It was the third anniversary of my shoot down, and I had just got the message, swept out with strokes as my ten comrades, one at a time, scrubbed their toilet buckets: "Here's to Cag for three great years. We love you; we are with you to the end." And I said to myself: "You are right where you should be; thank God for this wonderful life."

Holmes was more eloquent about what he learned and what he still believed, as written on page 24 of the book above:

"That the joy of living is to put out all one's powers as far as they will go; to pray, not for comfort but for combat, to keep the soldier's faith against the doubts of civil life; to love glory more than the temptations of wallowing ease, but to know that one's final judge and only rival is oneself with all our failures in act and thought, these things we learned from noble enemies in Virginia or Georgia or on the Mississippi, thirty years ago; these things we believe to be true."

Jim Stockdale
15 September 1993

(*Note:* Vice Admiral James Bond Stockdale, Senior Research Fellow at the Hoover Institution, Stanford, California, served on active duty in the regular Navy for thirty-seven years, most of those years at sea as a fighter pilot aboard aircraft carriers. Shot down on his second combat tour over North Vietnam, he was the senior Naval Service prisoner of war in Hanoi for eight years: tortured fifteen times, in leg irons for two years, and in solitary confinement for four years.

During his naval career, his shore duty included three years as a test pilot and test pilot instructor at Patuxent River, Maryland; two years as a graduate student at Stanford University; one year in the Pentagon; and two years as president of the Naval War College.

When Vice Admiral Stockdale retired he had the distinction of being the only three-star officer in Navy history to wear both aviator wings and the Medal of Honor. Besides the MOH, he earned twenty-six combat decorations, including three Distinguished Service Medals, two Distinguished Flying Crosses, four Silver Star Medals, and two Purple Hearts.

His writings have been many and varied, but all converge on the central theme of how people can rise in dignity to prevail in the face of adversity. His most recent books are *A Vietnam Experience: Ten Years of Reflection,* winner of the 1985 Freedom Foundation (Valley Forge) Honor Prize for Books, and *In Love and War,* coauthored with his wife, Sybil, and published by the Naval Institute Press. In early 1987, a dramatic TV presentation of *In Love and War* was viewed by more than forty-five million Americans.)

Preface and Acknowledgments

This book was designed to be the first ethics text for newly commissioned officers; to provide true instances of ethical dilemmas faced by junior officers of the armed forces of the United States. The contributions of hundreds of officers are acknowledged, for they provided the details surrounding the ethical issues in which they were involved.

Leadership requires an officer to be expert in many areas, with this volume attempting to provide insight as to modes of thought that may be used in arriving at ethical decisions. Other aspects of leadership are covered in two companion volumes: *Naval Leadership: Voices of Experience,* and *Fundamentals of Naval Leadership,* both published by the U.S. Naval Institute.

To General Wallace M. Greene, Jr., USMC, goes credit for the inspirational suggestion to produce an ethical guide for junior officers and have it take a case book approach that details the situation, ethical considerations, and what happened.

The editors thank Lieutenant Commander Daniel G. Donovan, JAGC, for his expert advice in dealing with legal and ethical crafting of issues enumerated herein. To Lieutenant Rosalind Richmond, USN, goes our appreciation for coordinating and preparing inputs providing insight into situations dealing with equal opportunity themes. We acknowledge the case contributions of Dr. John Johns and his pioneering efforts in bringing the study of ethical issues to the fore in military discussions.

While we take full responsibility for the contents of this book we thank Ensign Jeffrey R. Oettle, USN (USNA Class of 1993), and A. Duane Googe for their word-processing and computer expertise in setting type and format for this volume. We thank Effie Dawson for proofreading assistance, and Lieutenant Scott C. Herbener, USN (USNA Class of 1987), for his computer expertise, editing skills, and attention to detail.

The following provided leadership in acquiring cases on which this book is based: Admirals Leon A. Edney and Charles R. Larson; Vice Admiral John A. Baldwin; Rear Admirals Brent Baker, George W. Davis, John E. Gordon, Andy Granuzzo, Theodore E. Lewin, Thomas T. Matteson, USCG, James E. Miller, Richard D. Milligan, Joseph C. Strasser, William L. Vincent; Lieutenant General Charles C. Krulak; Major Generals James A. Brabham, Thomas V. Draude, and Raymund E. O'Mara. We are also indebted to Drs. Michael Burowsky and

Don Fujii, as well as Master Chief Petty Officer of the Navy Duane R. Bushey, USN, and Sergeant Major of the Marine Corps Harold G. Overstreet, USMC, for assistance in case procurement.

Special thanks is owed to Captain Gordon H. Clow, USNR, who as the Project Manager for the Class of 1964 was involved in every phase of the project from review/revision of issues to final proofreading and all coordination activities between the United States Naval Academy and the Class of 1964. To Robert W. Marsh, USNA '64, who, among other pursuits, indexes books professionally, we are deeply indebted for his expert preparation of the index.

For their contributions of articles to this volume, we thank Admiral Leon A. Edney, Vice Admiral James Bond Stockdale, Rear Admiral T. C. Lynch, USN, Rear Admiral Robert Sutton, Captain Arnold E. Resnicoff, CHC, Commander Richard Cataldi, Commander Randy Large, Commander William P. McBride, and Captain Gary E. Brown, USMC.

To Admiral Arleigh Burke, is paid special recognition for his article "Integrity," which is the basic writing on this subject in the Naval Service.

PREFACE AND ACKNOWLEDGMENTS

Military Ethics — A Concept

It has been said that the situation determines whether an action, or lack thereof, is ethical in nature. For officers, the acceptance and retaining of a commission establish the values that bound the expected behavior under which they operate. While values can and do change over time, leaders must unambiguously inform all subordinates of those changes, and officers must either accept them or resign their commissions. The commission carries with it an obligation to act ethically at all times, not just when in uniform; for we are responsible and accountable for our actions 24 hours per day in both our official and personal lives. *That* is what accepting a commission means!

It is not possible to anticipate every circumstance that officers will face during their service career, yet they may apply a simple test to ensure the action they have taken or will take, or the act they didn't perform or won't undertake, meets the ethical standards expected of an officer. If you are prepared to talk about your actions, or lack thereof, in front of a national audience, made up of all of your seniors, peers, subordinates, and friends who share the same professional values, and whose opinions you value, then your behavior was/is probably ethical in nature.

This book includes a variety of situations that *have* involved officers. Sometimes their actions were ethical, sometimes they were not. Sometimes an ethical action taken by an officer hurt that officer or others. That is the price we **agree** to pay when we accept a commission. In all cases where an unethical approach was taken, someone, some organization, or the nation itself was hurt.

Generally, officers who act unethically know that they are doing so. Their unethical action is usually taken with the thought that their senior wants it, or no one will be hurt, or they or someone else will benefit. *These situations will clearly show that there are not "victimless unethical acts" when it comes to serving in the Armed Forces as a commissioned officer.* In accepting and retaining their commission, officers make the conscious decision to be judge and jury of their own actions.

The following quotation from *Naval Leadership: Voices of Experience* is remarkable in its simplicity and truthfulness:

First you find yourself overlooking small infractions that
    you would have corrected on the spot in the past.
Soon, you are a participant in these infractions. "After
    all," you say. "Everybody's doing it."
All too soon you find yourself trapped: You no
    longer can stand on a favorite principle
    because you have strayed from it.
Finding no way out, you begin to rationalize, and then
    you are hooked.
The important fact is, the officers who travel the path
    outlined above have misused the very basic quality
    and characteristic expected of a professional
    officer, or any other professional for that matter:
They have compromised their integrity.

A valuable ditty, along the same lines, applies:

Sow a thought, reap an act,
Sow an act, reap a habit,
Sow a habit, reap a lifestyle,
Sow a lifestyle, reap a destiny.

This book may be read from start to finish to provide the new officer with an expanded ethical concept base. Or the reader may refer to the indices to locate case studies that provide guidance to ethical thinking.

After reading the situation and other factors influencing the situation, come to a tentative decision as to the right thing to do. *After* making that determination—turn to the referenced page to read about what happened.

Ethical decisions are not always easily arrived at; gray areas can trip up any well-intentioned officer. When an officer needs ethics counseling as to the action required, the matter should be discussed with subordinates, seniors, peers, and the JAG and Chaplain Corps.

This book was developed for junior officers, and all who read it are invited to send constructive suggestions and/or additional situations to: Professor Karel Montor, Luce Hall, 112 Cooper Road, U.S. Naval Academy, Annapolis, Maryland 21402-5022.

15 September 1993

This ethics book is presented to you, the junior officer, by the U.S. Naval Academy Class of 1964. This project was chosen by the Class of '64 Executive Committee after several candidate projects were presented to our Class. Once the Executive Committee approved the project, the concept was presented to the Superintendent, Rear Admiral Tom Lynch, also a member of the Class of '64, who concurred.

The Class was primarily interested in sponsoring a project which would professionally benefit our future Navy and Marine Corps leaders in some way. You collectively comprise that future leadership and, as you embark upon your first tour of duty, you will be presented with choices as a commissioned officer which, on occasion, will present an ethical dilemma. Your choice, be it in a professional, social or even an academic setting will probably be observed and will contribute to that intangible known as your "service reputation" which is developed over time. Likewise you have observed—or will observe—observe the actions and decisions of others in similar circumstances and form impressions of them. The choices presented do not always yield a clear course of action and, on occasion, a situation will even require an immediate response on your part. The actual case studies in this book will not cover every situation with which you might be presented and certainly will not guarantee that you will make the right choice. However, each of the actual cases carries a lesson with it and, in each, you will see the course of action chosen and the results thereof.

What a wonderful career each of you has ahead of you as leaders. Your country has invested much in you and has high expectations of a strong return on their investment. As commissioned officers, we really are held to a higher standard of conduct and accountability than our civilian counterparts. The Class of '64 sincerely hopes that this book may help each of you to live up to that higher standard. The Honorable John H. Dalton, Secretary of the Navy, also a member of the Class of '64, frequently refers to a quote from John Paul Jones when speaking of his expectations of our Naval leaders:

> "It is by no means enough that an officer of the Navy should be a capable mariner. He must be that, of course, but also a great deal more. He should be as well a gentleman of liberal education, refined manners, punctilious courtesy and the nicest sense of personal honor...."

The Class of '64 is deeply indebted to Professor Karel Montor for his dedication in assembling this book—he helped the Class transform a vision into reality—and to Captain Gordon H. Clow, USNR (Ret.), our project manager.

Good luck and God speed,

Robert Sutton, RADM, USN
President, Class of 1964
U.S. Naval Academy

Rationale For Acting Ethically

In the military we are trained to sustain combat, instability, destruction of resources, and death—along with other arduous situations, both in times of peace and war. The purpose of this training is to get the job done. During World War II, Admiral Arleigh Burke violated procedural doctrine in certain Pacific battles. One might argue that in so doing, he was acting unethically. However Admiral Burke had the experience and knowledge to recognize that the enemy knew what he was supposed to do, and by his not doing that, he threw them off balance and thus prevailed. It should be noted, however, that his seniors and our ships knew of his plans and fully supported his actions.

An exception to the rule, however, does not disprove the rule; rather it establishes that further consideration is warranted. Although some actions in war are necessary, the concept of doing what is right, when it is right, has full value, both in war and in peacetime.

There are many reasons to act ethically. Among these is that when an officer fails to act ethically, it reflects adversely on the command and the officer's associates. Officers in the chain-of-command are expected to know what is going on in their organizations. If you act unethically, your senior will suffer because it will be assumed, rightly or wrongly, that too much authority was delegated, not enough responsibility was exercised, and a climate for wrongdoing was probably traceable back to the senior. When officers do the right thing and avoid the wrong, they will establish a command climate that encourages all members of the command to be ethical.

An officer may act unethically thinking the greater good of mankind is served, that doing things "right" counts more than "doing the right thing." This is a rationalization, for it is usually impossible to act unethically without someone or something being hurt.

Further, when subordinates see unethical action as a way of doing business; they too will decide which rules to obey and which rules to ignore. Everyone is hurt when an officer acts unethically because it casts doubt about the entire officer corps in particular and the military in general.

When someone is suspected or found to have acted unethically, then the country and civilians, to whom we dedicate our lives, and those for whom we work, suspect us of operating illegally on more than the occasion during which we were found out.

Being prepared to die for one's country is noble. Being prepared to lose one's career to protect the integrity of the military is often of a higher calling. A professional is prepared to be ethical even if it means losing his or her career. A careerist is only prepared to be professional if it doesn't mean losing a career.

Pressure

One's professional reputation with others starts the day you first meet them as an officer candidate, and is renewed each day you meet them again as an officer—even if it is ten minutes after being commissioned.

And with the acceptance of a commission as an officer comes the responsibility to be held accountable for your actions. Accountability can never be delegated and thus represents a fundamental reason for an officer to act ethically.

You may have acted unethically before being commissioned, and it will take time to live that down. But if your performance as an officer is above reproach, from the moment people first see you with that bar on your shoulder, they will continue to see you that way throughout the future. Each act you perform must be an ethical one to further build your reputation as an honorable person who has integrity and is accountable for actions taken.

At times officers will be presented with a difficult decision because of pressure from others to do something that the officers might not otherwise be willing to do themselves. Whether it be a senior, peer, or subordinate who is making the request, the officer must keep in mind that in the long run, things that are done improperly are eventually found out, with resultant distrust of all future efforts by the person who committed a wrong in the first place.

An officer who comes to realize that a given act was unethical must then question what to do. The activity should be immediately ceased *and* the more difficult step of reporting yourself to your senior should take place. Telling a senior will result in your having done the right thing and letting the senior know that you can be trusted. Owning up to a mistake that no one else would have known about is usually considered when the extent of censure or punishment is being determined.

There is no place to hide when the truth is finally found out. Officers must realize that all those who tried to persuade them, through pressure, to do something wrong will either be nowhere to be found, don't remember the matter as the accused officer does, or are themselves under investigation and thus will provide no help.

An example might be that you find yourself serving as a member of an Administrative Discharge Board. Your decision is supposed to be based upon the evidence provided—without consideration of your commanding officer's evaluation of your judgment should your decision not agree with the command's position. An intimidating strong-willed CO can cause subordinates to decide the future of a person based on what they think the command wants, and over concern with what will happen if they go against the will of their senior. Be ready to challenge anyone who tries to influence your decision.

Usually, doing the right thing the first time requires more time to consider all of the alternatives and why it is, in fact, the right thing to do. Doing the wrong thing will seem to be very simple, and others will tell you that you have to be "practical," "realistic," "supportive of the boss," and a great many other slogans whose significance will soon be forgotten.

While more time will be required to do the right thing in the beginning, far less time will be required to justify that proper action should an investigation ever occur. Investigations, besides adversely affecting one's career, are great time consumers, whereas the rewards for doing what is right are threefold: (1) you can live with yourself; (2) you do not lose a lot of precious time later concocting stories, trying to remember what you told to whom, etc.; and (3) your integrity is never questioned.

Seek the Truth

As officers we have special responsibilities, one of which is to preserve the practice of telling the truth. If one suspects that a subordinate is lying, then it is the responsibility of the officer to ask for clarification. One of the ethical responsibilities of an officer is to set an example and to encourage others to be truthful. Doing nothing when a subordinate lies sends two messages. First, that it is okay to lie to a senior—thus encouraging it to happen again. Second, that the senior really wants to be lied to; that is, he or she approves of improper conduct but doesn't want to formally okay the transgression.

If you think you are being lied to by a peer or senior, you have a responsibility to question what you are being told. Tact and diplomacy are good habits to practice with peers and seniors, as well as with subordinates. It is important to ask for clarification for several reasons. First, you may not have understood what was said to you; second, your own information may be faulty and so your interpretation of what was said may also be faulty; and third, you must not assume that a peer or senior would deliberately lie to you. They may actually believe what they say to you. Thus, by bringing the matter up, all hands can be brought on board as to what the truth actually is.

If you are positive you are being lied to, as opposed to not being told all of the facts, which might happen as a result of your not having a need to know, then you need to remind yourself of what the officer corps is all about. We are dedicated to serving our country, even losing our lives. What may be more difficult is to lose one's career. If an officer is not so prepared, then a faulty program may be pursued, because no one had the moral courage to speak up.

If all attempts fail to resolve the matter, and you feel that you are being lied to by a peer or a senior, then you have no alternative but to confront that individual in front of their senior. Rarely will you be so involved, yet preparing mentally for the future is as important as doing the right thing today.

You need to make the conscious decision that your honor and integrity are important. If you are being told a falsehood, you have no choice. That is what is meant by: Duty, Honor, Country!

Subordinates

Officers are not only required to act properly in accordance with "Standards of Conduct" regulations, they are expected to know them *so well* that they can recognize unethical behavior in others. When the subordinate of an officer is seen acting unethically, and the officer appears to know what is going on, then the assumption is made that the officer both condones the unethical act *and* is deliberately looking the other way so as to allow the improper behavior to continue.

One contributor to unethical behavior by subordinates is their belief that they are being treated unethically and thus may give back treatment in kind. If officers are fair, compassionate, and forthright with their subordinates, then those subordinates will positively respond to demands, for they want to return that loyalty.

Avoid treating subordinates unethically, not because they will in turn report you, but because treating them fairly, with compassion and in a forthright manner, is the right thing to do.

When individuals feel they've been treated unethically, they may well hold a grudge if they are not able to immediately respond in kind. Their retaliation may take the form of failure to act, unethical conduct, or reporting the senior to the chain-of-command.

When a subordinate or peer suggests your actions may be unethical, you are best advised to pay some attention, because either that individual or someone they may have talked to may well file a formal complaint.

Just because a formal complaint or an appeal to a higher authority is not promptly made, an officer should not become complacent. In time, the complaint may be filed, and in the meantime, one's reputation is being hurt as others think about the wrong that has been done.

Officers who allow an unethical action to be taken by one of their subordinates, or are slow to act with regard to them, are subject to censure, including failure to recognize an unethical act.

Officers *are* responsible for subordinates's activities insofar as they affect official paperwork and records. (Such responsibility may take the form of up to a $10,000 fine.) An officer must recognize that events themselves may sometimes lead the "weak" person astray. Knowing your people as individuals is as important to ensuring ethical conduct as knowing their technical capability on the job.

An officer must also guard against the halo effect wherein an outstanding operational performer is also assumed to be totally ethical. Unfortunately, high performance on the job does not guarantee ethical conduct, though deviance is less likely.

Officers have to be ready to act quickly when an unethical action has been taken, is being done, or is being contemplated. Officers must be seen to uphold the principles on which our profession is based. Their subordinates must know in advance—as evidenced by the officer's words and actions—that their senior will neither tolerate nor condone unethical action. The reputation and actions of a unit, no matter how small, are the result of the leadership of the commanding officer.

As officers go about their daily business there is also a need to consider whether they apply double standards to their own behavior as compared to those of their enlisted subordinates.

For an officer, being late by one hour without reason might go without comment, while an hour late by an enlisted without reason might end up as a matter going to Mast. Enlisted are expected to be at work on time while officers should generally be working more hours than their troops.

Health, comfort, and berthing condition inspections are other areas where enlisted may be held to much higher standards than officers, yet the officers quarters are sometimes seen by some of the enlisted, giving rise to the perception of double standards for officers.

There should not be a lower sense of accountability for officers and consequences for infractions should be fair, if not equal. The reason for this is that officers are *expected* to conform to rules and regulations with little or no supervision.

Each person, whether an officer or enlisted, must be held accountable to obey the rules. Officers must be the role models, for if double standards exist, the leadership loses credibility.

Organization

While this course's primary purpose is to discuss leadership situations that will help junior officers better understand how to meet their responsibilities, it also addresses the issue of managerial competence, which is needed if leaders are to ensure that an ethical work environment can exist.

Ethical conduct is facilitated by good organization. Generally, the two work hand in hand. When disorganization is evident, ethical behavior is also affected. Individuals often begin to take shortcuts to get things done, perceiving themselves as part of a hollow, disorganized force with a thin infrastructure.

When you first join a unit, study the quality of the ethical climate, and for those areas over which you have control, make changes that will improve ethical actions. If supplies are hard to get, instead of going around the system, try to work with the supply officer to see how materials might be made to move more efficiently and effectively.

When channels of communication and movement of materiel are not facilitated properly, then nonstandard, possible unethical ways to accomplish mission objectives often result.

Know the Rules

Since an officer who is not a member of the Judge Advocate General's Corps cannot be expected to know all of the laws governing the actions of federal employees (military personnel, in particular), the advice of a JAG officer should be sought in all instances where an individual is not positive that what they are doing is ethically correct.

Of interest is Section 1342 of Title 31, United States Code, which prohibits an officer or employee of the federal government from accepting voluntary services, except for emergencies involving human safety or the protection of property. The purpose of the statute is to prevent future claim for services being made against the government, and to limit liability caused by injury while these services are provided.

The temptation is strong to accept help from members of the local community, as they want to help our military do its job. Such help must always be discussed, in advance, with a JAG officer to ensure that the proposed assistance complies with the "Standards of Conduct." Always doing the right thing may not be fully obvious, and that is one of the reasons why the JAG Corps exists.

An annual review of the Standards of Conduct instruction is required and will remind the officer of what is wrong and enable the leader to give thorough briefings to ensure subordinates know the rules.

The "Standards of Conduct" provide that military personnel will scrupulously avoid any action, whether or not specifically prohibited, that might create the appearance of impropriety.

For example, giving a civilian friend a ride on a ship when others aren't accommodated will undoubtedly be resented by others *and* the crew, who realize they are being "used."

Buying a civilian friend food at the commissary is another example of bringing adverse attention to and involving the military in an unethical as well as an illegal act. The people of this country authorize commissaries for military personnel, and would not understand why a privileged few received special help.

Likewise, two married officers living together cannot both draw full housing allowances. Failure to note a mistake in pay and hoping no one else will notice is not just an oversight, it is wrong. Use of government phones and copiers for private business is another example of unethical activity.

Some responses to accusations of unethical conduct have been based on lack of knowledge. For this reason an officer should not merely rely on briefings to know what is right or wrong. It is as much a part of an officer's reading program to understand the Standards of Conduct and the Uniform Code of Military Justice requirements as it is to know about the specific activity for which responsibility exists.

In addition to knowing what the rules and regulations require, an officer should also be guided by a JAG officer during any investigation, so as to avoid compromising the process through improper actions or words.

RATIONALE FOR ACTING ETHICALLY

Additional Points

This course is meant to serve as an overview as to what officers are expected to do and as a reminder of things not to do. While "The Officer's Code of Ethics" at the end of this article and the "Bedrock Standards of Conduct," provide valuable guidelines, they should not be thought of as all-encompassing or absolute. So-called common sense, which can not be codified, is also useful to an officer who wants to do the right thing. Additional points worthy of remem-bering are:

• Carelessness and inefficiency can easily give the appearance of impropriety.

• Soliciting town merchants for gifts to auction on base to raise money is unethical in that it carries with it the suggestion that if one "cooperates" with the military in some extra way that the military will give something back. We are here to serve the nation to the limits of our capability and in accordance with executive orders. No one has to pay for our services, we give our all freely.

• When you change duty stations, leave your government-provided property behind.

• Use "Sensitive—For Official Use Only" in double envelopes clearly marked so as to preclude inadvertent disclosures to mail room personnel—this is important!

• Try to use the chain-of-command to resolve problems. Remember that complaints to Congress enter the hotline program.

• An indifferent attitude by officers toward alcohol and drug abuse cannot be tolerated. It is a command/senior responsibility to ensure that adequate education and training is conducted.

• Command climate can adversely affect all aspects of operations and spill over into member's personal lives.

• Religious, racial, sexual, and ethnic biases have no place in the American military, whether they are the basis for positive or negative personnel action.

• Treat others as you would like to be treated.

John Paul Jones' admonition not to give even the appearance of a violation still applies today and is particularly important with reference to sexual misconduct. Here, the finest sense of ethical behavior is required. At times official duties will strain relations between individuals, and an officer must not confuse personal feelings with official duties and position.

In exercising impeccable behavior, even the perception or appearance of wrongdoing will be avoided. Officers are expected to be positive role models for those in their command, whether they be senior or subordinate in rank. There is no place in the military for officers to abuse their position by making sexually suggestive comments and/or physical contact, whether on or off duty.

In this same vein, racist remarks about any member of the command or other individuals are not only inappropriate but also an ethical violation. Being a racist is not compatible with being an officer in the Armed Forces.

The *perception* of wrongdoing will have the same effect on the command as if there *is* substantiated wrongdoing. Officers have an obligation to expose corruption wherever it is discovered, examples of which include advancing friends and awarding undeserved medals. If one does not take action, then morale is *negatively* affected.

It is also a lack of common courtesy and a violation of the "Bedrock Standards of Conduct" to talk negatively about enlisted personnel and officers in front of their peers, especially when they are not present.

Enlisted personnel and officers need to appreciate the authority commanding officers do have, even though it sometimes results in a subjective command decision or involves command prerogatives. Personnel will therefore understand that a decision may be against *their* best judgment but does not constitute unethical conduct.

The rewards of an ethical approach to commissioned service are many, including the self-satisfaction of having exercised leadership in a positive manner, knowing that one is contributing to the job satisfaction of others and the knowledge that one is upholding the highest traditions of military service.

AN OPEN LETTER TO GRADUATES AND FRIENDS
OF THE UNITED STATES NAVAL ACADEMY

In your hands you hold a remarkable book. Thanks to its contributors and its editor, you will find here a discussion of concrete ethical problems, dilemmas that actually have occurred--and that will continue to occur--in the real world of service in the Navy and Marine Corps. As you live and work in this real world, you will have to meet ethical challenges of your own: all of us do. One of the primary goals of the Naval Academy is to develop in its graduates the moral character necessary to meet the challenges that lie before them; this book is a new tool in that preparation.

In this volume the point is made that no one of us is perfect, even though all of us in a critical moment are capable of heroic and sacrificial action. Service in the Navy and Marine Corps does not require an impossible perfection. But it does require personal honor and integrity--which make us willing to be as honest about our failures as about our successes. Service in the Navy and the Marine Corps also requires courage--the courage to defend the rights and the dignity of others, the courage to speak out and take action against impropriety and injustice, and the courage to put ourselves "on report." And, finally, service in the Marine Corps and the Navy requires commitment--to the highest standards of conduct, of performance, and of care for the men and women with whom we serve. We must never let ourselves forget that our commitment to these ideals defines our readiness to defend our comrades-in-arms and our country: lives beyond our own depend upon our adherence to these ethical standards.

Of course, it is easier to talk about ideals than about our real difficulties in living them out. But whether we are midshipmen, or junior officers, or seasoned professionals, or senior leaders, we all live in the tension between what we know in our minds and hearts to be right and the compromises we feel our situations may demand. This book encourages us to consider who we are and what we would do at moments like these. Read these cases, as I have, and ask yourselves the question I have asked myself: how can I help to build a Navy and Marine Corps team in which--faced with these dilemmas--men and women will have the strength of character to respond according to the highest standard? Ask yourselves that question, and then work in your own situation to make the answer real.

I am deeply proud to be a graduate of the U.S. Naval Academy and a member of the Class of 1964. I am proud that my class decided to contribute this book to the ethical development of our officer corps. I am grateful to have been asked to take part in passing this book along to you. And, most of all, I am honored to join with you in serving the country that we love.

John H. Dalton

Computers
(Issue 1)

An officer assigned to an administrative position at a shore command decided to supplement his military income by operating a private business on the side. A judge advocate officer advised that it was legal to do so as long as it did not interfere with the officer's professional responsibilities.

At one point the officer requested emergency leave, stating that it was needed to take care of a personal family matter. In fact, it was so that he could make a trip to enhance his business. A coworker who was aware of the officer's success made a "hotline" report that was subsequently investigated.

What was being done wrong that led to a complaint?

The coworker noticed that the officer was using a government computer to help in his personal business and thought it unfair for him to use equipment solely intended for use on government projects.

Further, the officer was observed interweaving his personal business with that of his military responsibilities during regular working hours. In addition, the officer also received personal business telephone calls during government working hours.

This officer made a number of ethical mistakes, not least of which was lying to his senior. The use of government equipment, services, and facilities for other than official government business is a violation of the Standards of Conduct and is also a waste of finite government resources.

One basis for these rules is to avoid putting those in the civilian sector at a disadvantage. If the assignment of the officer was such that it did not require a full-time performance, then that fact should have been disclosed to the senior who could possibly have combined it with some other assignment.

While some shore-based officers may temporarily have the luxury of an eight-hour day—and thus have time to supplement their military income by taking second jobs with their commanding officer's approval—the general rule is that an officer is available for duty during any or all of the 24 hours in a day. Not many officers can complete all of their responsibilities in an eight-hour day, and most officers find themselves with ever-increasing ones.

When an officer considers secondary employment, the first consideration has to be whether their extra time should really be devoted to their military job; so that the service and country can possibly be more effectively and efficiently served.

The concept that we are in the military 24 hours per day is partially based on ours being a profession rather than just a job. At sea, an officer may work 18 hours per day, and sometimes longer. In an increasingly complex world, the responsibilities of the American military can be expected to grow. Therefore, what we have to do will have to be done with less people, requiring more of us to work longer. The same is true for those who work in industry.

Turn to page 181 to find out what happened.

Every violation of truth is not only a sort of suicide in the liar, but is a stab at the health of human society.

—Emerson,
Essays, First Series: Prudence.

COMPUTERS

Travel Orders
(Issue 2)

An officer with 11 years of service and admired by junior officers was stationed overseas on an unaccompanied tour. Having been recently married, he decided to resign from the military because of pressure from his new wife, who was living alone back in the United States. Personnel Headquarters, however, required him to complete his full overseas tour (he had only completed one year of a three-year tour) before permitting him to leave the service.

He decided that he needed to have a face-to-face talk with his wife and was granted leave to do so. He tried to secure a seat on a Space-A flight to the United States, but Space A was full. He next tried to obtain priority as a courier, although he did not have that status. This attempt also failed to secure him a flight.

Further overseas telephone conversations with his wife made it apparent the marriage was threatened, and he needed to go home and discuss with her the advantages of finishing his 20 years of service.

What are all his options?

The officer, under severe emotional pressure, decided to commit an offense *he considered very minor* and undetectable. He also thought that if by some remote chance his actions were discovered, his seniors would consider his past contribution to the service and the necessity of his going home. This, he felt, would bring understanding and mitigation of any punishment.

It is useful to note that "a minor ethical violation" is at the heart of many situations wherein an individual rationalizes that actions taken really don't hurt anyone and the good gained far outweighs any possible harm to anyone else.

Once we rationalize that the discovery of a violation is what is really important rather than the violation itself, we are put in a position of having to evaluate every decision on the basis of whether it will or will not hurt more people than it helps.

Officers of the U. S. Armed Forces must set the example. They cannot take it upon themselves to obey only those rules they think are worthwhile. If an officer judges a rule to be wrong, then action should be taken—through the chain-of-command—to have changes made based on a thorough review of the matter.

In this case the officer needed help. That is why all personnel have a senior to whom they can go and appeal for help. While the matter might eventually have required a resolution by the area commander, that at least would have provided a *workable* solution.

Turn to page 181 to find out what happened.

This is our special duty, that if anyone specially needs our help, we should give him such help to the utmost of our power.

—Cicero,
De Officiis, Book i, Chapter 15, Scene 49.

Command Readiness
(Issue 3)

You are the commander of an aircraft squadron embarked on a carrier scheduled to conduct task group night sea-air operations. The admiral's pre-operation brief stressed the importance of the exercise going well, in order to demonstrate the task group's accomplishments and present level of capability.

Shortly prior to aircraft launch you find that: (1) the copilot in the lead aircraft failed to attend the previous night's operations brief; (2) the lead pilot and copilot have not flown together, nor did they have time to brief each other plane-side; (3) you are aware that neither person has ever been involved in a safety mishap during their thousands of flight hours; and (4) you have received a message from the admiral telling you to ensure that your part of the operation starts on time.

What do you do?

You realize that failing to execute the operation on time will affect the admiral's view of your competence, others in the squadron, and the unit's ability to conduct complex, extended operations. Further, you feel from your own experience that once the pilots are in the air, they will have time to brief each other, as experienced pilots have done in the past; and since these pilots have never been involved in a mishap, the risk of one occurring is almost nonexistent. You realize that the only way to be sure of never having a mishap is to keep aircraft on the ground.

There is a gamble in this reasoning: First, lives and aircraft are important to the military and neither should be risked unnecessarily. Second, one of the reasons we train is to minimize uncertainty, mishaps, and accidents.

Several failures indicated in this scenario include: (1) when operational tempo is increased, preparatory training should also be increased; (2) monitoring all operations should be increased as the complexity of the mission increases; (3) record keeping needs to be improved; (4) preparation for night operations should be treated differently from day exercises; (5) pressure—whether real or perceived—is not permission to abandon good judgment or orders; and (6) not having time to do something properly is not acceptable as a valid reason after a mishap has taken place.

What makes this an ethical matter is the combination of several people, by their lack of action, *choosing* not to follow rules and regulations. That is, failure by the operations officer to ensure that all briefings were properly conducted, lack of coordination training of the full crew, and lack of discipline to make sure things are done right the first time. Not following NATOPS and failing to use appropriate checklists are invitations to disaster. Included in being ethical is undertaking the appropriate pre-flight checks (though no one may know you do) if by doing so an accident is avoided. NATOPS has developed over the years from lessons learned following the investigation of mishaps, including those accompanied by loss of life and aircraft. The question might be: Why is there never enough time to do the job the right way and always enough time to do it over?

Turn to page 181 to find out what happened.

To choose time, is to save time.

—Francis Bacon,
Essays of Despatch.

The Party
(Issue 4)

At a party hosted by military personnel, an excess of alcohol consumption led to some personnel acting in a criminal fashion, to the annoyance and anger of some of the guests.

A subordinate of a senior military official at the party complained the next day, without further elaboration, that there had been a wild affair the night before.

The senior, who had a great deal on his mind, listened to the brief remark but took no action until three days later, when the subordinate went into further detail, which indicated that matters had gotten out of hand and that further action was required.

Was there a senior or subordinate communications failure?

The first question to be considered is: Who is responsible for one person receiving a communication from another? It is generally held that the sender is responsible to see that the message is sent in terms that the receiver will understand, and that the sender should look for feedback to ensure that, in fact, the message was received as intended.

In a military organization the completeness and accuracy of communications lie with seniors and subordinates. On the one hand, the senior needs to create a climate so that all subordinates feel free to speak, even though they know that the senior may not like or want to hear what they have to say.

If the boss (or "Emperor") isn't wearing any clothes, as in the case of the children's fairy tale, the junior must speak up. It is the responsibility of the senior to ensure that all subordinates know that they will not be "shot" just because they are the messenger bringing bad news.

Conversely, subordinates have a responsibility to their seniors to ensure that the latter understand what is going on and to recognize that a busy senior may not be paying full attention to nor understand the significance of their remarks.

If the senior is extremely busy, then it is necessary for the subordinate to find an alternate way to ensure that the senior is paying attention and understands what they are being told, along with the implications and expectations that derive from that knowledge.

A senior is expected to be responsible and reasonably prudent enough to recognize the significance of violations of the UCMJ and *not* look the other way. In addition, the senior should attempt to draw out details and not be distracted by other matters.

SECNAVINST 5520.3A requires immediate reporting of major criminal offenses to the Naval Criminal Investigative Service. Thus officers need to consult the JAG to define, identify the nature of, and determine the degree of an offense so that proper handling can be determined.

When a subordinate is trying to reach a senior and is put off, they should *demand* to get through if the situation is critical enough.

Communication is also an ethical responsibility of both seniors and subordinates, with the former making the command climate possible and the latter insisting, as necessary, to be heard.

Turn to page 182 to find out what happened.

God is with those who persevere.

—*Koran, Chapter 8.*

THE PARTY

Software
(Issue 5)

This issue concerns a civilian contractor spending government research and development funds to develop software for an existing government computer. It's possible that workable software may already exist and be owned by the government. After the contract was let to the civilian firm, a highly competent programming JO was assigned to the project as assistant to the military project officer.

On the one hand, the JO felt that there might be software the government owned that could be used and thus cut research and maintenance costs, and delivery time for that system. On the other hand, when approached with this cost and timesaving idea, the contractor rejected it, not wanting to renegotiate a lower-priced contact, as well as not wanting to lose follow-on maintenance contracts.

The project officer in charge had never worked with this system and knew very little about it. It appeared that the JO posed a threat to the project officer because the JO was able to give guidance to the civilian employees, work the budget, outline project parameters, and give general and specific requirements for the project.

The relationship of the JO to the rest of the command was excellent—professional and productive. The personnel within the command found the JO to be easy to work with and a truly resourceful individual.

When the JO approached both the contractor and the project officer with ideas on how to save money, they advised the JO not to upset the apple cart. The JO was made to realize that the contract was set in stone and waves were not to be created.

What should the JO do?

Factors in favor of the JO pushing ahead and determining what software might exist include: (1) loyalty to the government and fellow officers who would be affected by the system; (2) integrity of knowing that the system could be produced less expensively, safer, and better; (3) mission accomplishment—taking advantage of the JO's expertise and thus doing what the service had assigned the JO to accomplish; and (4) avoiding a possibly inferior product.

The arguments for not rocking the boat, include: (1) a senior officer was against seeking out and determining if software already existed, (2) the military service should present a unified front to the civilian contractor; (3) a fruitless investigation of ethical practices of the contractor and some senior officers might result; and (4) the whole business would be a negative reflection on the individuals who originally made the basic contract for programming services.

For the JO to pursue the matter might be taken by some senior officers and the contractor that the JO was merely being a troublemaker. Long hours and extra work, along with extensive travel and research, would be necessary before the JO could make a case. Certainly the JO had to consider the possibility of being marked down on the next fitness report by the reporting senior.

As this officer told the editors: "A person has to do some real soul-searching in order to make any decisions that may affect one's life and the lives of others.

Turn to page 182 to find out what happened.

I praise you when you regard the trouble of your friend as your own.

—Plautus,
Mostellaria, Line 151, Act 1, Scene 2.

Rescue Mission

(Issue 6)

You are the 0-5 CO of an aircraft squadron embarked on a carrier off the coast of a nation that has illegally imprisoned Americans. Word comes down from the task force commander that your unit will fly cover for a rescue mission to start in 48 hours, and that your report to area command, indicating your unit's readiness, must be filed within two hours via the chain-of-command.

In reviewing aircraft status you ascertain that all requisitioned repair parts have not been received, and some of those that are missing are critical for meeting the mission readiness required for the task. The ship's supply officer determines that parts won't be delivered for at least 72 hours.

You send your report stating your unit will not be fully ready because of delayed parts. Within minutes you receive a call, over a secure circuit, telling you to revise your report to say your aircraft are ready. As the task force commander explains, a few aircraft one way or the other will not have a significant effect on the mission.

You refuse to change your report, but within the hour you find out that your report was changed, over your signature, saying that your unit *will be* ready to fly, and the report was sent on to area headquarters. You know for a fact that the area commander personally selected your admiral to command the task force, and by his past words has shown great confidence in this person.

What do you do?

In his article "Integrity" (Appendix A), Admiral Arleigh Burke makes the point that: "Keeping our own integrity up to par is problem enough. We are responsible for our own conduct; we are not responsible for another's integrity." This would be an appropriate time for the reader to consult Appendix A, for more than a few sentences are needed to convey all of Admiral Burke's thoughts on ethics and integrity.

After reading Admiral Burke's article in Appendix A
turn to page 183 to find out what happened.

Dealing With A Vendor
(Issue 7)

A civilian working for a commissary officer had been delegated authority to make command purchases. The commissary officer made sure that all qualified vendors were able to bid on contracts to provide goods and services.

The sales agent for the company that won the award was polite, personable, and generally a pleasure to do business with. On one occasion when he was making a delivery, he congratulated the government purchasing agent, whose wife just had a baby.

By this time, the civilian and the vendor salesman had become good friends, and thus it seemed only reasonable that the vendor gave the civilian some baby food at the birth of his daughter. The food was still good, but it would have been out of date before it could be properly delivered to other stores.

What were the responsibilities of the commissary officer?

The basic guideline is that government employees may not accept gratuities from contractors or businesses that are engaged in (or desire to engage in) financial dealings with the government. Taking free baby food from the salesman constituted the acceptance of a "gratuity"—something for which the government did not pay fair retail market value. It was the responsibility of the commissary officer to emphasize to subordinates the intent and provisions of the Standards of Conduct and Government Ethics.

In this case the civilian felt that he would be personally insulting the salesman if he did not accept baby food.

Turn to page 184 to find out what happened.

Reason and judgment are the qualities of a leader.

—Tacitus,
Annals, circa A. D. 90.

Component Parts
(Issue 8)

A vendor made a "hotline" complaint because he felt he had not been given a proper opportunity to bid on material required by the military. An investigation indicated that instead of putting the material itself up for bid, Navy procurement personnel elected to purchase the material's component parts individually, thus giving the impression that the requirement for full and open competition had been circumvented.

Was anything done wrong?

"Hotline" complaints are usually made by those who are trying to ensure that the government and the people of the United States are treated fairly. The first step in ensuring that command personnel don't mistake actions taken is to advise them in advance of why any action that might seem inappropriate to the uninformed is taken.

In this case, since equipment normally cannot be broken down into component parts to avoid competitive bidding, it would have been best to make sure that all command personnel connected with the transaction knew why it was being handled as it was.

Second, since the action might be misinterpreted by non-command personnel, it would have been a good idea to check with the JAG and base supply personnel to ensure that everything was being done properly.

Finally, to avoid vendor misunderstanding, it would have been a good idea to let local/regional vendors know what was being done, in advance of contracting out so that they would know that they were still actively being considered for all procurements.

Taking this additional step might also have uncovered the existence of a second supplier who might be relied upon in the future. In any case, we must never forget that we are agents of our government and thus represent what the people have determined to be a proper way of acting.

Turn to page 184 to find out what happened.

Training Supervision
(Issue 9)

A squadron needing a pilot for a mission assigned one of its newer members, who had come to the unit with a fine reputation and had shown a great willingness to participate in all evolutions. The tempo of operations was quite high. The training officer's records on the pilot were not complete, but the pilot assured everyone that he could handle the mission without difficulty, and was eager to contribute his share to the squadron's operations.

After considering others who were qualified to fly the mission, the training officer, under the pressure of manpower shortages, okayed the flight. He received yet another affirmative answer when he asked the pilot whether he was sure he had all the necessary training for this particular aircraft evolution. The training officer then asked the CO for authority to send the pilot on the mission.

What should the pilot's CO do?

Enthusiasm is not a substitute for knowledge, and the pilot's commanding officer must make decisions based on facts rather than feelings. What makes this an ethical matter is that the CO has to consider what is best for the squadron. There is an inherent risk in flying, and every senior has the responsibility to provide subordinates with safe opportunities to show what they can do, and thus further their career development in the military.

The question is, how much can commanding officers be expected to know about the capabilities of each of their subordinates? Must every commanding officer be expected to know how every one of his or her subordinates will operate under every situation?

In a high tempo operation, it is especially tempting to assume that everyone knows what they are supposed to. Unfortunately, most people do not have full knowledge of what others know or don't know.

Turn to page 185 to find out what happened.

Submarine Inventory
(Issue 10)

The supply officer (0-3) of a *Los Angeles*-class nuclear-powered, fast-attack submarine received orders to detach from submarine duty and transfer to a new command. Although excited about the new orders, the lieutenant knew that executing them would be difficult since the sub was scheduled to commence an extended deployment on the same day as his detachment.

In addition, due to the rigorous underway schedule, the new supply officer would be unable to report aboard until just five days prior to the lieutenant's departure. This demanding schedule allowed just four days for the new officer to relieve the lieutenant of all accountability and assume all duties and responsibilities as supply officer.

This problem was even further exacerbated by the fact that the four day relieving window overlapped a holiday weekend. The major portion of the relief process was the required inventory of all subsistence items for which the lieutenant was accountable. Normally, this would be a relatively simple process; in this instance, however, it would be an arduous task indeed.

In preparation for the upcoming extended deployment, a full loading of food had just been completed, bringing the sub's subsistence inventory to just above the required 90-day endurance load. As a result, the inventory and the following reconciliation of stock records were certain to take all four days. Anticipating the situation, the lieutenant prepared a plan and presented it to his commanding officer for approval. The CO later called the lieutenant to his stateroom and told the 0-3 not to conduct an inventory.

What do you do?

The supply officer asked the CO for his reasons not to conduct the inventory and was advised that first, it would be too difficult and would take too long due to having a full deployment load on board. Second, in order to support both the required pre-underway ship's maintenance and the inventory/reconciliation, a "port and starboard" (two-section watch bill) would be required.

The lieutenant informed the CO that government regulations required a full inventory during the relief, since the supply officer is held personally accountable for the provisions. The CO was not persuaded at all by the legal argument and stated that conducting the inventory would require him to "hydro-test" his crew on a predeployment holiday weekend, something he simply refused to do.

The CO ended the conversation by giving the supply officer a direct order specifically not to perform the inventory, which the lieutenant wanted and his relief had requested. The junior officer decided that the CO had issued an illegal order; together with the relieving supply officer, the two were forced to make a difficult decision. The lieutenant felt that most of the burden was his, and that he had only three viable alternatives.

1.   Proceed with the inventory as was required (which was certain to elicit the full wrath of the CO by ignoring his order).

2.   Force his relief to sign a "paper inventory" based on the current stock-record card balances.

3.   Notify the submarine squadron supply officer of the problem and seek his advice/assistance.

Turn to page 186 to find out what happened.

The man who does something under orders is not unhappy; he is unhappy who does something against his will.

—Seneca,
Epistulae Morales ad Lucilium, 63 A. D.

The "Experienced" Officer
(Issue 11)

Jack F. enlisted in the Coast Guard and within seven years had attained the rank of chief boatswain's mate. He was an extremely proficient sailor, displaying superior skills as a small-boat coxswain and conning officer on a medium-endurance cutter. A tough taskmaster, his people worked hard and respected BMC F. because he worked hard right beside them. He also worked very hard at enjoying liberty.

After a year as a BMC, F.'s performance was rewarded with an appointment to OCS, and he was commissioned an ensign upon graduation. His superior performance and liberty habits continued. Ensign F. worked his way through assignments until, as a lieutenant commander he took command of a seagoing buoy tender (WLB). For the first time he served with female crew members aboard his ship. His immediate supervisor was the district aids-to-navigation officer, who also evaluated (rated) three other WLB commanding officers.

What could go wrong?

By hook or crook, enlisted BMC F. could get necessary supplies, support to better his unit, and work done. This carried over into liberty. On the beach, BMC F. could drink and carouse with the best. He never got into trouble with the law, mainly because his friends watched out for him.

His command didn't care what BMC F. did on liberty as long as it didn't embarrass the command or affect his work performance. In fact, chiefs were expected to be hell-raisers at times. His supervisor sometimes overlooked minor idiosyncrasies because of BMC F.'s overall superior performance.

Although older and slower, LCDR F. continued his unabashed liberty antics. For example, after a few beers, he enjoyed showing off the propeller tattoos on his rear end. To get a cheaper rate at a military hotel, he had his yeoman type an illegal set of permissive orders. In addition, he was somewhat abrasive to his crew members and some of the females interpreted this as harassment.

His supervisor heard rumors of LCDR F.'s behavior but didn't act until the District Command Enlisted Advisor told him of a complaint received from one of the female crew members.

Turn to page 187 to find out what happened.

Maintenance Supervision
(Issue 12)

A cargo aircraft was being towed at 3-5 miles per hour, from one location to another at 0730 on an air base. While the plane was making a gradual turn, one of the enlisted maintenance personnel fell from the aircraft, where he had been sitting with his legs dangling over the edge of the cargo door. He was killed as the rear wheels of the aircraft ran over him.

Was the maintenance officer responsible?

Is it reasonable to hold every officer directly responsible for anything and everything that happens to subordinate personnel? Since the scope of an officer's duties may well be vast, it may be argued that personal supervision cannot be exercised at all times. Thus, it would seem that in this case the maintenance officer, while responsible for subordinate personnel, should not be punished or reprimanded for this unfortunate incident.

Leadership by example is not just a phrase: it means not only setting the example but ensuring that it is being followed. All officers need to take the time to ensure that all safety regulations are being followed and that subordinate personnel are sufficiently observed to ensure that they know what they are doing, how to do it, and under what circumstances they are to do it.

Turn to page 187 to find out what happened?

The degree of criticism varies in direct proportion to the distance from the point of responsibility.

—Brigadier General W. M. Fondren, USA,
At Quarry Heights, C.Z. 1962.

Fund Raising
(Issue 13)

A church in a town close to a military base burned down. Members of the congregation secured items from various merchants in town to auction and approached the base commander to see if there was some service the military could provide that might be given away to the community, and thus become another item for auction.

The base commander asked the JAG for an opinion and received a carefully crafted five-page statement. The CO read the full opinion, which concluded with the comment that the decision was up to him as to whether or not to give away the service in the form of a ride on one of the base's vehicles.

A "hotline" complaint resulted. Why?

The base commander read the JAG opinion quickly and relied on the last sentence, which implied that the final decision was up to the CO. The main body of the memo, however, when carefully studied, indicated that the CO could probably be in violation of written instructions if he permitted this type of an auction.

The basic principle is that officers may use government equipment in the performance of their job, but they are not the owners, even though they are responsible for its care, maintenance, and may be held pecuniarily liable if something happens to that equipment.

Our actions are always subject to review and censure because we are servants of the people. While we choose to work for less than what we might make in the civilian sector, and accept the risk of death without reservation, we must meet standards. Recipient of the Medal of Honor, Admiral John Bulkeley, USN, was awarded France's highest medal, the Legion d'Honneur, for "Spearheading the Normandy Invasion and the Liberation of France." The admiral put it best in his dedication to the book *Naval Leadership: Voices of Experience.*

"For in my mind there is but one honorable profession. It requires the daily attention of all faculties, the persistence of a bulldog, the compassion of a man of the cloth, foresight entrenched in previously learned lessons, the willingness to sacrifice for the good of the service all that has been personally gained or earned, and unyielding belief that it is better to preserve peace than to wage war, the self force-feeding of knowledge and new technology, the ability to blend confidence and humility, and the unyielding conviction that it is far greater to serve one's country rather than oneself. These requirements demand a foundation, and that foundation is, inescapably, experience.

The naval officer is truly unique, for he must have the capacity to simultaneously love his country, his service, his family, his shipmates, and the sea. He needs each of them unquestionably as each of them needs him. And the demands which each place on him never diminish, they only grow.

Beyond all the words and phrases of a naval officer's dedicated service, honor and professionalism must remain his past, present, and future. That, sir, is why it is **"The Honorable Profession."**

Turn to page 188 to find out what happened.

A man of character in peace is a man of courage in war. Character is a habit. The daily choice of right and wrong. It is a moral quality which grows to maturity in peace and is not suddenly developed in war.

—General Sir James Glover,
Parameters, "A Soldier, His Conscience," September 1973.

Quarters Competition
(Issue 14)

A newly reporting officer was selected to be a flag aide while still awaiting quarters assignment. Knowing that the position would require long hours and occasional separation from family, the aide mentioned to the housing officer that the couple was living in an expensive rented home off-base awaiting quarters assignment.

While the matter was under consideration, the officer assumed the responsibilities of aide to the flag and quickly became known throughout the command as an effective, efficient, and influential officer.

What is appropriate action by the housing officer?

The housing officer recognized the importance and influence of the aide's position. In looking over the waiting list for quarters assignment, it was determined that the aide would have to wait six months before quarters would become available.

In trying to decide what to do to help the aide, the housing officer thought about the inconvenience and even risk that was attendant with leaving the aide in civilian quarters. At times, for example, the spouse might be left alone at night. Further recognizing that the aide had to be on call around the clock, and thus should live on base, the housing officer moved the aide to the top of the waiting list so that the couple could move in right away.

The aide thanked the housing officer and, as a result of having on-base housing was even more efficient in providing assistance to the flag. The flag was also appreciative of the courtesy shown the aide and commented so to the housing officer after learning that the aide was now on post.

This seems to be a fairly straightforward case of recognizing the needs of the service and helping a fellow officer do a better job.

All officers have influence by reason of their rank, and some, because of their assignment, receive more cooperation and consideration than others. Actually, all hands should help everyone do the business of the military without regard to who "is in favor" at a particular moment in time. This does not mean that a flag aide shouldn't be cooperated with—for the aide works for and speaks for the flag, but it does mean that officers with such additional influence must not abuse the trust that is put in them.

Turn to page 189 to find out what happened.

Ejecting to Avoid Disaster
(Issue 15)

The CO wanted to help a junior officer become qualified in an aircraft not previously flown. The CO received assurance from the pilot that all NATOPS requirements had been met. When a mid-air equipment failure occurred, the crew felt obliged to eject.

How might this aircraft loss have been avoided?

If the pilot had not been fully trained, the overall squadron coordinator of training is responsible.

Indeed, a "discipline of ethics" requires an officer to search out all information that might be needed for the successful completion of one's assignment. This is not just limited to a cursory examination of applicable parameters but includes a thorough check with other more knowledgeable personnel as to possible conditions that might lead to a mishap.

NATOPS is the result of years of investigations into what factors contributed to various mishaps. In addition, there are many generally available magazines, specific to one's particular community, that all officers should consult. Careful reading of these can help personnel avoid problems that even the most experienced leaders might not anticipate or be totally familiar with.

Turn to page 189 to find out what happened.

War is not an affair of chance. A great deal of knowledge, study, and meditation is necessary to conduct it weil.

—Frederick the Great,
Instructions for His Generals, 1747.

EJECTING TO AVOID DISASTER

Request for Transfer
(Issue 16)

As the officer-in-charge of a Family Service Center, you report directly to the CO and XO of a naval station. You have been at your present duty station for two years, but because of some conflict with the XO, you have struggled in your current position. You have recently requested an early transfer, which your XO has verbally agreed to, but the Bureau of Personnel has delayed in issuing your reassignment orders. Upon contact with your detailer in Washington, D.C., you learn that your XO has misrepresented the job scope of your current position and said it does not warrant department head credit.

What should you do?

One principle of ethical conduct is for seniors to let juniors know where they stand. If a senior is recommending an action against a junior, the latter should be advised so that he or she may provide amplifying information if so desired.

In a situation such as this, the OIC should schedule a meeting with the XO to find out why the XO has done what he has. After that meeting, the officer should request a talk with the CO if unable to get the XO to change his position and correct the situation. If this does not resolve the matter, the officer should advise the CO of intentions to file a formal complaint to the Bureau of Personnel through the chain-of-command.

Another course of action for the OIC would be to file a formal written complaint directly to the Bureau of Personnel. Taking this approach would not effectively use the chain-of-command, but this handling of the complaint creates the least immediate disturbance in the daily operation of the unit, though its long-range effect will be more disruptive.

Filing a written complaint through the CO would keep the chain-of-command informed, which would reduce ambiguity while simultaneously increasing the likelihood of justice being served.

Turn to page 190 to find out what happened.

Government Equipment and Services
(Issue 17)

A civilian friend of a commanding officer, an 0-6, was accorded unusual access and deference by the command. An 0-3 assisted the friend by making copies of computer programs with the thought that it would please his senior officer.

What ethical concepts are involved?

Since taxpayers make all the things we have in the military available, it may not seem inappropriate for military personnel to share some of what we have, especially when doing so does not seem to increase the cost of doing business.

In this case the civilian friend of the commanding officer provided a wide range of contributing activities to members of the command, all of which were legal.

The command had purchased several business type computer programs which they used in their daily operation. Therefore, when the civilian friend asked for a copy—which would seem to take nothing away from the command—he was so obliged. The data printed was on paper supplied by the civilian friend whose own printer broke down.

The issue to be considered revolves around who is authorized to use government equipment. From an ethical standpoint it is not fair to give one person special access when it has not been authorized by Congress for all. An example of ethical activity would be an air show where all of the public can come on the base and enjoy activities as part of a public relations program.

In this instance, only one person benefited from the use of government equipment and services, a venture that was both improper and not within the minds of Congress when they authorized expenditures to make goods and services available.

Turn to page 190 to find out what happened.

Motivation Isn't Everything
(Issue 18)

A squadron commander noticed that one of his pilots seemed to have an attitude/performance problem that apparently stemmed from concern over his engagement. The CO discussed the pilot's social life with him and determined that although the pilot's thoughts did wander to his girlfriend, and he was not totally concentrating on his flying duties, the pilot definitely wanted to keep flying.

How should the CO handle the matter?

Officers are able to timeshare their thoughts between two or more areas. It is in fact this ability to avoid sensory overload which ensures their being able to react under stress.

In this case the CO decided that the pilot, although experiencing concerns about his social life, was committed to being a good pilot and gave every indication he was motivated to do things correctly. Thus he decided to allow the pilot to fly.

There is no question that all factors in life cannot be quantified and that a senior officer has to rely on judgment and experience. The question is whether an officer has to rely solely on his or her own judgment or should the thoughts and records of others also play a significant role? For example, checking with the flight surgeon, or other appropriate medical personnel, to ascertain the pilot's state of mind, as well as reviewing recent performance records held by the operations and training officers, would have provided the CO with additional useful information. In addition, one of the many functions of an executive officer is to provide a sounding board for the commanding officer.

Just as officers might question another's judgment, so must their own determinations be subjected to self scrutiny. Not facing the possibility of fallibility in their own decision-making process is an ethical failure based on not wanting to admit that they might be wrong. Look for truth, and if all other opinions confirm an officer's judgment, so be it, even if events later show that other factors were involved. At least the officer has tried to obtain all pertinent information in order to make the best decision.

Turn to page 190 to find out what happened.

Overpayment
(Issue 19)

As officers move from one station to another, the possibility exists that through administrative error they will be paid more than they are entitled to receive. Complicating the situation will be the necessity for the officer to "hit the deck running" after arriving at the new station: he or she may be hard-pressed thereafter to find time to reconcile differences with disbursing personnel.

In this instance an officer found that overpayments were being regularly made to his bank account, but the press of high-priority operations distracted him and delayed his bringing the matter to the attention of the finance officer.

What could possibly happen?

Officers are paid for duties carried out in their official capacity. They are expected to know, to the penny, pay entitlement, allowances, and travel.

An excess payment is, in actuality, an unauthorized transfer of funds from the government to an individual. While an agent of the government may have made an administrative mistake in issuing the excess funds, the officer is expected to realize that the money is not really his or hers and consequently, as with finding someone else's wallet, the officer should immediately see that the money is returned.

Turn to page 191 to find out what happened.

Public office is a public trust.

—Grover Cleveland

OVERPAYMENT

The Drug Test
(Issue 20)

An E-5 nuclear submarine technician who has been a good solid performer comes to his division officer following random unit-sweep urinalysis. He claims stress at home caused him to use cocaine for the first and only time in his life, and he deeply regrets it. The results of the urinalysis subsequently turned out to be negative.

What should the division officer do?

There is insufficient evidence here of drug use. Maybe he didn't do cocaine, but is really asking for help. On the other hand, what signal does inaction give to other sailors? If the sailor did use drugs but wasn't "caught," might he try drugs again?

The division officer has to consider the E-5's job as it relates to security and safety. He also has to realize that if sailors can't trust their officers with their problems, they may not open up at all.

As hard as we all try, we all make mistakes. Maybe this individual will be scared enough by this close call to avoid any drug use in the future. But the zero-tolerance policy should have been enough of a scare to signal that drugs are not the answer to *any* problem.

Turn to page 191 to find out what happened.

Any man can make mistakes, but only an idiot persists in his error.

—Marcus Tullius Cicero,
Philippics, 44 B. C.

Stress at the Bingo Point
(Issue 21)

A certain pilot had a history of suffering from task overload. Because of sea conditions, he had been given three carrier wave-offs, was low on fuel, and found himself at the bingo fuel state (that point where a pilot has only enough fuel left to get from the current position to a shore landing field).

There were multiple transmissions between the carrier and the pilot: questions asked, directions given, advice offered, and the pilot again experienced sensory overload.

What should the squadron CO have done?

Some people are known as good problem solvers, and this may have been the case with the CO, who had to decide what to do with an airborne pilot who was low on fuel and confused as to what he should do next.

However, being a good problem solver is not always enough; each officer has to concentrate on being a good problem avoider. While we may say someone is a good problem solver, we might also ask why do they have so many problems to solve.

There is never enough time in the day to do everything we want, and that is certainly true of those who have chosen careers as officers. Although there is nothing that can be done after the fact, there is usually more that could have been done to avoid problems in the first place.

There is always a human desire to give everyone a chance to both train and prove themselves. It is at times like these that command becomes a lonely thing. Yet flying high-performance aircraft is not suited to everyone; thus, the more challenging the assignment, the closer attention a CO must pay to the capabilities of subordinates.

A CO does not have to face all such decisions alone, however. A flight surgeon can be consulted, as well as others who have flown with a particular pilot or interacted from ground communication points.

The ethics of being someone's senior means that you are responsible for what happens to them and what they do performing their job. Command can be lonely at times, but not as lonely as having to write a spouse, parents, or others expressing regret that their loved one has died.

Turn to page 192 to find out what happened.

The Christmas Gift
(Issue 22)

A Civil Engineer Corps officer working in construction on a contract in Italy returned home one day and found on his doorstep an unsolicited Christmas gift from an Italian construction contractor. The basket of fruit and other food and drink items was worth approximately $200.

The outright refusal of such a gift would constitute a personal affront to the Italian contractor with whom an excellent working relationship on an important project had been established.

What do you do?

Gifts like these are common in the construction industry, especially overseas, but officers are subject to the "Standards of Conduct" and government ethics and are not allowed to accept such gifts.

The "Standards of Conduct" and ethics information is provided to all construction contractors in bidding documents and is reiterated to successful bidders during pre-construction conferences.

On the other hand, it was a very nice gift, difficult to turn down, and no one would have been the wiser if the gift had been kept since it had been delivered directly to the officer's home. Further, the officer knew that the contractor knew the gift would not influence the officer's decision-making process on the construction project in progress or on any future work. The contractor's gift was the result of a sincere, friendly gesture.

The officer considered that the headquarters' legal counsel might determine that the gift would have to be returned, thereby tarnishing the working relationship between the government and the contractor.

The task was to properly dispose of the unsolicited Christmas gift in a manner that would not jeopardize the working relationship between the government and the contractor, but would satisfy the "Standards of Conduct" requirements, which are in place to prevent undue influence on the government by any particular contractor.

Turn to page 193 to find out what happened.

Drinking Contest
(Issue 23)

You and several officers have decided to supplement your income during off-duty hours by operating a bar in town.

During the course of one evening a drinking contest is undertaken by the patrons, which eventually leads to several of the customers becoming legally intoxicated.

<u>Assuming no fight ensues, have you done anything wrong</u>?

(*Note:* Off-duty work should only be undertaken after consulting SECNAVINST 1700.11C and discussing the venture with the base JAG officer. You also need the approval of your commanding officer.)

As an officer in the American military you are, in addition to any other specialty, a public affairs officer representing your particular branch of the service. As an officer in contact with the civilian sector the entire military is judged by your appearance, conduct, and words.

Alcohol problems are of great concern to the military, as they are to members of the civilian populace, for accidents on and off the job are often traceable to excessive alcohol consumption. When one accepts a commission they are tacitly accepting a position as a role model and included therein is the responsibility to maintain good order and discipline, as well as to obey the law of the state and nation within which one resides.

A number of establishments that dispense alcohol have breathalizers available for both patrons and operators of the establishment to determine whether they have exceeded the legal limit of alcohol ingestion.

The concern, which is a matter of law in a number of states, is that if a customer becomes legally intoxicated, then torts or crimes committed by the inebriated individual may be traceable to the operators of the establishment that served the liquor that caused the patron to go over the legal limit. In that event, the operators of the bar can be held liable for damage resulting from the action of the customer who became intoxicated in their bar.

<u>Turn to page 193 to find out what happened</u>.

Responding to an Emergency
(Issue 24)

A pilot had been used to flying a helicopter when he volunteered for and transitioned to a fixed-wing aircraft. There are significant differences between flying the two aircraft, both in the procedures and terminology used. For example, when one wants another to leave a helicopter the command is "get out," while "eject" is appropriate for the fixed-wing aircraft. The procedures for a stall recovery require exactly opposite reactions in the two forms of aircraft.

An emergency condition developed as the aircraft went into a stall, requiring immediate egress of all hands from the fixed-wing aircraft.

What should have been done differently and why?

When the pilot realized that they all had to exit the aircraft, he reverted to his longstanding memory of what to do in an emergency in a helicopter and gave the command for everyone to "get out." Unfortunately, the others in the plane were confused by this nonstandard order, and repeated yelling of the same command had no effect.

Following this confusion the pilot tried to recover from the fixed-wing aircraft stall by using the procedures he had practiced many times in a helicopter—which had the opposite effect from that intended.

In this case, the pilot had relatively few hours of flying the fixed-wing aircraft. While he could land and take off and fly level, he was not adequately trained and prepared to act in an emergency situation.

What makes this an ethics issue is the failure of the pilot's senior to take personal responsibility for all that the pilot was doing. It is common knowledge that helicopters and fixed-wing aircraft are different craft to fly; when a pilot switches from one type to the other, the old habits have to be unlearned and the new habits learned. Going from one aircraft type to another takes more time and "behavioral" training than transitioning from one fixed-wing model to another.

Turn to page 193 to find out what happened.

TREAT YOUR SHIPMATE AS YOURSELF:

The Golden Rule as a Guideline for Equal Opportunity Goals
by

Captain Arnold E. Resnicoff, CHC, USN

As officers—that is, government representatives *and* military leaders—we are pledged to support equal opportunity (EO) goals. So important is this requirement that today's fitness reports specifically rate our EO performance.

But equality is an elusive concept. People are different, and differences count! As officers, we rate others based on differences within a highly competitive environment: differences that will qualify and disqualify our personnel for countless opportunities and rewards.

Moreover, even if we limit EO goals to specific minority categories, it is not really *equal* treatment that is our goal. After all, *My Fair Lady*'s Professor Henry Higgins boasted that he treated everyone equally: equally shabbily! Our goal is to treat others with respect and dignity, which is the same way we want to be treated by others.

Based on this concept—one that a variety of religious and nonreligious traditions teach as one version or another of the famous golden rule—the Navy's Bureau of Medicine initiated the "T.E.A.M." program: "*Treat Everyone As Me.*" But in a military environment where rank accentuates differences in power and authority in both personal and professional relationships, can the golden rule serve as guide?

Yes, it can. "Treat your shipmate as yourself" can help us develop an ethical framework for dealing with military and civilian personnel based on concepts of *individuality, mutuality,* and *responsibility.*

INDIVIDUALITY

We all want to be treated as individuals: equal in terms of basic rights, but unequal based on ability and drive. Ironically, we want just enough equality to allow us to pursue opportunity based on individuality.

In other words, we are not "equal" in the sense that we have no differences, but *equal in our right to be treated and judged as unique human beings*—with individual strengths and weaknesses. Our race, sex, and beliefs are a part of our identity, but they are not all-defining, and we have the right to be judged based on our actions alone, not on those of others with whom we might be lumped together at the expense of our individuality. And with the right to be judged on our actions alone comes the responsibility to be held *accountable* for those actions. As officers we take an oath to support and defend the Constitution, but the "vision statement" that precedes and frames that document is the Declaration of Independence. There we proclaim our belief in an equality based on "inalienable rights," including such basic rights as life, liberty, and the pursuit of happiness. These same "core values" apply to all persons as part of a "human family." Our actions, and our dealings with others, must pass the test of inalienable rights.

A respect for *individuality* means that standards be set based on job requirements, not social groupings. Our responsibility is to ensure that our personnel have an equal opportunity to rise to as high a level of responsibility as possible, dependent on individual talents, capabilities, and diligence—not on differences in color, gender, or creed.

Desert Storm/Desert Shield news coverage provided many civilians with their first opportunity to see the "face" of today's military, a face that showed the success of our EO efforts. Of all our wars, the military's battle against prejudice and racism has included some of our most significant victories. Continuing that fight is one of our greatest challenges as naval officers.

MUTUALITY

We treat our shipmates as ourselves when we imagine, as some native Americans used to say, that we are walking in their moccasins. The golden rule is not as much about the relationship of the moment as it is about our continuing relationships as human beings.

This is the idea the Muslim teacher and mystic Al-Ghazali had in mind when he taught that we refrain from lying by imagining how we feel when someone else lies to us. Similarly, when Confucius was asked what principle could guide all conduct, he answered "reciprocity": that we should not do to others what we would not want them to do to us. Therefore, we should treat our parents the way we want our children to treat us, our teachers the way our students should treat us, and so on.

Judaism stresses the applicability of the golden rule by noting that it can even apply to the relationship between executioner and the person sentenced to death! "Love your neighbor as yourself" in such a case, Jewish tradition advises, *by making the death as quick and painless as possible.*

We cannot forget our rank and position, but we can always imagine "the shoe being on the other foot" and then carry out our responsibilities with the same consideration we might hope would be shown *if the roles were reversed.*

RESPONSIBILITY

An officer enjoys the "special trust and confidence" of our nation, its citizens, and its leaders. We are entrusted with the responsibility to safeguard our nation's freedoms. Our responsibility as officers does not end with obeying the law; we must do our best to teach, inspire, and lead others to live by the values we are pledged to protect and defend.

A modern speaker has said that there are three answers to three basic questions. The three answers are:
- do right
- do your best
- treat others as yourself.

The three questions are:
- Can I trust you?
- Can I count on you?
- Do you care?

We must treat others equally—without regard to race, religion, sex, or national origin—not only because it is the law; *it is the right thing to do.*

We must treat others with dignity and respect, reflecting our commitment to equal opportunity to the very best of our ability. *Others have put their trust in us.*

And we must treat others as ourselves *because we must never lose touch with their humanity, fears, and aspirations—or with our own.*

Billet Assignments

You have only been on board for 15 days as the ship's executive officer when two new seamen report aboard. One is a minority member and the other is not. Your task is to assign them to a working billet. Most of the minorities on board are in the supply department as cooks, stock control, etc. Most non-minority members of the crew are in operations. In the best interest of the Navy, the ship's crew, and each individual sailor—

What assignment should you give to these two men and why?

Being new on board, and realizing that a decision needed to be made fairly soon, you might follow the example of the previous executive officer and assign the new personnel in accordance with their racial make-up so that they would be comfortable on board.

This approach perpetuates the Navy's past discrimination practices, however, further eroding the morale of minority members of the crew who see themselves in dead-end jobs. By handling the case this way, you would send a message to the rest of the officers, as well as the crew, that certain people have to be kept in their place.

Turn to page 194 to find out what happened.

We hold these Truths to be self-evident, that all Men are created equal, that they are endowed by their Creator with certain unalienable Rights, that among these are Life, Liberty, and the Pursuit of Happiness.

—U.S. Declaration of Independence

Official Travel
(Issue 26)

You are a very hard-working officer who works long hours and puts the good of the service before other needs. At times you spend your own money to purchase supplies to enable you to do your job better.

Recognizing the importance of physical conditioning to the military officer, you regularly work out and are very proficient in a sport you first excelled at in college. Because of your prowess you have been invited to participate in a sporting event in a distant city. The group sponsoring the event does so for charitable fund-raising purposes and does not have funds to defray your expenses in going to the event.

How do you get to the event?

Because officers are considered available for duty 24 hours per day, the area of what is personal and what is official may seem clouded regarding any required action. In this case the officer was stationed close to a military air base and the distant city at which the event would take place was also close to a military airfield.

In addition to pay, officers receive medical care, shopping privileges in post exchanges and commissaries, and a large number of other services, such as offices and computers, which cost a great deal and are used in the furtherance of their official duties.

Since aviators are expected to periodically train and hone their skills, they often find themselves doing cross-country hops to maintain their qualification level and skills. Since the pilot often has the option of choosing which city to fly to, then someone wanting to go from one city to another might ride along with that pilot without causing additional expense to the government.

Turn to page 194 to find out what happened.

Labor to keep alive in your breast that little spark of celestial fire called conscience.
—General George Washington

Briefed Altitude
(Issue 27)

A two-seat aircraft was on a mission. Prior to takeoff, both pilot and copilot were briefed on the minimum enroute altitude at which the aircraft could fly. Yet these experienced aviators flew the aircraft into a mountain.

Could this mishap have been avoided?

For the preceding 72 hours all that transpired in the lives of the mishap aircrew was investigated.

Being ethical means obeying the rules even when one doesn't believe in them. If a rule needs to be changed, then an officer should so recommend, via the chain-of-command.

Could this mishap have been avoided? Probably, if the officers and all who knew them had put the good of the service before themselves. The selection and training process for aviators is complex, rigorous, and long. During this extended period, every pilot is observed by many experienced aviators. It is not easy, but when an individual exhibits a lack of self-discipline, then others should do or say something both to the individual and that person's senior officer, as appropriate.

We each need to review our performance and our motivations, and if we find something that we are or are not doing that we wouldn't be too proud to let others know, then we need to change. Being ethical means to do the best that you can.

Turn to page 195 to find out why it happened.

Discipline is summed up in one word—obedience.

—Lord Admiral John Jervis,
Earl of St. Vincent.

Systems Acceptance
(Issue 28)

An 0-6 project manager who had recently visited a contractor's plant for update performance testing, directed a subordinate military officer project engineer to travel to the same facility to sign the acceptance papers for the system.

Upon reaching the plant and conducting an evaluation, the project engineer found he had 36 typewritten pages of serious discrepancies.

What do you do?

The project engineer (PE) was faced with a dilemma. Should he reject the system, thus both defying his boss and, by implication, suggesting that his boss didn't know what he was doing by sending the PE to the plant to accept the system? Or should he accept the system, over his own objections, because he knew his boss wanted it accepted?

Also to be considered is that the boss did not do his job properly and would be pleased that the PE discovered the discrepancies.

On the one hand, our bosses do not always have the time to tell us all the reasons they may have for their actions. The military runs on trust, so to do other than what was directed might be seen as an attempt to impugn the integrity of one's senior officer.

Against that background of military expectations between seniors and subordinates must be considered the fact that one swears allegiance to the Constitution and not to a particular boss. Further, conditions may have changed or the contractor misled the 0-6 when the latter was at the plant.

When officers sign something, they are attesting that to the best of their ability, they know that what is on the document they have signed is correct and complete.

Turn to page 195 to find out what happened.

Sensible initiative is based upon an understanding of the commander's intentions.

Soviet Army Field Service Regulations, 1936.

The Canteen Corks
(Issue 29)

A stateside installation and its new commanding major-general, who holds the Medal of Honor, was picked to be the first Marine Corps site to implement a new Table of Organization, with an emphasis on logistical responsiveness to generated needs.

After World War II the officer had been charged with reclaiming Marine Corps property still in supply dumps on islands bypassed as the war moved west. Being a frugal farm boy, he managed to reclaim all government property regardless of service affiliation, with the Marine Corps as temporary custodian. It was his application of his General Orders to "Take charge of my post and all government property in view."

The new CG conducted personal inspections of every unit down to companies within battalions in his division. One minor item to be accounted for (there are no minor items in a legitimate supply system, however) was the lowly canteen cork. It is an item costing a few cents but one which is vital to the well-being of the individual in the field, who survives on water. If a canteen lacks a cork to secure the water, vital drops will be lost as the active Marine runs through the field.

One day the commanding general came to inspect an individual company, and in response to the CG's question, the company commander was able to truthfully answer that he had all the canteen corks he was supposed to have.

What was wrong?

During prior conversations with company commanders, platoon leaders, and individual Marines about the status of canteen corks, the CG had found out that the picture was bleak—back orders were more than six months old.

During his regular inspections, the CG had asked company commanders, platoon leaders, and individual Marines about the status of canteen corks in his company, platoon, or among his individual equipment. The system wasn't responsive when it should have been.

Canteen corks were an item in short supply because the contracts for ordering them were not a high-priority item among professional supply officers, who were more concerned with ordering big-ticket items. But to the Marine in the field, a canteen with a properly fitting cork was a necessity.

On the day of the inspection the company commander knew that he was ready and felt that the possession of canteen corks by each Marine in his company would reflect well on his personal leadership.

Turn to page 196 to find out what happened.

Inter-Aircraft Communications
(Issue 30)

This situation involves two aircraft flying a formation flight in hazardous mountain terrain. Neither pilot had previously experienced a mishap. During flight, the two aircraft collided and both aircraft were destroyed. Fortunately, no one was injured.

What do you think went wrong?

Both pilots forgot that every day they train to be better officers as well as pilots. Attention to detail is a matter of ethics, for without it, we are faced with mishaps waiting to happen.

These pilots didn't enjoy the paperwork, procedural follow-ups, and constant attention to detail required of all officers. In failing to remember that they were officers first, and pilots second, they failed themselves, their squadron mates, their seniors who had put confidence in them, and the taxpayers.

This was not a sudden mishap that could not have been prevented. It was a disregard for the rules governing being a good pilot and a good officer. As officers we have a special trust and confidence put in us, and we are often left on our own to enforce that trust.

Turn to page 197 to find out why it happened.

For nothing goes for sense or light, that will not with old rules jump right.

—Butler,
Hudibras. Part i, Canto 3, Line 135.

Shortage of Funds
(Issue 31)

A senior enlisted, with more than 20 years of service, decided that additional income was required to maintain a desired life style. A number of options were open to increase income, but they would severely limit free time for off-duty recreation.

What approaches are available to tackle this problem?

When personnel in the military take action they have to be concerned with its effect on the public, their command, and the ethical and legal consequences of what they do.

Depending on the economy, the holding of a military position may be financially more rewarding than a civilian job. One principal reason individuals are in the military is to serve their nation. In that capacity it is the receiving of psychic income which helps offset real dollar limits.

Psychic income refers to the satisfaction received from knowing one's presence means something, is filling a need in the defense structure of the nation, and means the ability to pay oneself an amount of satisfaction for things accomplished. One is able to take pride in repeated contributions to others and their country.

How we seek real and psychic income makes the difference as to whether our actions are judged ethical and legal.

Turn to page 197 to find out what happened.

The reward of a thing well done is to have done it.
—Ralph Waldo Emerson,
Essays: Second Series, Realist, 1844.

Fraternization
(Issue 32)

You assumed command of a Personnel Support Detachment about a month ago. Your predecessor gave you a good turnover, but you have uncovered a rather disturbing situation that exists in your command. Your XO, an 0-4, has recently married a female ensign assigned to your command. They have been married at least three months. This is a direct violation of the Navy's policy on fraternization.

What action is appropriate to take?

Your initial response to the situation is to call your executive officer in for questioning. At that time you determine that the integrity of the chain-of-command has not been compromised. Both the XO and the ensign have performed responsibly throughout their courtship and subsequent marriage. Further investigation uncovers no apparent change in morale or possible current repercussions throughout the enlisted ranks due to this infraction of Navy regulations and standards. You may not be able to see it, though the prejudice to good order and discipline is there.

You could contact the detailer and have the ensign assigned to another command. Daily operations seem to be running fine however, and you consider counseling the couple and taking no further action.

Turn to page 197 to find out what happened.

Pardon one offense and you encourage the commission of many.

—Publilius Syrus,
Sententiae. circa 42 B. C.

Air Show
(Issue 33)

An experienced pilot who was also a NATOPS evaluator was scheduled to perform short-field runway landings at an air show. Prior to the day of the show, the pilot briefed his copilot on how the mission would be flown, including the steepness of the approach to the runway.

The day of the air show the pilot made an extremely steep approach to the runway, possibly trying to impress other pilots as to just how short a landing could be made.

What might have gone wrong and why?

In this case the copilot failed to provide comment in advance as to reservations held on the steepness of the approach. Being ethical does not only mean that one doesn't lie, cheat, or steal. There is more to it than that. While writing or saying something that is false is wrong, withholding comment about the approach to be used on a mission, fearing that another's feelings might be hurt, is also wrong and suggests a lack of ethical "guts."

Officers have many responsibilities, and one extremely important trait that needs to be exercised is showing loyalty to others by letting them know what you think when doing so might make a difference.

Safety is one of the biggest concerns we have in the military; thus, each officer owes it to all others and the nation to speak up when they think that something may lead to a mishap or other unwanted action.

It is not easy telling others what they may not want to hear, but ethical loyalty demands that we do. In the long run, the person we tell will be grateful, and disappointed if we don't when they realize that they could have stayed out of trouble if someone had said something to them in advance.

Turn to page 198 to find out what happened.

An officer should make it a cardinal principle of life that by no act of commission or omission on his part will he permit his immediate superior to make a mistake.

—General Malin Craig, U.S.A.,
Address to the graduating class, West Point, 12 June 1937.

The Gift
(Issue 34)

In a government program office, for as long as anyone could remember, the support contractor furnished a caricature of the departee as a gift when military personnel were reassigned or civilian personnel retired. The artwork presentation was the high point of the ceremony since the artwork included references to the awardee's personal and professional life.

The financial manager (FM), a newly assigned officer who had completed a tour in an Inspector General's office, questioned the propriety of such a gift. Office personnel, including the program manager (PM), assumed the gift was relatively inexpensive since similar caricatures could be purchased for under $75 and that the gift was part of the normal public relations work of the contractor. The PM considered this practice to be an important morale booster for the office, and even if it was marginally "incorrect," there was no reason to stop the practice.

The FM investigated and discovered that the contractor had been providing these gifts for at least 13 years, at a cost of nearly $400 per gift, and that the contractor charged the gift against contract work. When the PM was advised of this, the decision was made to discontinue the practice.

Within a week of this decision one of the division heads decided to retire on short notice. This man was considered an office icon, with over 35 years of government service, and virtually all of it in the same program office. Immediately, his division personnel began to make plans for the imminent party, the high point of which would be the presentation of the caricature.

When they contacted the contractor, they were informed that the contractor was told by the new financial manager to discontinue the practice. This caused an office uproar that culminated in a meeting in the PM's office. The gist of the argument was that even if the practice had to be stopped, this supervisor was special and should be the last one.

The PM decided that office morale would suffer if this particular supervisor did not get the caricature and that the size of the office precluded raising $400 to pay for the present. Therefore, as long as the present FM did not feel that the practice was illegal, as opposed to unethical, one more caricature would be allowed, but the practice would end with this one. The contractor then completed the artwork for $270.

The contractor did not charge the work against the contract, but took the charge against corporate profit.

What could possibly go wrong?

This particular program office had been the subject of scrutiny prior to this incident. The program manager, in order to correct practices that he felt were ethically marginal, had sought a financial manager with a background in the Inspector General's office to investigate this type of practice. This was one of many practices that were discovered and corrected during the tenure of the FM, which made the relationship between the support contractor and the program office more professional and less personal.

While civilian support personnel had been with the office for many years, the contractor and military personnel had changed many times. This produced a general uneasiness, bordering on animosity between civilian and military personnel. It was within this context that the PM felt that the effect on office morale was a consideration in allowing one more "gift." This was reinforced by the FM's advice that the gift was clearly *unethical,* but since the contractor apparently concurred in the giving of the gift, it was not clearly *illegal.*

(*Editor's note:* Contractors are in the business of landing and keeping contracts. It is for that reason that the government should not accept gifts. Even if it doesn't influence contract awards, there is often the presumption by industry, and others, that it did in effect have an influence, thus creating an image of a corrupt governmental operation. Perception can be everything in some situations. Even "the appearance of impropriety" can be construed as "illegal" or questionable ethical conduct.)

After the decision had been made, it appeared to be the correct one from an office morale standpoint. The retirement party was a success and the awarding of the caricature was indeed the highlight of the event.

Turn to page 199 to find out what happened.

The morale of the force flows from the self-discipline of the commander, and in turn, the discipline of the force is reestablished by the upsurge of its moral power.

—Brigadier General S. L. A. Marshall,
The Armed Forces Officer, 1950.

Working with a Contractor
(Issue 35)

An officer involved with the procurement of government equipment found that repeated visits were necessary to the contractor's place of business. Because the meetings were conducted over the course of two days, overnight accommodations were required.

What could go wrong?

It must be remembered that the livelihood of people doing business with the government depends on their ability to please the customer—in this case the military—and thus every effort is expended to provide the government with a good product.

A number of companies are usually capable of providing different goods and services. Thus, there are times when a vendor will try to go the extra mile not only to please the customer (the government) on the current contract but also to help them secure other contracts.

It is imperative that those who represent the government in negotiations with civilian concerns keep an arm's-length arrangement and do not engage in any actions that might give special benefit to the contractor and compromise the position of the government.

Turn to page 199 to find out what happened.

Every compromise was surrender and invited new demands.

—Emerson,
Miscellanies: American Civilization.

Letter From Home
(Issue 36)

Two aircraft were scheduled to fly a formation flight together. Because the aircrew had worked together before, they comprised a good team for this particular mission.

On the day of the flight they were well briefed. Nothing unusual happened before the briefing session, nor was the brief itself particularly unusual. Both aircraft were in good condition and the aircrews were in good spirits.

What could possibly happen?

The copilot of one of the aircraft had not had enough sleep. It certainly is impractical to monitor everyone around the clock—and ethically speaking, each individual crew member is responsible for themselves, as well as what goes on around them. It is unfortunate that: (1) no one else noticed that the copilot was tired after a hectic schedule; and (2) no one said anything to the copilot about his reading a personal letter during the preflight brief—a clear violation of NATOPS, aviation discipline, and professionalism.

Turn to page 200 to find out what happened.

I blurt ungrateful truths, if so they be, that none may need to say them after me.

—J. R. Lowell,
Epistle to George William Curtis.

Equal Treatment
(Issue 37)

You are a senior lieutenant stationed at a small naval base. You've just reported in, following consecutive sea tours. A "hard-charger," you have enjoyed the many challenges of sea duty and look forward to a new set of challenges on shore. Still getting a feel for the command and your current job, you have encountered some issues that have made you uncomfortable.

As administrative assistant to the commanding officer, you have been afforded insight into how the command operates, and at this point you are concerned about some recent incidents. You have overheard conversations that have not been very flattering toward women. Having been at sea, you are accustomed to some of these remarks, but these recent conversations have left you uneasy. You have also noticed your male counterparts playing jokes on some of the female lieutenants, and recently your CO has shut down the only female lavatory in your building.

As a naval officer, what are your responsibilities?

Officers must ensure fair and equal treatment of all personnel; in addition to being responsible to their commanding officer and fellow shipmates.

With a view to doing what is right, the senior lieutenant might try to handle the situation at the lowest level by confronting the male lieutenants and voicing concern that perhaps the women are not enjoying the current excitement as much as the men, and they should consider discontinuing practical jokes and inappropriate comments. This approach might further perpetuate the harassing behavior, however, along with increasing the incidents of alienation towards female personnel.

Turn to page 200 to find out what happened.

Professional courtesy and good manners should be carefully integrated parts of your command and leadership principles, both up and down.
—Major General Aubrey "Red" Newman,
Follow Me, 1981.

EQUAL TREATMENT

The Disbursing Officer
(Issue 38)

An ensign assigned as an afloat disbursing officer at a forward deployed site required a large on-hand balance of U.S. and foreign currency at all times (approximately $300,000 to $500,000). Documentation of transactions was excellent, as were procedures for turning over money to the cashiers and balancing out accounts after completion of check-cashing/currency exchange.

When handling this amount of cash and making large numbers of transactions, it is inevitable that sooner or later someone will come up short or over. On a couple of occasions, the ensign had come up short by approximately $20-$50, which is not a lot when the total amount of cash being handled is considered. On both these occasions, the ensign chipped in the money out of her own pocket to cover the loss. Because she felt personally accountable for the money, and the dollar value was relatively small, she chose not to report the losses.

It should be noted that both the supply officer and the assistant supply officer were extremely level headed individuals and looked upon disbursing as a business, just as they viewed the other accountable jobs in the department. They understood that people make mistakes and as long as a verifiable audit trail existed, and an organized approach to problem solving was used, they could live with human error.

On one occasion, the ensign purchased additional foreign currency to what she usually had on hand and simultaneously had to revalue the exchange rate. She was in a hurry and did the calculations quickly, which involved five decimals. In her haste to get the money line open, the ensign transposed the fourth and fifth decimals. The line was open for approximately 20 minutes before she realized her mistake. She had already lost about $100. Had she reported the loss, she would not have been allowed to cover the loss out of her own pocket and close the matter. (A report results in an evaluation or, if necessary, an investigation by SECNAV). Because the error was due to inattentiveness on her part, the ensign felt obligated to personally cover the loss.

One time after the situations described above, the ensign had just gone through her cash after a payday and come up about $1,000 short. She scrutinized both her books and her safe for three days. She could not find the problem. She reflected that with the exception of the small shortages reported above, she had always successfully resolved the discrepancy.

What should she do?

The number of cash transactions was significantly higher on this tender than those on stateside tenders due to limited sources for check cashing off the ship. Paying agents were trained to handle check-cashing and foreign currency exchanges. Naturally, the ensign felt badly about the losses because she was always extremely meticulous in her methods for handling money. She was reluctant to report what were considered nickel-and-dime losses because, in the event she came up short by a significantly greater amount in the future, she would feel compelled to report it, and she would not want to have an established track record of losses.

The CO was also extremely level headed, so in actuality, the ensign had nothing to fear, but her desire to be viewed as being "squared-away" prevailed and she did not report the losses.

On certain occasions the ensign did come up over instead of short. On both occasions, she reported the overages (approximately $100 to $200) in accordance with established procedures.

The only other times the ensign's operations experienced losses were due to errors made by other people handling her money as agent cashiers. She had always emphasized to the cashiers that they had nothing to fear about letting her know that they had a problem with their cash. On both occasions, they never found the money (shortages were approximately $100 to $200 each) and reported the shortages as required, which involves a letter to SECNAV via everybody else in between. The ensign's entire chain-of-command handled these incidents professionally and neither she nor her people suffered retribution. In fact, even with these documented overages and shortages, her operation received a grade of "outstanding" (the highest possible) for the two Supply Management Inspections (SMI) they went through while the ensign was the disbursing officer.

Since three days had already passed, the ensign did not feel right about sitting on what she had viewed as a potential problem. She went to see the assistant supply officer and told him she suspected she was short about $1,000. While they talked he remained completely calm, and after the conversation sent her back to recount. Since she had already gone through the cash and books thoroughly, she was not optimistic about finding the money.

Turn to page 201 to find out what happened.

NATOPS Check Flight
(Issue 39)

A flight was arranged so that a pilot could increase his proficiency in a particular aircraft. The flight was approached by the evaluating senior pilot as a "pilot appreciation" hop between friends who knew each other socially, as opposed to the scheduled NATOPS check flight it was intended to be.

What was wrong in this situation?

When one becomes a designated aviator, one also takes on a great number of responsibilities, including acting professionally. The barnstorming of the early years of aviation has been replaced with precision flying. Groups such as the Thunderbirds and the Blue Angels are not stunt flyers; they are disciplined aviators—the best of the aviation community—recognized for their ability to do precisely what the flight plan spells out without making it a social event.

The ethics involved include: (1) doing what the rules say you are supposed to do; (2) being professional at all times; (3) regarding the trust placed in an officer as sacred; and (4) remembering that everything an officer does affects others in the military, as well as affecting what non-military personnel think about the military.

Turn to page 201 to find out what happened.

The military profession is more than an occupation; it is a style of life.

—Morris Janowitz,
The Professional Soldier, ix, 1960.

The Fitness Report
(Issue 40)

0-4 rankings during the annual October fitness report cycle are perhaps one of the most competitive and influential set of marks received in the course of a career. It is this set of marks which carries the major determination on who is, and is not, selected for 0-5 and command. This is even more critical for an officer who is a senior 0-4 and preparing to go before a selection board.

This particular situation involves a squadron that had nine 0-4s assigned as department heads (DHs). Based upon the size of the year groups present, the numbers are five in year group "A" and four in year group "B."

For year group "A" the October fitness report ranking was to be the last one prior to the 0-5 selection board, which convenes in the spring. The squadron CO was faced with the realization that the ranking and report of fitness on the five DHs would make or break the majority of Group "A's" chances for selection, yet the instruction was quite clear: DHs must be ranked, and reported, from 1 to 9.

The squadron CO, who had worked with each of these officers on a daily basis, felt that each one was more than qualified to be an 0-5. Based on their performance, they warranted selection. The CO also knew that promotion rates would be approximately 60-65 percent for year group "A" and probably less, next year, for year group "B."

Revisiting available options, the CO considered a plan to take care of each DH. By ranking the DHs competitively only within their year group, and then double-ranking both within the year group and between year groups, the CO could ensure that each of the year group "A" DHs were ranked as number 1 or 2. The CO further knew that by sending in the fitness reports piecemeal, instead of as a group, the chances that his system would be detected would be greatly reduced.

What do you do?

The squadron CO has the best opportunity to observe the DHs on a close daily basis and thus might be considered most qualified to determine who is and who is not promoted. Historically, if one is not ranked number one or two as a DH, chances for promotion are greatly reduced.

The inability of the selection board to detect a single CO when considering multiple rankings reduces the fear of being caught. The misplaced loyalty to their CO of subordinates who process the fitness reports might further reinforce the CO's decision.

The reduced promotion opportunity means that a CO who does do the right thing when ranking DHs has penalized such officers. Morale is also decreased, while the military loses the services of some of its ablest officers.

There are basically three courses of action:

1.   Cheat and thus compromise the integrity of the promotion system and influence the leadership of the service. Those promoted will be the ones whose COs can cheat best.

2.   Reinforce and improve the current system requiring COs to submit all FITREPs at the same time and returning any piecemeal submissions.

3.   Overhaul the rating system in the military service so that cheating won't work. This approach assumes, however, that cheats will not be able to figure out a way to beat any system. It might be better to change the thinking of some raters to be more ethical in tone than to try and outsmart those whose way of life is outsmarting the system.

Turn to page 202 to find out what happened.

Oh, what a tangled web we weave, when first we practise to deceive!

—Sir Walter Scott,
Marmion, 1808.

THE FITNESS REPORT

65

Transportation
(Issue 41)

You are a senior officer at a base who, over time, has developed many friendships with members of the civilian community. You are also quite popular with your junior officers as a result of your concern for their welfare and the challenges they face in their jobs.

It is not uncommon for you to compliment personnel who work for you as a result of their outstanding performance. One of your friends in town, who is slightly disabled, has entertained members of your organization without charge, as a goodwill effort. He has also opened his home for overnight guests who were visiting members of your group.

You are approached by this civilian friend to help move his belongings sometime at the convenience of the motor pool and your personnel. About the same time, your JOs ask to borrow a government van for use in a morale-building night out.

What do you do?

In reflecting on both of these requests, you realize that your own success at the base has been due in large part to the morale-building effort of your civilian friend and the devotion to duty and extra hours worked by your JOs.

You determine that a government van will be available on the evening scheduled by the JOs, and that even if an additional requirement comes up, there will be extra vans available that could be used. Another call to the motor pool establishes that a truck could be made available on the day your civilian friend wants it and that other back-up trucks will also be available if needed by someone else.

The remaining question to be resolved is how to provide the base's civilian friend with the manpower necessary to make the move since the amount of household goods is too bulky for the friend to handle.

Turn to page 202 to find out what happened.

The Flight
(Issue 42)

A flag officer decided to attend a high school reunion with his wife, as they had both gone to the same school. Unfortunately, the school was located many hundreds of miles away, and the flag, who had an extremely busy schedule and was expecting important visitors the day after the reunion, would not have enough time to drive back from the distant city.

One of the flag's subordinates, hearing of the situation, arranged for one of the airfield's officers to take a check flight that would go from the flag's base to an airport close to the reunion. The subordinate, after making arrangements, told the flag officer that another officer would be flying back late that night which would enable the flag officer to arrive back in time to meet the next day's visitors.

The flag thanked the subordinate for the trouble taken to find out about the flights that could be used. The flag officer and his wife utilized the check flight to attend the reunion and returned without incident to meet the next day's visitors.

Did the flag officer do anything wrong?

Arranging a flight to take a senior to a private function was wrong, both on the part of the subordinate and the pilot who made the trip. Government funds are allocated to provide the means for the military to meet its mission requirements. It might be argued that making a senior feel good would help morale in the command, in general, but this is not a valid reason for utilizing a government aircraft for personal convenience.

For one thing, there are regulations to "avoid flights open to misinterpretation by the public." The subordinate and the pilot were clearly in violation of this regulation. Realizing what the ethical/legal violation of the senior was, however, requires more insight into what it means to be an officer and the power officers have.

Above all, seniors are expected to know all the regulations that govern their behavior, as well as to ensure that they follow all the rules. Thus, not knowing there was a specific instruction about avoiding flights that might be misinterpreted is not a valid excuse.

Second, the more senior one becomes, the greater the realization and sensitivity one is expected to have that their behavior and use of government funds are constantly under scrutiny and review.

Third, a senior must be aware that just asking a question sometimes leads a subordinate to assume that that senior wants them to "make it so". All officers have a desire to please their seniors and make things happen in furtherance of the seniors' wishes. Other than the civilian leaders of the military, no senior can become a senior without having first been a junior. Thus, all officers should remember how they felt and acted as they went up through the ranks.

Turn to page 203 to find out what happened.

The wise man is informed in what is right. The inferior man is informed in what will pay.

—Confucius

The Bus to Liberty
(Issue 43)

As your unit's Morale, Welfare, and Recreation officer you are constantly on the alert for opportunities to provide the officers and enlisted with pleasurable off-duty opportunities.

A survey of the unit's members indicates a great number of them would enjoy an outing at a family theme park that is several hundred miles away. You put out notices as to departure and return times for a bus, along with incidental costs that will be incurred. The bus will be drawn from your own motor pool and filled at the pool pump before departure.

On the Saturday the bus is to leave, you show up a half-hour early before an 0700 departure, thus ensuring that everything is ready when the service personnel and their families arrive.

By 0730 there is still only one couple there, a more senior officer with spouse and children. At 0745 the senior officer asks what the delay is and when the bus is going to leave. It is obvious to all that you, your spouse, and the other family would be the only ones who would be going.

What do you tell the senior officer?

The senior officer is an extremely hardworking individual who, together with spouse, does a great deal for the enlisted in the command. You know that they have been looking forward to this trip and have changed some significant other plans to be able to go.

The use of the bus for a MWR trip was an approved evolution because of its benefit to the troops. At this point you don't know why no one else is there, but are positive, as is the senior officer, that everyone received the word.

In trying to decide what to do you are not unmindful that the senior officer is also your fitness report evaluation senior.

Turn to page 204 to find out what happened.

The Hotel
(Issue 44)

You are a hardworking officer who has a brother who works for a motel chain, though he is not an official of that chain. Upon receiving transfer orders, you find that your brother's motel chain has special rates for military who are on PCS orders.

You mention to your brother that you are going to be traveling from the East to the West Coast and how nice it is that you will be staying at your brother's motels because of the special rates available to all military personnel.

Several days before you and your family are to travel across country, you receive word from your brother that if, when you check in at each motel, you mention a special code number, you will be able to receive an additional 25 percent discount. That is his special discount number and you are free to use it.

What do you do?

The issue here is one of whether special treatment is being accorded beyond that which you are entitled as a military officer.

The motel chain is in business to make a profit for its owners/shareholders and thus their granting of a special discount to military personnel represents a reduction in their level of profit as part of their awareness of the contribution made by the military to the United States.

Second, the motel chain tries, as do many companies, to reward its own employees with discounts for using their own services/products. Since rooms are occupied and have to be cleaned the following day, providing this discount also reduces the profit of the motel chain as they try to show their gratitude to their employees.

The question to be considered is whether the combining of these two discounts is ethical. Does the brother have the authority to offer the additional discount and does the officer have the authority to accept it?

Turn to page 205 to find out what happened.

THE HOTEL

Standards
(Issue 45)

You are the legal officer of an aviation squadron, due to transfer in four months. It has been a frustrating and tedious job, and your assignment has included many challenges and obstacles. Your executive officer has established policies that have been questionable, and you have been involved in at least a dozen cases of administrative separation of enlisted personnel that under other circumstances, would have been handled at much lower levels.

You have seen a pattern in administratively separating minority personnel, and have admittedly been involved in processing them out of the Navy.

Your replacement, a black female ensign, fresh out of legal officer school, has recently reported on board. You have been further concerned by events that have occurred since her arrival. Your XO has verbally abused her on several occasions and has assigned her as assistant legal officer. The XO is currently attempting to send a pilot to legal school to take your place before you transfer. You have managed to ignore the previous injustices but have decided that something must be done this time, feeling guilty about having compromised your standards.

<u>How can you possibly make a difference in this instance?</u>

Although you have been involved in many situations at your present command that have caused you to question your own integrity and real purpose in the Navy, you consider tactfully approaching your XO to ensure that no further harassment occurs.

This situation further highlights the message contained in the article by Admiral Arleigh Burke dealing with integrity (Appendix A). The possibility exists that speaking up now will end your own career, for in not challenging your senior, when he was acting unethically, and not standing up for what was right, you have made yourself a part of the problem, rather than the solution.

The entire officer corps depends on trust. By pledging your oath to support the Constitution, you have placed yourself in an untenable position, but not an impossible one. Your obligation is also to all who observe you. As the legal officer, you are supposed to be setting a standard. If you don't stand up for what is right, then many others will realize that their doing so is almost impossible.

On the other hand, you consider that by taking a stand for what is right now, you may end your own career. Unfortunately, you have compromised your own personal standards to the point where you hesitate to challenge any authority, reasoning that since you know what is right, the service will be better with you than without you.

Turn to page 205 to find out what happened.

Never for an instant can you divest yourselves of the fact that you are officers. On the athletic field, at the club in civilian clothes, or even at home on leave, the fact that you are a commissioned officer in the Army imposes a constant obligation to higher standards than might ordinarily seem normal or necessary for your personal guidance.

—General George C. Marshall,
*Selected Speeches and Statements of
General of the Army George C. Marshall, edited by Major
H. A. Deweerd, 1945.*

STANDARDS

Pay Day at Sea
(Issue 46)

Married less than a year, you are the assistant supply officer on a ship deployed to the Pacific. After four and one-half months at sea, you are reunited with your spouse in Hong Kong for ten days of leave. Along with other crew members who have arranged for their spouses to join them overseas, you are looking forward to an enjoyable mini-reunion with your spouse.

A day and a half into the leave a typhoon was forecasted as heading straight for Hong Kong. Telephone calls went out to all crew members to return to the ship for further instructions. Upon returning to the ship, the CO told all who had spouses in Hong Kong they could continue on their leave and were to join the ship in a week at Subic in the Philippines.

You realize payday will occur during this period of time and that direct deposit and allotments are not used by any within the command. As the ASO you are also the disbursing officer. The responsibility of ensuring the officers and enlisted are paid is yours. If you remain on leave, how will the crew be paid? As ASO you begin to wonder whether the desire for a reunion with your spouse should take priority over responsibility to the crew and ship?

What do you do?

With so many things to be concerned about, the CO would probably not think to ask the ASO to stay on board; somehow the troops would have been paid by one of the other officers.

This was the ASO's spouse's first exposure to service life, and after traveling 10,000 miles to join the ship only to be separated again within 36 hours of arriving, would be devastating. The apparent message that would be sent to the spouse by staying on board to pay the troops created anxiety for the young ASO.

Pondering whether to raise the question with the CO or supply officer, the ASO hoped to reach a resolution prior to the ship's departure for the Philippines. If a resolution could be achieved prior to the ship getting under way, the ASO might be able to take care of the ship as well as continue leave in Hong Kong.

By not discussing the payday situation prior to the ship getting under way, the ASO would be assured of staying in Hong Kong although the crew might have been paid late.

Turn to page 206 to find out what happened.

Team Spirit or Lack of Courage
by
Commander Richard Cataldi, USN

At AOCS (Aviation Officer Candidate School), officer candidates are taught teamwork as they train together for nearly twenty weeks. They survive their drill instructor's intense indoctrination together. They complete their academic education together. They successfully run the regiment as officer candidates together. They experience emotional stress, physical exhaustion, joy, and achievement together. And they go on liberty together.

One such class came forward, with less than a week to go before graduation and commissioning, to inform the chain-of-command that one of their number had a drinking problem. A follow-on class, which had the same personnel situation, did not report it. Both classes had seen the results of their respective classmates' drinking problems. Both classes had, as good teammates, covered for the hangovers, late returns from liberty, and failures to carry out normal duties for many weeks.

In the first case, with the drinking problem that was reported, an evaluation found the OC to be physically and psychologically alcohol dependent. The OC had been drinking since age fourteen and had experienced memory loss on more than twenty occasions. Most of the OC's college life had been spent intoxicated. Although found fit for duty, he was to undergo Level III, in-patient treatment before going on to follow-on training. The OC was graduated and commissioned. The OC went on to successfully complete treatment, as well as flight training, and earned "wings of gold."

In the second case, no one ever came forward. No one had the courage to even talk to their classmate about the drinking problem. Shortly after graduation and commissioning, all the classmates were reunited for a memorial service. After a late-night binge, their classmate had died in a car crash, so drunk he didn't know what hit him.

Part of becoming an officer is to recognize your areas of responsibility. Your first oath of allegiance is to the Constitution, with loyalties to seniors, peers, and subordinates—in that order. Team spirit does not mean covering up for another, especially when failure to act as an officer may lead to death and the obvious effect on those who survive their loved one's demise.

The Weak Lieutenant
(Issue 47)

A newly promoted Marine Corps first lieutenant was freshly assigned to deploy overseas on a Navy ship with a small complement of Navy and Marine officers who had been working with one another during routine training events over the previous six months. As the newest member of a well-established team, he was subject to close observation by other officers in the team.

The CO of the Rifle Company, a Marine captain, was a well-intentioned individual who lacked a definitive rapport with his subordinates. This was possibly because the company XO, a Marine first lieutenant, lacked confidence in his own leadership abilities, and was unduly influenced by a sincere desire to have his peers and subordinates respect and like him. In time, the XO lost the ability to discipline the other lieutenants. In order to appease the common gripes and complaints of his peers, he began to bad-mouth his commander.

Another of the Marine lieutenants in the Rifle Company, a picture-perfect Marine who was big, athletic, and imposing, had a truly impressive presence and bearing that afforded him an immediate good first impression on those he met. As time progressed, it became apparent that this lieutenant's fundamental professional knowledge was weak at best, but over time he had begun to manipulate the XO in a variety of ways to suit himself.

As the deployment continued, the unethical and weak lieutenant, who told stories of "college pranks" (criminal episodes) and taking advantage of women, split the Marines into three groups: (1) those who were opposed to whatever he said; (2) others who simply condoned it; and (3) those officers who found it easier not to get involved.

Finally, the unethical and weak lieutenant confided that when he stood duty in garrison, he would sort through his commander's personal files and belongings in order to see what the captain was "up to." He had found the personal notebook used by the CO to track his subordinates' performance. Thus, the weak lieutenant knew every event and personal reflection and decision made by the CO regarding his subordinates' fitness reports.

<u>As the newly assigned junior first lieutenant, what do you do?</u>

Whenever you criticize or accuse anyone, you run the risk of having your own deficiencies brought out in the open. Young officers often have an unwritten code by which they "stick together." This is a fine concept, for it adds to morale, esprit-de-corps, and camaraderie.

In the Marine Corps, it is called the LPA (Lieutenants' Protective Association). It is a philosophy whereby young officers who are inexperienced will work together and try to help or aid a fellow officer who may find himself lacking in a few areas. Yet such a system should not be used to hide, mask, or condone poor performance, judgment, or behavior. Such actions make all parties equally as guilty as the actual offender.

The lesson here is that we must police our own ranks, and simply because you are not perfect does not mean you do not have the right and duty to police your peers and subordinates. Small lapses in judgment or performance do not equate to another person's criminal behavior.

Interestingly, at least one officer did try to approach the weak lieutenant and confront him with the many problems on the ship that were due to his poor performance. He would not hear of any criticism, however, and immediately tried to verbally and physically intimidate the other lieutenant. He also immediately began to try and wreck the other officer's reputation and credibility by making snide remarks at opportune times to selected individuals to try and ostracize the other officer from his peers.

Many young people in the military view friendship and loyalty as two of the most important values they can hold. How many times would one say, "He's my friend; I'd do anything for him"? Or, that someone might cover for a friend out of loyalty. There is no friendship or loyalty when one considers behavior or performance that may endanger the collective unit.

So where does one draw the line, determining to abandon loyalty and friendship for greater imperatives? This is up to the individual and the situation, but someone imbued with a good ethical and moral set of values will be able to arrive at an appropriate solution.

Turn to page 207 to find out what happened.

Not always right in all men's eyes, but faithful to the light within.

—Oliver Wendell Holmes,
A Birthday Tribute.

THE WEAK LIEUTENANT   77

Certification
(Issue 48)

You are a lieutenant assigned to a Pacific-based aviation squadron. You are the tactical coordinator as well as the mission commander for your crew. As such you have overall responsibility for the accomplishment of the mission.

Your plane is presently involved in an Annual Mining Certification Readiness Inspection. So far, the mining run has been without error. As you near the end of the run, you release a mine, but the computer errs and drops the last two mines in unison into the designated target. Your department head, a senior lieutenant commander, is currently in the process of becoming certified to take over as mission commander. As he stands over your shoulder, he indicates that no one would be able to detect the error, and because it was your second-to-last drop, your score would remain 100 percent.

How do you respond?

Your aircrew has received outstanding marks in prior inspections. You feel that an error of this type would not be detected by the current radar and besides, your department head has been around long enough to judge this situation better than you.

As mission commander, you have the overall responsibility for the aircraft. Regardless of rank, in the air you are in charge. You are accountable to your seniors, to your crew, and to yourself for successful mission performance.

Turn to page 208 to find out what happened.

Responsibility is the test of a man's courage.

—Lord St. Vincent

Food For Friends
(Issue 49)

As an officer who lives off base, you find that your family has made many good friends in the community. At times, when your spouse has been sick, your next-door neighbor has taken your children to school and has even picked up items for you at the local grocery store.

Your families often go to the beach together. The older teenagers engage in wholesome activities with each other, and the parents enjoy their weekend evenings together playing cards and talking.

While you have your military life and a strong supporting spouse, you do recognize that there are differences between the two families because of the differences in pursuits.

After you have been living in the neighborhood for over a year, one of the adult members of your neighbor's family has to leave on an extended trip. The spouse who stayed behind has become sick and unable to carry out the many daily chores. You are now the one asked to help take the children to school with a request the next time you go to the commissary, to pick up food. The sick spouse provides you with money with which to do the shopping.

What do you do?

You were already on an extremely busy schedule and the added burden of taking the children to school, as your spouse does not drive, along with a request to help with the shopping, makes it almost impossible to go to more than one place to buy the food required for both families.

The store your neighbor shops at for food is in the opposite direction from your military station. Feeling that military personnel should also be good neighbors, you do the shopping for both families at the base commissary.

Your neighbor's spouse is most appreciative, and their teenage children show their appreciation by cleaning up your yard, something you had planned to do the next Saturday morning. Needless to say, you are delighted at the opportunity to sleep in late on the weekend.

Although everything seems to be going fine, your spouse expresses concern over the help given to the neighbor.

Turn to page 208 to find out what happened.

Assignment of Officers
(Issue 50)

You are the executive officer when two ensigns report aboard. One is female and the other male. As XO, your task is to assign them to a working billet. Two billets need to be filled: an administrative billet and a damage control assistant billet. In the best interest of the Navy, the ship's crew, and each individual officer—

What assignment would you give these two officers and why?

The XO needs to consider the complexity of the two billets available. The Damage Control Division involves a lot of manual labor as well as comprehension of some complex technical information.

The female ensign recently transferred from an administrative billet where she did an extraordinary job. The XO realizes that it is his responsibility to develop young officers and utilize their maximum potential. Not only is assigning the best person to a job important, but also not perpetuating past Navy stereotypical assignments, further eroding the morale of ambitious female officers and enlisted crew members who desire more technical positions.

Turn to page 209 to find out what happened.

He saw with his own eyes the moon was round, was also
certain that the earth was square, because he had journed
fifty miles, and found no sign that it was circular anywhere.
                                                    —Byron,
                              Don Juan. Canto v, Stanza 150.

Take-Off Time
(Issue 51)

You are an Air Force captain and the flight examiner who administers flight evaluations at one of the major Air Force commands in Europe. To be considered on time, flights can take off at zero minutes early or up to two minutes late. On this particular day, there is a mechanical failure, and one crew member has to transfer to a spare airplane, resulting in a take-off that's six minutes late.

You radio the command post reporting take-off time as 0606 hrs. A voice replies "change that to 0602." You respond that there was a mechanical failure, that the crew did a highly professional job of changing planes, but that take-off was 0606. Again, the response is, "change that to 0602."

What do you do?

Knowing that correct reporting is a requirement of your job, you insist that the take-off time be entered correctly in the log and ask for the name and rank of the person who is on the other end of the radio link. You are advised that it is an Air Force corporal who says he has been given instructions that all times will be listed within the prescribed limits.

You advise him that you are an Air Force captain and that you refuse to report something that isn't true. There is a pause in transmission and then a colonel comes on the line and advises you to report as instructed if you know what is good for you. Further, the colonel advises that the reporting time is within the authority of his responsibility and therefore, you would do well to respond immediately so that they could go on with more important matters.

You recognize that while you probably have more time in service than the corporal, the colonel not only outranks you but also has greater experience than you. You ask for an explanation of why the wrong reporting is to be done, and the colonel tells you he doesn't have time to explain: "Just get on with it if you know what is good for you."

Turn to page 210 to find out what happened.

The Combination
(Issue 52)

During a West-Pac deployment, an incident occurred that questions the practice of ethics by two junior officers. These two officers circumvented security procedures by obtaining both of the combinations to a security container that was used to transport COMSEC (Communications Security) material.

Both officers obtained the second combination as a convenience for times when they required access to the material, or other items stored with the material, and a person to open the second lock was not around. This enabled each individual access to material that required two-person integrity. This was a clear violation of COMSEC procedures.

At a time when you are working in a communications center, you notice an officer opening a security container that was designated for opening by two officers.

What do you do?

The ethics involved are the safeguarding of classified material. The choices are supposed to be clear. On one side there are the rules and regulations that govern the use of COMSEC material; on the other, there may be the belief that as long as no one knows, it's okay to bend the rules now and then.

It is hard to believe that the officers involved did not know that what they had done was wrong because one of them was the new command security manager and had recently completed Communications Management Security School.

Memorizing both combinations was a deliberate act, not a chance happening because one of the officers had seen the other opening the second lock so many times. To memorize a combination, and use it, one has to make a conscious effort to do so, it doesn't happen by accident.

Some of the factors that contributed to this incident were the poor state of COMSEC education and the lack of refresher training. This led to an overall atmosphere of complacency with regard to COMSEC material. Thus, another consideration has to do with whether the officers should be held responsible if they had not received as much education and training as they should have at Navy schools.

It is known that neither of the officers who had traded combinations had ever been in trouble before and that they were hardworking individuals who spent more time on the job than most. There was never a hint or suspicion that either officer ever used security information for other than the purpose that was intended.

Turn to page 210 to find out what happened.

The Performer
(Issue 53)

A junior petty officer was part of a twenty-one person work center on a ship deployed to the western Pacific. The PO had a hard life growing up. Now on board ship, the PO was recognized as an outstanding performer, although he had problems getting along with fellow workers.

As a result of performing above and beyond peers on cruise, the PO was advanced by the command to the next higher pay grade. After this action the PO's performance started to decline.

Counseled by an 0-2 for indebtedness, lateness, and lack of interest in assignments, the PO went UA (unauthorized absence) in Australia. The PO was placed on report upon return to the ship and sent to Captain's Mast, awarded a fine, restriction, and reduction in rate (grade).

This was followed by more violations and further UA incidents.

What do you do?

There are two areas of consideration involved in this incident, first the junior petty officer, and second the balance of the twenty-one person work center, as well as the perception of the rest of the crew.

It is apparent that the PO had the capability to do well, but for some reason the motivation to do so had changed. Although repeatedly counseled, the PO did not change, and the rest of the ship was closely watching what would be done to this errant enlisted member of the crew.

Individuals are the key to the military service; although they all bring different backgrounds to their assignment, there is a need to require the uniform compliance to various rules. The 0-2 officer doing the counseling felt that the PO had to be treated like anyone else even though the PO had been advanced and had received other awards for superior performance.

The officer made sure the enlisted knew UCMJ regulations. Although the JO wanted to give the PO a few breaks because of past outstanding work, the JO felt that the PO was pushing the system too far.

The question is how much counseling is enough and how far could the JO let the PO's performance slide before it had an effect on the rest of the work center crew and the ship as a whole.

Turn to page 211 to find out what happened.

You are a brand-new Deputy Commander for Maintenance in a fighter wing in Europe. After you have been in your position for a few weeks, you uncover the fact that your midnight shift in job control has been submitting a daily report at 0300 to higher headquarters showing more aircraft in operationally ready status than actually are in that status at 0300.

When you question this practice you are told that this has been going on for a long time. This helps the wing commander look good to higher headquarters and, normally, between 0600 and 0700, the minimum number of operationally ready airplanes to maintain the wing at a fully operational ready status are, in fact, available for training (or combat) missions.

<u>What do you do?</u>

You recognize that while operational procedures are relatively constant throughout the worldwide sphere of Air Force operations, it may well be possible that individual variances are being made at local commands.

Your first step is to check all of the next lower echelons to see whether this late reporting has been engaged in throughout the command and for how long. You find out that this has been the standard operating procedure and further confirm with the Commander for Maintenance that he knows of this practice and the Wing Commander also knows what is going on.

While you would not have instituted such a policy yourself, you also realize that fighting the system at this point may well jeopardize your career by stirring up a lot of fuss over what appears to be a rather innocent disobeying of the rules. Further, when you discuss the matter with your boss, he indicates that it is best to leave the matter alone as operations have never been affected by the misreporting.

<u>Turn to page 213 to find out what happened</u>.

I would lay down my life for America, but I cannot trifle with my honor.

—Admiral John Paul Jones,
Letter to A. Livingson, 4 September 1777.

Off-Duty Employment
(Issue 55)

You are a lieutenant colonel and the Director, Personnel and Community Activities at a state side Army post. Your deputy, a major, has leased a building in the nearby community and opened an antique shop, which his wife operates. You know of this operation because your wife bought and sold several items there. You also know that the major is a conscientious, hardworking, and loyal officer.

Last night, with you in the audience, the Post Commander spoke to a group of local business and community leaders about contributions the post is making to the local community. During a question-and-answer period, a local antique dealer accused your deputy of hurting his business because of unfair competition.

The Post Commander received a letter several days later signed by two antique dealers alleging that the major attracts customers from the post by using his official position and contacts. It is further alleged that while on TDY trips, the major buys and sells antiques, and sometimes wears his uniform while carrying on transactions with customers.

What do you do?

You check with the base JAG officer and determine that it is legal for an officer to have an outside interest in a business, as long as it doesn't interfere with assigned military duties.

Notwithstanding the legality of what the major is doing, there is the question of the appearance of wrongdoing that is the cause of the complaint by the local antique dealers. The JAG officer points out that it would be improper if, in fact, the major is actually soliciting business and is wearing his uniform while carrying on transactions.

You are faced with the dilemma of what to do since the major is one of your hardest workers and is an inspiration to his subordinate troops. You call the major in and ask for his side of the story, and he lets you know that he needs the money for sending to sick parents. He knows of others who are involved in business, and he wonders why he is being singled out for special attention.

Turn to page 213 to find out what happened.

Grievance Hearing
(Issue 56)

A junior officer was asked by the unit's executive officer to make statements against the commanding officer during an article 138 grievance hearing. Prior to the beginning of the investigation, the CO had assembled his officers and asked for their loyalty and reminded them he would eventually find out who spoke against him.

The junior officer felt the CO (1) was: by far the worst he had ever served with; (2) fell short of many of those qualities he had learned a leader should possess and strive to exhibit; (3) was the contributing factor to low unit morale caused by his negative, unfriendly, and condescending treatment of unit members; and (4) his testifying would provide support to the XO.

On the other hand, the JO felt that the CO was technically proficient and always accomplished the unit's mission. In addition, he felt that testifying against the CO would: (1) be an act of disloyalty to the CO; (2) probably result in a less favorable fitness report from the CO; (3) possibly bring adverse attention to the unit; (4) potentially create an uncomfortable work environment since he risked having his statement shown to the CO and others; (5) possibly result in his being labeled an outcast (not trusted) by juniors, seniors, and peers. After all, the JO thought, maybe his analysis of perceptions of the CO was incorrect.

Not making a statement on behalf of the XO would provide the minimum risk to the JO's career.

What should the JO do?

If the JO chooses not to make a statement in support of the XO, three events may occur.

First, he would be faced with a tremendous amount of guilt: guilt for not doing what he thought was right; for letting down his country, the military, and his family; for not demonstrating the moral courage to stand up and be heard; and for taking a "careerist" approach to leadership and in meeting his responsibilities.

Second, he would be contributing to a bad situation. If enough support for the charges was not substantiated, the case could be lost and the CO could continue to perpetuate unethical behavior and conduct. Not only would the current unit suffer this lack of leadership, but the CO's future units would as well. His failure to testify would be an endorsement of the CO, who would conclude that his conduct was proper and could continue.

Third, he may be contributing to the demise of the XO. If the XO's allegations are correct, and those who could substantiate the charges fail to do so, the outcome could be that the allegations are found to be unsubstantiated. This could adversely affect the XO's career and reputation.

The junior officer is faced with a classic ethical dilemma: to decide to disavow loyalty to the CO and possibly to his branch of service or to choose the greater loyalty, that of loyalty to supporting the ethical conduct expected of a military officer.

Turn to page 214 to find out what happened.

No man can serve two masters; for either he will hate the one, and love the other; or else he will hold to one, and despise the other.

—*Bible, Matthew 6:24.*

Flying a Scheduled Mission
(Issue 57)

Assigned to fly a particular mission, two fighter aircraft were conducting air combat maneuvers (ACM) against each other. During a roll, the senior of the two aviators, who was also the second most senior aviator in the squadron, lost sight of his wingman.

As this senior pilot continued into a rolling pull-up, he attempted to regain visual contact with his wingman. When contact was regained, the senior pilot attempted to re-engage, despite being nose high and at a very slow air speed. Additionally, the senior pilot noticed his aircraft's wings rocking. He then attempted to recover from this in-flight condition. Although he recognized his situation, he was too low to effect a recovery; he ejected. The pilot landed safely while the aircraft was destroyed on impact. The flight data recorder, electronics, and tape were unrecoverable due to fire and impact damage.

A mishap review board determined that the ejection sequence was normal. The aircraft departed flight due to slow air speed, high nose attitude, and high angle of attack, with the stall warning signs disguised by a destabilizing configuration of external fuel tanks. The pilot took off in a flight configuration which exceeded the center of gravity for air combat maneuvering because it was known to aggravate high angle of attack hang-up situations and disguise stall warning. This particular situation was known to be evidenced by rocking of the wings and might aggravate a hang-up situation.

What went wrong?

The basic question in this situation has to do with who schedules a mission and does a pilot have the authority to change the mission once it has been scheduled by the commanding officer.

In this case the mishap pilot was an 0-5 known for his over-bearing, oppressive personality, while the mishap pilot's wingman was a young lieutenant with insufficient moral courage to stand up to his senior officer.

An investigation determined that the mishap pilot was not current in air combat maneuvering, as he had not flown for 18 days prior to the mishap. NATOPS requires flight within seven days in this particular aircraft.

It was further determined that the mishap pilot, as mission commander, briefed and flew an unauthorized flight since an air intercept flight had been scheduled on the squadron flight schedule as opposed to the air combat maneuvering flight that was actually flown.

Turn to page 214 to find out what happened.

The Thief
(Issue 58)

An officer was caught shoplifting at the base exchange, causing a good friend of the thief to wonder whether that person might also have been responsible for thefts from officers in the unit over the past two years. Items reported missing from individuals in the unit included credit cards, money, wallets, and other personal effects.

The good friend was, in fact, the officer's best buddy and a friend of the family as well.

What should the good friend do?

If the friend doesn't ask the thief about the other missing items, then it may be possible to retain the friendship, as well as regard for the individual, assuming this was a one-time transgression.

If the friend does ask the thief about items missing from other officers, that is in effect saying that the best friend is a long-time thief, not just someone who made a foolish mistake one day. By confronting the thief with such an accusation, it will also remove the friend as someone who might otherwise be called upon for help.

On the other hand, by not confronting the individual, all other officers in the unit remain under suspicion as having been the person who stole the missing items.

Turn to page 215 to find out what happened.

Every rascal is not a thief, but every thief is a rascal.

—Aristotle,
Rhetoric. Book ii, Chapter 24, Scene 5.

Humor
(Issue 59)

You are the executive officer at a remote command to which you reported almost two years ago. The command has been a fine organization to work with, and the job has been a challenging one, though you felt that the old CO was rather demanding. A new, less demanding CO recently reported on board, and you welcomed the change in leadership.

Recently, however, some events have significantly disturbed you. The new CO is easygoing and likeable but at times his humor can be slightly inappropriate and almost embarrassing. You've made note of several occasions when the CO has made rather overt statements to newly reporting female lieutenants and today your command master chief had a private conference with you about several female enlisted in the office indicating that they felt very uncomfortable working around the new CO.

The Command Master Chief was not specific about what made them "feel" uncomfortable; he simply felt obligated to mention it to you, as XO, because one of his top performers—a yeoman, first class—was rather disturbed about a recent incident that had occurred in the CO's office.

As XO, what are your responsibilities?

The XO's primary responsibility is to ensure mission accomplishment. In addition, the job involves facilitating harmonious working relations both up and down the chain-of-command.

There had been no written complaints of wrongdoing, and the XO thought that perhaps this matter did not need immediate attention. From personal experience he realized that comments can often be misinterpreted, and the women might have had a tendency to be oversensitive to issues concerning gender.

Turn to page 216 to find out what happened.

Everything is funny as long as it is happening to somebody else.

—Will Rogers,
The Illiterate Digest, Page 131.

Missile Test Firing
(Issue 60)

An important test firing of an air-to-air missile had been delayed a number of times and was now scheduled for launch on 30 September with a 1 October back-up date. The shot was funded by O&M,N one-year money that was to expire on 30 September.

On 27 September, a meeting was held to decide whether, if the shot didn't get off on the thirtieth, to shoot on 1 October anyway and backdate the range and telemetry costs.

The test was important and new money was not available in the next Fiscal Year. All the local players (Range Director and Test Director) were willing to go ahead with the backdating plan.

What should be done?

There was no natural constituent who didn't want the test to take place. The Navy testers, the missile's builder, and even the Range Directorate stood to gain something from the test.

The O&M,N money was meant for this test, so why turn it back for want of a single day's delay? The decision was made by two 0-4s, one 0-5, and two GS-13s to proceed on 1 October if necessary, and "adjust" the accounting.

Turn to page 217 to find out what happened.

God grant that men of principle shall be our principal men.

—Thomas Jefferson

Submarine Pictures
(Issue 61)

A Supply Corps food service officer (ensign) was on his first retrofit prior to cruise on an FBM submarine patrol. His CO needed 100 pictures of the submarine, which its submarine tender was to provide. This was a very hot issue for the CO, and the new ensign was eager to please.

The ensign approached the tender's Ship Superintendent who was responsible for all maintenance, repair, and photo requirements. The Ship Superintendent was quite pleasant, but he indicated that he didn't think that he could provide the number of pictures in accordance with the ensign's schedule. He added, however, that two bags of shrimp would undoubtedly expedite the process.

The Supply Corps ensign knew that it would be no trouble for him to get the shrimp—the crew probably wouldn't even miss it—and it was a small price to pay to keep his CO happy.

What do you do?

The ensign realized, as a very junior officer, that he should try to maintain low visibility and get the task accomplished without making waves. Further, he was positive that no one would ever know the shrimp were missing.

The ensign also had to consider that taking an ethical stand with the Ship's Superintendent could result in his refusing to provide the pictures and jeopardizing the maintenance and repair schedule.

In considering what to do, the ensign also had to figure out whether his CO would appreciate his standing on principle over two bags of shrimp, and whether the failure to get the pictures would in turn embarrass the CO with his seniors. Would the CO decide that the ensign was just too immature, by making an issue of what must have been a somewhat standard practice with the Ship Superintendent?

Turn to page 217 to find out what happened.

Communication
(Issue 62)

A strong lack of communication and distrust existed between an 0-3 and an immediate senior enlisted E-8. This realization made the chain-of-command difficult for subordinates to use. While the 0-3 was aware of the problem and actually often exacerbated already uneasy feelings between the two, no action was taken to ameliorate this tension.

The inaction of the 0-3 encouraged the E-8 to also do nothing to resolve the problem. The lack of communication between the senior enlisted and junior officer resulted in routine fiascoes and a breakdown in control.

The ethical climate lacked the element of leadership by example, which was required for this training command—as it is for all military units. You are the commanding officer of the unit and know what is going on and are concerned about the message that is being sent to officer candidates who are training with the unit.

What do you do?

Communication between individuals who work closely together is necessary and should be automatic. The need for the services to work with the minimum number of personnel needed to do the job is important because national defense resources are limited and there is a general need to maximize both the expenditure of dollars and the accomplishment of personnel.

Teamwork in the military is the key to all that is done; each member of the team is expected to know not only their own job but also to keep an eye out for others so that they may be helped when the need arises.

In the final analysis, ultimate responsibility for activity, or inactivity, as the case may be, rests with the CO. Trouble in an organization is generally considered to be from the top down as opposed to the bottom up. At every level of command, it is the responsibility of those senior in the chain-of-command to know what is going on below them and to take steps for improvement where necessary.

Although they probably didn't really know each other and didn't try to understand one another, the CO did determine that the 0-3 and the E-8 had feelings toward each other that bordered on hatred.

Turn to page 218 to find out what happened.

The Junior Officer
(Issue 63)

A JO is a new member of a 15-person aircrew. He is in charge of BOQ/BEQ reservations at the unit's TAD site. He makes necessary advance reservations and is confronted by senior and junior crew members who insist: "We don't stay on base—just in hotels in town." "We don't reserve ahead of time so that quarters are filled when we arrive." "The former JO did it the 'right' way, and other crews do it. It's an unwritten rule."

The advance-reservation practice directly affects the amount of dollars received by each crew member. The JO notices that the CO turns his head, he doesn't want to know, and seems to be saying that what the CO doesn't know won't hurt the command.

What would you do?

Per written guidelines, JO should make early BOQ/BEQ reservations to keep TAD cost and per diem cost low, as government quarters/messing would be available and rental cars would not be required.

By living up to the regulations, the JO would: (1) avoid compromising his personal pride; (2) ensure his future reputation as an honest officer characterized by integrity; (3) not undermine his ability to lead/discipline later, as he did not compromise his ethics; (4) accomplish the changing of the command/crew climate to one that is more ethical; and (5) experience personal satisfaction himself.

Insisting on exactly following the rules and continuing his practice of making advance reservations, however, means that the JO will be assured of: (1) a reputation as one who rocks the boat of both crews and the command; (2) reprisals by peers, seniors, and juniors; (3) winning this particular battle but "losing" the war; (4) costing everyone dollars; (5) making certain that no one would have a rental car to have fun in; and (6) making sure that the aircrew all had to stay in government quarters vs. a nice hotel.

The ethical course of action makes this JO stronger in the long run, personally. It may change the command climate by bringing out ethical behavior in others. It can definitely enhance this officer's reputation for years to come.

On the other hand, he risks being shunned by peers, juniors, and many seniors. The CO would probably be forced to adhere to ethical policies and would be foolish to enact recriminations with a poor FITREP, and probably would not do so. Actually, the CO may appreciate the command's cleaning up its act and view the JO as a leader.

Turn to page 219 to find out what happened.

Lack of Courage
(Issue 64)

An 0-3 had a commanding officer whose personal behavior had a negative impact not only on the wardroom, but also throughout the command. The CO had a history of failed marriages, womanizing, excessive drinking, and fraternization with both female enlisted and junior officers.

Although technically proficient, it was his personal behavior on deployment that caused him to be late or miss morning briefs that were the result of many early morning hours of work and effort by his personnel.

His fraternization with certain enlisted members of the command, as well as select junior officers, began to create a deep malaise that threatened to rip morale and camaraderie apart. In time, some of the other officers of the unit took on the example set by the CO. Those who did not participate felt particularly in the middle, for they had a loyalty to the skipper yet an obligation to their troops.

What should the 0-3 do?

Everyone in the Navy is a sailor, regardless of rank or time in service, and thus has an obligation to meet professional standards of performance and discipline in both their personal and professional lives. While the armed forces do not prohibit drinking, they do expect responsible behavior by their members.

Senior enlisted expect their officers to set an example for the troops. Failing to do so further complicates their job in maintaining discipline and ensuring that all evolutions are carried out in a timely and efficient manner.

As a direct result of the CO's behavior, respect for him waned, and discontent become rampant throughout the command. Disenchantment comes easily to a young sailor, even a junior officer, and the troops felt betrayed by the behavior of men they had previously held in high esteem.

The command previously had an enviable operational record, as well as having been deployed in support of wartime operations. All personnel felt that if the matter was reported, the ensuing headhunting and recriminations of a full-scale investigation would hurt the command more than what was occurring. At least that was the consensus of those in the middle, who were careful to avoid any actions that smacked of mutiny.

With every passing incident, the morale of the nonparticipants dropped. Officers who did not carouse felt their fitness reports would be negatively affected. Male enlisted felt threatened that their female counterparts were sexual liaisons for the men they swore to obey. Some officers who normally would have bridled their behavior, felt no compunction in mimicking many attitudes and actions of their leader—the CO.

As a commissioned officer, the 0-3 knew that the behavior of the others was a reflection on the entire officer corps. Powerless to rectify the situation and to restore the morale and confidence of the troops, the junior officer contemplated alternatives.

The 0-3 considered talking to the XO since the intervening department head was also involved, but wondered whether the XO would be too afraid about his career to act. Also taken into consideration was the fact that the CO was a very likable person who was incredibly dynamic and full of life.

Turn to page 219 to find out what happened.

The higher in rank you go the more people look to you to set examples.

—General Maxwell D. Taylor,
The Field Artillery Journal, January/February 1947.

LACK OF COURAGE

Extra Labor & Equipment
(Issue 65)

An 0-4 functioning as a Department Head at an overseas installation had supervisory responsibility for a labor and equipment division. This division had, among others, an automotive group who worked on government vehicles and a group of laborers who performed maintenance services, including care of the grounds.

The ethical climate established by both the commanding officer and executive officer was one of "look the other way," and did not involve oversight of the 0-4. There was a general feeling that being in an overseas environment required less attention to details.

What might go wrong?

There is an implication in this case that the rules of ethics might be different in the American armed forces when personnel serve overseas. This is, of course, fallacious; if anything, Americans should be on their best behavior when being viewed by other nationalities.

It is important to remember that standards of ethics and integrity vary from one culture and country to another, but American service personnel must always uphold the highest of standards. By the actions of our personnel our country is judged. There have been times during past deployments when service personnel have brought some shame on our country as they engaged in activities that were prohibited.

It is well to consider that leadership by example means that at whatever level an officer is, there will always be those who are subordinate and will take their guidance from the senior. The military runs on trust, and while a CO or XO may not be paying close attention to what goes on, that is no excuse to bring discredit upon one's country by taking advantage of this lack of close control. Even if the culture of the country allows "shady" dealings, by engaging in them the worst of messages is sent to those more junior than the perpetrator in our own military.

Turn to page 220 to find out what happened.

Personal Integrity
by
Commander Randy Large, U.S. Navy

A friend once described a sly technique for boiling a live frog. The problem that must be overcome when attempting this task is that the frog usually senses that the water is warming up to a dangerous level and jumps out of the pot before the water gets hot enough to boil and thus cook the frog.

My friend explained that first you must place the frog in a big pot of cold water so that it will feel comfortable. Next place the pot on a stove and ever so slowly turn up the heat, increasing the temperature one degree at a time. Let the frog become accustomed to the warm water before increasing the temperature. Then before reality sets in, the warm water will make the frog so weak that jumping out of the pot is no longer a possibility.

Once the frog is incapacitated, you can turn up the heat and warm the water as fast as you want. If you turn up the heat too fast, before the frog is weakened, the frog will notice the danger and jump out while still strong. The key to the effort is to make the frog lose the ability to detect the dangerousness of the situation.

This story has a strong parallel with personal integrity. Some individuals operate in a "gray area" and at times compromise their integrity until they lose the ability to tell right from wrong. They operate in the gray area until it becomes the norm and can't tell when they are losing their integrity.

The boiling frog story has a special meaning to me. I began my Naval Special Warfare career in the Underwater Demolition Teams, the Navy's "Frogmen." In the NSW teams, junior officers are placed in positions of responsibility normally filled by naval officers with far more experience and seniority. One trap that junior officers can fall into is adopting the modus operandi that "it's okay to cut corners on the small things" or "everyone does it," when, in fact, they are basing their decisions on what people say rather than what those people do.

The majority of naval officers do not cut corners or cheat the system. They work hard to make the system work. Most officers take for granted that people operate with integrity; it is assumed that naval officers have personal integrity beyond reproach. Consequently, there are severe, usually career ending penalties for being involved in unethical behavior.

Early in your career, there will probably be an instance when a peer or a junior will propose that you participate in a shady deal. Usually this scheme will involve only small benefit or personal gain, but your decision then will set the tone for your personal approach to the integrity issue.

As a newly commissioned officer, you will be placed in positions of increasing responsibility and be given special trust and confidence. You will be in positions where your actions will go unchecked. Your seniors assume that you will make decisions impartially, and in the best interests of the government. Just because you are not under a written honor code does not mean that integrity is not important. It is assumed that you live by it.

As you have learned in high school and college sports, the way you practice is usually the way you will perform in the game. The same applies with integrity. You cannot cheat the system or bend the rules on little things with the intent of making the correct decisions on the big deal, the high visibility project, or when you get to be more senior. By continually losing focus on the difference between right and wrong, that difference will become clouded. You will operate more in the gray area and, just like the frog, become more and more comfortable with it until you can no longer tell the difference between right and wrong. Making shady deals and operating in the gray will become a way of life. Then, sooner or later, you run a very high risk of making bad decisions.

A story that really shocked me was that of the respected 0-6 aviator whose retirement was delayed while the Inspector General investigated several false travel claims that had been submitted. As the officer-in-charge of a specific type of aircraft, he had free access to one of the planes, in which he would routinely fly to Washington, D.C. to conduct official business. He would use the opportunity to spend the night with a brother (which is perfectly legal), except that later a false hotel receipt was submitted along with false hotel expenses. The officer had been doing this for some time and had not been caught.

Finally, while reviewing a routine travel claim, an auditor noticed something unusual. The 0-6's retirement was suspended, pending the investigation, and the officer was threatened with courts-martial and possible loss of a military pension. All of this discredit and shame to an otherwise illustrious career was the result of this officer trying to secure a few extra dollars. He had lost the ability to tell right from wrong.

This story is not unique. You hear stories all the time about intelligent and successful people in responsible positions (military/civilian/private sector) who abuse the special trust and confidence that has been entrusted to them.

I recently completed a tour for a covert program wherein personal integrity was a prerequisite for my assignment. Once in the program, I was placed in a position of incredible trust and confidence. One of the most satisfying moments of my career is having been placed in this elite position. My lifelong personal integrity was put to the litmus test and I passed.

Occasionally, I realize I have inadvertently misled someone. When this happens I always go to the appropriate person and say: "I'm afraid I left you with the wrong impression. What I really should have said was . . ." or "I filled out this form erroneously. I need to change it." I find people are amazed at my efforts to go back and correct my previous actions. It really bolsters their confidence in me and my ability to do the right thing. It also provides me with a redefined focus as to what is right.

When planning a military evolution, some senior officers say that if you develop an overall plan and then worry about the little things later, the big things will take care of themselves. This philosophy will also work with personal integrity. I am highly sensitive to small, everyday personal integrity issues, and by being so I have found that I automatically make the correct decisions on the larger, more complex integrity ones.

One of my favorite posters hangs in a small room in the Pentagon. It pictures an American eagle and the caption states: "Eagles are not found in groups, they fly by themselves." So it is with integrity issues. Just because everyone does it, or we've always done it this way, doesn't mean it is correct. Sometimes you have to set your course, follow your convictions (regardless of what those around you choose), and fly by yourself.

The Competition
(Issue 66)

Tactical air training and competition often take on a life of their own, and "train like you will fight," and "war is not a fair game" are two common themes of the aviation community. It is often a matter of doing everything within your power to destroy a target (or win a competition).

Winning a competition depends a great deal on eliminating "First-Time-Itis," ensuring the aircraft systems are fully operational, and understanding the nature of the target.

Prior to an annual bombing derby, the squadron CO and operations officer of an A-6 crew launched on a functional check flight—which is an authorized evolution—to ensure the aircraft was ready for the competition flight.

How could they increase their chances of winning?

The ethical issue is gray. It is too easy to say that a win-at-all-costs attitude will cause a squadron to act unethically. In combat, however, an aircrew is expected to do everything possible to get to the target and return. Anything less than that is a foolish and an unacceptable goal.

In tactical training and competition, it is going to be up to the individual to determine how far a pilot is willing to go to win. The question is whether everything that might be justified in combat is also justified in training. For one thing, we don't try to kill our teammates during training; for another, we aren't quite as prepared to die in training as we are in combat.

The point, then, is that in training, winning is important, but it isn't everything.

Turn to page 221 to find out what happened.

Nobody can acquire honor by doing what is wrong.

—Thomas Jefferson

Fraternization
(Issue 67)

A junior officer was sent to a Safety Officer School for five weeks of temporary duty. A BOQ room was assigned for the length of the stay. At the same time, an enlisted person of the opposite sex was on leave nearby the school. They met by chance, and the JO was told details of a serious personal problem that had resulted in the enlisted's spouse forcing the enlisted out of their house that very afternoon.

What should the JO do?

While helping another service member is to be accomplished wherever and whenever possible, the conscientious officer needs to keep in mind military fraternization policies.

All personnel in the chain-of-command are concerned with what happens to their people. Here, it would be appropriate to counsel the enlisted to contact their supervisor, the home Command Master Chief, or the home Family Service Center about problems experienced.

Also to be considered is the distance from the home command. One must be careful about becoming the personal caretaker of the enlisted and becoming emotionally involved.

Turn to page 221 to find out what happened.

Am I my brother's keeper?

Old Testament, Genesis, iv, 9.

The Exam
(Issue 68)

You are an officer student at a service school and you want to take leave to go home for four days to attend your sister's Saturday wedding. Your grades, however, are not high enough to qualify you to meet normal standards for leave.

In addition, a big exam has been scheduled for two days after the wedding. This requires review of classified materials that cannot be taken from the base, and you have not completed studying for the exam.

What do you do?

Because your sister's wedding is important to you, it might be worth trying to obtain leave despite the probability that it would be turned down. Possibly, though not necessarily, your request for leave would be approved upon your assurance that you would improve your overall approach to studying. If you are turned down, however, you will have brought attention to yourself and you definitely will not be able to leave over the weekend.

You recognize that if you just take off, no one would probably miss you over the weekend. You could fill out study logs, stating that you studied all weekend long, and this falsification would not be discovered because the logs are not required to be countersigned. You might well rationalize that you are merely certifying that you were studying, but not that the studying had taken place at school, even though that is what would be presumed by your signed statement.

You feel that you deserve the time off and that although passing the exam is important, so is your sister's wedding.

Turn to page 222 to find out what happened.

Faults done by night will blush by day.

—Robert Herrick,
The Vision to Electra.

Inflated Readiness Levels
(Issue 69)

During flight school and subsequent assignment to a flying billet, officers are educated as to the requirements for attaining training proficiency. An 0-3, newly assigned to a squadron, found that more senior officers were inflating individual aircrew readiness levels so as to reflect high squadron readiness levels.

Both short-and-long term effects were felt at the aircrew squadron levels. The individual aircrews suffered from lack of adequate training and the squadron's performance levels were poor. The ethical climate of the command was such that the result was wholesale acceptance of the concept "that's the way it is."

What do you do?

This ethics issue deals with false reporting of aircrew readiness levels. Instead of bringing aircrews up to standards, effective training of aircrews was sacrificed by failure to perform numerous basic training evolutions, while recording that they had been accomplished. This was done to reflect high squadron readiness levels.

Senior and intermediate-level personnel further compounded the situation by accepting certain readiness levels regardless of completion of required events. This set an example that was followed by all in the command.

With their seniors accepting less-than-required results, junior officers succumbed to the seniors' influence. They followed their examples and allowed this situation to continue. It is noted that there were written instructions governing what the required training should have been.

Turn to page 223 to find out what happened.

The measure of life is not length, but honesty.

—John Lyly,
Euphues: Euphues and Eubulus.

Souvenirs
(Issue 70)

Officers and enlisted personnel were preparing to return from an extended overseas deployment. Some were married and many thought it would be nice to bring their spouses and friends gifts from the various countries they had visited.

After returning to the United States, the entire unit had a reunion party and presented their gifts to spouses and friends. All the gift recipients were extremely happy, as were the officers and enlisted personnel. They felt appreciated for their service to their country, and they valued the warm welcome they had received at home.

What could be wrong?

Members of the military are generally paid less per hour than their civilian counterparts. To some extent the Federal Government compensates its military by providing medical care, commissaries, retirement pay, and a few other amenities in recognition of the hardship and sacrifice of our fighting forces.

There are limits as to what can be brought in to the country, the same as with bringing produce in to California from another state. A law in California bans fresh produce from being brought in to the state, and state officials inspect all vehicles as they come across state lines.

Because traffic is so heavy entering the state, and it is so easy to hide small amounts of fruit within a motor vehicle, it is possible for someone to smuggle in fruit. This is both illegal and unethical because it endangers the fruit production of California and the nation, as well as avoids fines for violating the law.

It is also relatively easy for service personnel upon return from overseas assignments to hide items from custom agents.

Turn to page 223 to find out what happened.

The law is the last result of human wisdom acting upon human experience for the benefit of the public.

—Samuel Johnson,
Miscellanies, i, 223.

Video Harassment
(Issue 71)

You are a lieutenant stationed on board a destroyer deployed in the Mediterranean. You have been on board a little over two years and are currently nearing the end of your tour. Recently, the electronics division used a personal camcorder to record a skit that made fun of the only African-American in the division. You have seen the video and found it to be distasteful and in contradiction to current Navy policy on equal opportunity. You present the matter to the XO, who dismissed it as a matter not deserving disciplinary action.

What do you do?

One of the major questions to be faced is whether you have fulfilled your responsibility upon informing the executive officer. It is a question of whether it is the lieutenant's responsibility to ensure equal opportunity issues are made known to the CO, especially when there is concern that the XO is not handling them in an appropriate manner.

Turn to page 224 to find out what happened.

A prejudice is a vagrant opinion without visible means of support.

—Ambrose Bierce,
The Devil's Dictionary.

The Lone Ranger
(Issue 72)

In your particular command, junior mission commanders are asked to "pencil whip" crew qualifications so the squadron's readiness will look good to the wing.

While knowing this is wrong, you come to realize that others in the squadron who certify crew qualifications are falsifying records. Ironically, upon completion of their assignment, many of these same officers receive "prime" orders for their next assignment.

As a junior officer, you are aware that reduced defense budgets are certain to mean fewer command slots in the future. You are also cognizant that receiving good orders, such as advancing to a department head job in an operational squadron, will be crucial if your career is to advance properly.

<u>What do you do?</u>

Longstanding practices are established by senior officers, and a JO has to consider whether limited experience will cause a shortsighted approach to doing one's job.

It may well be that time and experience have dictated procedural modifications in the best interest of the command. Certainly, when one individual thinks that everyone else is out of step, there is a need to do a certain amount of introspection to determine whether a realistic view is being taken.

The armed forces are built on trust, and for one JO to suggest that a particular squadron is failing in that area may require specific knowledge. Experience also would help.

In making a decision, the JO has to consider the effect of his actions on the good of the squadron. Might it not be better to bide one's time until higher rank has been attained and then make policy changes to prevent the perceived fudging of data?

<u>Turn to page 225 to find out what happened</u>.

All, as they say, that glitters is not gold.

—Dryden,
The Hind and the Panther. Part ii, Line 215.

The Parking Pass
(Issue 73)

You are an officer who wants a better parking spot, which would cost $55 per year. You decide that it would be a great prank, rather than a fraud, if you could somehow produce your own pass, for which you didn't have to pay.

To accomplish this purpose you borrow a legitimate pass from a friend and make several copies. Through careful work you are able to make one that looks exactly like the real thing. You show your handiwork to friends, and they compliment you on what a skillful job you have done. They warn you, though, that it is a fraud, and if you are caught, you might receive a significant punishment.

In considering what to do, you figure that if you don't use it every day and only at random times, you will not be caught. But your friends still advise against it. You are sure, however, that none of them will turn you in.

What do you do?

In considering what to do, the officer realized that the right path was not to use the fake pass for legal parking. The officer was far less concerned with being caught than about how friends considered what had been done. This is one of the early steps in the development of a sense of ethics: that is, when the opinions of others about your actions mean something to you.

In making the pass, the officer hadn't considered how much trouble might arise from the prank. In thinking about what had been done, there was already the realization that some friends would think less of the officer because of what had been attempted.

Turn to page 226 to find out what happened.

The easiest person to deceive is one's self.

—Bulwer-Lytton,
The Disowned, Chapter 42.

Marijuana
(Issue 74)

Four junior officers attended a concert together on a Friday evening. After the concert they decided to have a night on the town. One of the JOs was short of cash and asked to be driven to a bank ATM machine.

Upon returning to the car, the JO, who had secured the funds, found that fellow officers were smoking and passing around a pipe filled with marijuana.

What do you do?

Does a JO turn in fellow officers for committing an illegal act? Does friendship dictate that what one learns about friends during their off-duty hours should not be held against them? Another approach, consistent with taking responsibility, might be to confront the three friends and tell them of the disapproval of their act.

Safety is another consideration. Maybe the action to be taken is different if the friends are using the illegal substance prior to a flight evolution, thus possibly endangering the aircrew and others.

What are the circumstances in which it is okay for a friend to end another's career? Also, what will the effect on the wardroom be if an officer turns in friends? Will it breed mutual suspicion and distrust among the officers?

Another approach would be to confront the individuals and allow the offending JOs an opportunity to turn themselves in.

Turn to page 227 to find out what happened.

Laws are not masters but servants, and he rules them who obeys them.

—Henry Ward Beecher,
Proverbs from Plymouth Pulpit: Political.

Designation
(Issue 75)

Regardless of opposition by some key personnel, a command allowed some of its personnel to achieve their final designation as PPC (Patrol Plane Commander) or PPTC (Patrol Plane Tactical Coordinator) even though they did not demonstrate the necessary ability to fulfill these duties effectively.

In all cases these individuals completed their training events, but their performances were below standard. One individual was even made an instructor.

By allowing this, the command did not have to confront the individuals with their sub-standard performance, thus taking the easy way out—the path of least resistance.

You are one of the pilots who was fully qualified.

What do you do?

Confidence in a command is important and is enhanced by a high number of personnel passing their qualification exams. This in turn helps these individuals pursue a military career. ·

On the other hand, the validity and prestige of the designations is lost if exams are made invalid by passing unqualified persons. Safety is compromised, and there is an overall negative effect on unit morale.

Actually, the command would still look good for refusing to relax standards rather than being concerned with numbers.

The big question is whether one makes waves to insist on the hard, right decision or assumes that one individual cannot change the world.

Turn to page 228 to find out what happened.

A failure is a man who has blundered, but is not able to cash in the experience.

—Elbert Hubbard,
Epigrams.

Keeping Everyone Happy
(Issue 76)

The XO of a CV wrote to BUPERS shortly after the enactment of the "Aviation Career Incentive Pay" (ACIP) program, which bases flight pay on longevity in a flying billet. He wanted to credit some officers' "accounts" who were filling billets different from that which their OCR indicated. He also mentioned the names of officers who were incorrectly shown in those same flying billets.

An adjustment was made to credit those officers who had filled flying billets, while removing credit improperly given to officers filling non-flying ones.

When the CO found out about the change, he notified his XO that he, the CO, was going to contact BUPERS and ask for credit to be given back to those who had been assigned it in addition to the newer members who were now eligible.

As the XO what do you do?

The responsibility of the CO is to study and understand the new law both from the standpoint as to why it was enacted and how it should be administered. The CO had the additional responsibility of adjusting to the new pay law that ACIP created, and accurately seeing to it that his and Washington's records reflected the status of personnel assigned to his command.

The responsibility of BUPERS is to enforce the rules, even though it breeds dissatisfaction among those whose longevity status changes due to their now occupying a non-flying billet.

Fair treatment of all personnel within an organization is one of the responsibilities of command. Those who receive flight pay, but are not entitled to it, destroy morale, as favoritism is being shown.
Angering a CV CO is a matter of concern as well.

Turn to page 228 to find out what happened.

There are no tricks in plain and simple faith.

—Shakespeare,
Julius Caesar, Act iv, Scene 2, Line 22.

The Complaint
(Issue 77)

A junior enlisted approached an officer who was not within the enlisted's chain-of-command, complaining of harassment by another officer in the unit of the same rank. The officer being charged was held in high regard at the command.

What do you do?

Should the officer receiving the complaint forward it up the chain-of-command, report it to the officer being complained about, or do nothing?

Forwarding the complaint may hurt someone's career and family life. Doing nothing might be considered appropriate since you are not in the individual's chain-of-command and can't be held responsible for everything that goes on in the military.

Since the accused officer is highly respected in the command, reporting the incident could possibly alienate other officers within the command. Thus, not doing anything will maintain a greater degree of harmony in the unit.

Talking to the accused officer may avoid problems with fellow officers, though it does not allow the chain-of-command to know about a possibly serious problem. Thus, it can be argued that in not reporting the alleged offense one is failing the chain.

Doing nothing won't solve the problem either. In matters such as these, one helpful rule to consider is the chain-of-loyalty: ship-shipmates-self. While loyalty to our shipmates is important, and we might hope to never have to resolve conflicts between shipmates, our first loyalty remains to the ship: that is, our organization, command, and country.

Turn to page 229 to find out what happened.

Many free countries have lost their liberty, and ours may lose hers; but if she shall, be it my proudest plume, not that I was the last to desert, but that I never deserted her.

—Abraham Lincoln,
Speech, Springfield, IL, December 1839.

(Issue 78)

During flight training a student was having considerable trouble with the syllabus, and had flown five unsatisfactory graded flights. This was two beyond the allowable limit.

While you are debriefing a flight flown with the CO, an instructor enters and tells the skipper that the aforementioned student was marginal on the latest flight, and that was after two refresher simulator training sessions.

The CO, who is concerned with graduating enough pilots, tells the instructor to give the student "anything but another down."

<u>What do you do</u>?

To be considered is the effect on other students, both those who complete the program and those who attrite and go on to other careers in the service.

Passing this student by repeatedly giving additional opportunities raises in the mind of others whether influence or favoritism might have an effect. (Also, the CO may be "setting up" the JO for a future aircraft accident due to nonproficiency.)

Since pilots generally work in teams, the passing of a less-than-qualified student casts a doubt in the minds of those who are called upon to risk their lives. It is important that pilots have total confidence that their wingman will be there when needed and be able to meet all evolutionary requirements.

Another concern is that those who were washed out after three failures might also have passed if given enough extra chances. In your consideration as to whether to say or do anything, does it matter that the problem might be handled in such a way that no one else would know what was done and thus the special treatment would not be discovered?

<u>Turn to page 230 to find out what happened</u>.

That which among men is called favor is the relaxing of strictness in time of need.

—Favorinus,
Fragments, No. 81.

Training
(Issue 79)

As a junior officer who has recently joined a unit, you've been assigned responsibility as the training officer. You are well briefed as to the importance of your duties and the concept that "we fight as we have trained."

You are pleased to note, upon inspection of unit training records, that all departments and divisions of the command are training on a weekly basis and properly completing the Training Critique Form.

About a week after your arrival you decide that your position also requires you to observe some of the training so that suggestions can be made for its improvement, if that seems necessary. You watch one of the teams training and notice that they haven't gone through all of the evolutions required by the training plan. You wonder about the incomplete training but assume that the unit will probably complete the missing portions within a few days.

Upon inspection of the Training Critique Form, however, you realize that the unit has taken credit for having completed all of the required evolutions when, by your personal knowledge, you know that was not the case.

What do you do?

Training is done to enhance the crew's knowledge. You realize that the unit is probably less well trained than the completed reports are indicating to higher authority. What can happen with any documentation scheme is that completion of the form becomes the objective rather than completing the training. This type of thinking leads to what is sometimes referred to as "gundecking" and the mistaken principle that "training well documented is training well done."

You recognize that first training must be accomplished as prescribed and then, only after the first step is completed, should the critique form be completed. You understand that incomplete training documented as completed leads to a breakdown of the training process. In turn, this leads to a degradation of mission readiness and a general breakdown of unit cohesion.

As you look into the matter you find that there are a few other units that are also "gundecking" their training records. They are led by officers who have been with the command longer than you and are senior to you.

If you ride with the system you'll eventually be able to move on to another job. But if you make waves you may well find your career negatively affected by comments and actions taken by the other officers.

Turn to page 231 to find out what happened.

Lost Documents
(Issue 80)

An officer could not account for some classified documents that had been signed for. The officer actually believed the material had been destroyed, but the record of destruction had been lost.

Rather than admit that control of this material had been lost, the officer attempted to reproduce the destruction record. By reproducing this record, the officer would gain the needed receipt for the material believed to be destroyed.

As two signatures are needed to verify destruction, the officer attempted to solicit another individual to sign—knowing that the other person did not participate in the assumed destruction. The individual asked was a longtime friend and also an officer.

You are the friend. What do you do?

Reproducing this record is not an ethical choice because signatures verify that the material was destroyed by the individuals present at the time of destruction.

The friend who was asked was absolutely positive that the officer must have destroyed the material because it could not be located, and thought that the only possible explanation was that the receipt had been lost.

Although possibly good intentions were meant, as the individual in question honestly believed that the material was destroyed, what was being considered was an attempt to compromise someone else's integrity by asking them to falsify destruction for the sake of continuity of paperwork.

If subsequent to this falsification the material had turned up not destroyed, the officer's actions would have resulted in the complete loss of documentation control and the commission of a serious illegal activity that involved both officers.

On the other hand, if the officer came forward and admitted losing document control, there would be an investigation with resultant negative effect on the officer's career and possible legal action being taken against the officer. As time to resolve this dilemma was short, the officer felt that a quick decision had to be made.

Turn to page 232 to find out what happened.

Cowardice
(Issue 81)

The squadron XO was intimately involved with a subordinate officer in the squadron. Most of the squadron were familiar with what was going on and disapproved of the XO taking advantage of rank and position held within the command.

You are a junior officer in the squadron and start to notice that morale and efficiency seem to be going downhill.

What do you do?

In considering talking to the XO about what you consider unethical and unacceptable behavior, you consider the reputation of the XO as someone who is vindictive and who might unhesitatingly ruin your career if you speak out.

On the other hand, you realize that it is the right thing to do and consider speaking with the XO when the latter doesn't seem to be too busy. Further thought makes you realize that you would feel good for two seconds—until the hammer fell.

After discussing the matter with other members of the squadron, you come to the conclusion that the chances of a JO surviving the situation are virtually zero, yet you realize that something has to be done to lessen the unit's morale decline.

Turn to page 233 to find out what happened.

Duty-Honor-Country. Those three hallowed words reverently dictate what you ought to be, what you can be, what you will be. They are your rallying points: to build courage when courage seems to fail; to regain faith when there seems to be little cause for faith; to create hope when hope becomes forlorn.

—General Douglas MacArthur,
Address to U.S. Military Academy cadets and graduates,
12 May 1962.

The Munitions Case
(Issue 82)

During the Iran/Iraq War, an American governmental agency pressured a military officer to modify his recommendation that a particular munitions package not be delivered to Iraq. The officer believed that our country's providing the munitions package would result in Iraq's aircraft having the same capability as U. S. aircraft!

Pressure increased as the governmental agency pressured the officer's boss to have the officer change his written recommendation. The officer's boss made it clear to the officer that he, the junior officer, did not know all the facts and that he was acting on a principle that didn't even apply in this case.

What should the officer do?

On the one hand, officers will often find that they are directed to carry out orders they may not fully understand. On the other hand, by reason of education, training, and trust placed in them, officers are expected to have the intuition, common sense, and knowledge to recognize when orders may either be illegal or ethically inappropriate.

When an officer is in doubt, questions should be asked for clarification. If an officer's first reaction is that something improper is being proposed, it would be appropriate to try and prove the boss right. What is really wanted is truth, not necessarily something that supports the junior officer's concept of the military.

If, in trying to prove that the boss is right, it turns out that the boss seems to be wrong, then that latter determination should be discussed with one's senior, and an attempt at resolution pursued.

At times, officers will be faced with a decision that may require more knowledge and experience than they have. At such times they have—in addition to their senior—the base judge advocate, the chaplain, and their peers to discuss the matter with. Difficult decisions should always be talked over with others to increase the breadth and scope of thought.

Turn to page 234 to find out what happened.

THE MUNITIONS CASE

Trust: The Cornerstone of Ethical Leadership
by
Captain Gary E. Brown, USMC

(Editor's note: The following article is adapted from the one that won the 1992 CG MCCDC Leadership Writing Award. It appeared in the July 1992 issue of Marine Corps Gazette.)

All officers are placed in a position to influence those junior to them. How an officer does this in an age of declining moral standards is of utmost importance.

The Armed Forces of the United States has always been a reservoir of character—people who can be trusted. This attribute is fortunate, considering editorialist George Will's assertion that:

"...never before in this nation's experience have the values and expectations in society been more at variance with the values and expectations that are indispensable to a military establishment."

Americans, especially young Americans, are increasingly forsaking moral decency and civic duty to pursue self-gratification. The symptoms are distressing. Children kill children for their tennis shoes or "just to see what it is like." The average age for first-time drug abuse is 13 years old, and homicide is the leading cause of death in the 15- to 19-year-old minority youth group. Senator Dan Coats (R-IN) has observed that:

"Many Americans are no longer outraged by news of . . . ethical lapse. Convicted felons are no longer outcasts. They are celebrities. They are invited to elite parties. They write best sellers."

I believe that such attitudes, events, and statistics, combined with what Senator Coats called a "spectacular rise in all forms of crime, family abandonment, child neglect, suicide, wide-spread adoption of destructive behavior, and an exponential growth of drug and alcohol abuse," have caused an atmosphere of distrust to descend upon our country. The prognosis for improvement is poor because distrust prevents people from working together for the common good. I have noticed many of our newest E-1s displaying characteristics of the society from which they were recruited. Because of this observation, I have made trust the cornerstone of my leadership philosophy.

Two Traits

I believe there are two character traits a commander must foster in a unit before its members can trust each other without reservation. These traits are moral courage and respect for others.

Moral courage is the more complex of these traits. It is the reasoned choice to "do the right thing" despite personal consequences or pressures to do otherwise. Moral courage promotes trust throughout a unit by instilling in each individual the moral imperative to act in the best interest of the unit regardless of the personal costs. When service personnel can depend on each other to do the right thing without supervision, they can give themselves completely to the team's objective—preparing to prevail in time of peace or war.

I have identified three methods of fostering moral courage. First, a leader must ensure that all hands understand that right and wrong are absolutes. This concept may prove confusing to many new recruits. Our country has seen, according to Senator Coats, militant relativism that dictates that it is impossible to prefer one value above another, since all conceptions of . . . good are equally subjective. Many parents take exception to those who presume to teach morality to their children, even though they may find it inconvenient to fulfill this parental obligation themselves. As a result, many school districts have adopted programs that essentially say, "There is no right and wrong. We are going to throw out all these values and let children pick and choose between them."

It is time to take a stand on what is right and what is wrong. Military leaders, at all levels, are in a unique position to take a stand. Presently, some officers recoil from the idea of imposing a sense of morality on their subordinates. They feel comfortable forcing their troops to conform to the moral standards set by the Uniform Code of Military Justice and service orders, but there is a general feeling that imposing a personal sense of morality on one's subordinates is the highest form of arrogance. Something has gone terribly wrong if officers do not have faith in, and equate their standards with, general standards of conduct and, more fundamentally, with traditional altruistic American values. Leaders must have the courage to embrace these values as the essence of morality and the measure of character.

Leaders must recognize that young men and women may not possess traditional American values when they enter the Armed Forces.

As a company executive officer, I have been faced with a noncommissioned officer who did not realize that lying is wrong. As a staff platoon commander at The Basic School, I have also had to explain to a roomful of O-1s that killing a prisoner of war is wrong despite any situational twist. Leaders must be prepared for the challenge of developing "good people" as well as good warriors. Sir John Winthrop Hackett put it this way:

"What the bad man cannot be is a good sailor, or soldier, or airman. Military institutions thus form a repository of moral resources that should always be a source of strength within the state . . . the highest service of the military to the state may well lie in the moral sphere."

The second method of fostering moral courage is group leadership discussions. These discussions can be used to establish a common understanding of acceptable behavior. They provide an opportunity for the leader to communicate commitment to traditional American values and to encourage subordinates to exercise moral courage in defense of these values. If leaders are to develop a bond of mutual trust within their units, they must focus their authority and energy on the moral education of their troops. If you do not agree with this statement, ask yourself this question: "Can you trust someone you think is immoral?"

Finally, the commander must set the example. Moral courage must start at the top. Most officers have known a leader who made decisions based on selfish considerations instead of unit welfare. This form of betrayal stifles moral courage and removes the bond of trust in a unit. Conversely, I know of a company commander who displayed moral courage when reporting safety hazards in a newly renovated barracks to the base fire marshal after unsuccessfully protesting the impending move of troops into these barracks. The barracks was condemned, and my commanding officer was in an uncomfortable position with seniors, but the safety of the troops was ensured. This incident raised the level of trust in our unit and encouraged all hands to display moral courage.

Mutual Respect

While moral courage is a more complex concept than that of respect for others, both are equally vital to the establishment of trust. The ability to respect others requires one to recognize that every person is a unique human being with the potential to contribute to the improvement of society. It requires service personnel to look past different customs, languages, and economic classes to uncover each person's hidden attributes. Mutual respect promotes trust by removing the fear of unjust treatment, irrational prejudice, and the threat of physical assault. Some service personnel have been in units that have had racial incidents, or in units where there was overt denigration of military personnel both up and down the rank structure. Still others have been in units where leaders denied the professional and social worth of their troops by insulating themselves from their subordinates. These conditions indicate a lack of respect among the members of a unit and invariably lead to an atmosphere of distrust. The promotion of mutual respect will prevent these conditions from developing.

There are three ways to promote mutual respect in a unit. First, set the example by avoiding sarcasm and adopting a teacher/scholar approach to leadership. Second, prevent the formation of cliques within a unit while remaining sensitive to the pride service personnel have in their ethnic heritages. Unit assignments, training programs, and athletic events can be used to discourage cliques. Finally, seek the opinions of your subordinates and *listen* to what they have to say. It is all too common to see leaders go through the motions of soliciting the opinions of their subordinates without listening to what they say. These leaders create cynical subordinates who believe senior officers are not interested in their welfare. As Erwin Rommel said: "The ordinary soldier has a surprisingly good nose for what is true and what is false." Teaching troops to respect their fellow human beings can be difficult, but the advantages are well worth the effort.

Fostering the traits I have discussed will ensure that the Armed Forces continues to provide our nation with people of character and high moral standards. Each member of the Armed Forces must understand that the standards set by the services have utility outside of the military. Our standards are grounded on traditional American values. Our troops must be able to return to their neighborhoods and set the example for a generation in jeopardy. Until character building regains its preeminence as an American social priority, leaders must accept their moral obligations to send each of their troops into combat, peacekeeping, humanitarian aide, or back to society as better human beings—as citizens who can be trusted to do the right thing.

Confidential Information
(Issue 83)

An officer with a need to know was entrusted with confidential information about personnel in the command. By chance another officer in the unit overheard the entrusted officer repeating tidbits of information to several others at a party at the Officers' Club.

By the nature of the information it was apparent that the officer should not have disclosed what he had spoken about. The officer who overheard was junior to the one who was loose lipped, and by nature of the latter's position, would have the next assignment to be affected by the relationship between the two.

What should the junior officer do?

The concept of "need to know" applies to all information held by officers. In effect, it says that what you know may only be divulged to those who, by nature of the position and requirements of their job, have a need to know what you know.

This includes security information, of course. Secret information may not be disclosed to another individual, even if that person holds a "secret" clearance, unless they have a legitimate need to know certain information in order to be able to perform their assigned duties.

In the course of everyday working, we learn certain things of a personal nature about others. The concept of trust implies that what we learn, if it in no way affects the job the person is doing, should not be repeated to third parties, except in unusual circumstances-including criminal and self-destructive behavior. If, on the other hand, we feel that the information might affect the person's performance, then we have a military obligation to make the information known to the chain-of-command for their determination of what, if anything, should be done.

In this case the offending officer was the personnel officer of the unit and thus was entrusted with personal information. The question is whether the officer who overheard should: (1) ignore the situation since more senior officers had been at the Officer's Club and overheard what was said; (2) challenge the personnel officer as to how the job was being done—thus affecting the future of the junior officer, or (3) report the matter to the chain-of-command and risk adversely affecting the personnel officer if an investigation showed that the junior officer misunderstood what was said. The junior officer could thus look foolish jeopardizing future assignments.

Turn to page 234 to find out what happened.

A Friend?
(Issue 84)

The rule for pilots is that they should not drink within twelve hours of flying. You are the friend of a pilot who has just flown, yet had a few drinks at a party held eight hours previously.

You've known the pilot for many years and both of you know the rules that pertain to "from bottle to throttle."

What do you do?

While it is legally the right thing to report your friend—you realize that the rule was established based on extensive experience with aviation mishaps—you are torn between friendship and doing what you know to be ethically right.

You realize that if you report the incident, it will adversely affect the career of your friend. Further, you also know that the safety of others, as well as property, may be at stake.

On the other hand, you would like your friend to cover for you if someday you do something wrong, and since you know your friend knows the rules, you don't feel it is your job to play informer in this instance.

One of the possibilities is that you might counsel your friend on the risky violation of flight rules and point out that other lives were unnecessarily risked because your friend would not take himself off the flight schedule—something that would not have hurt his career.

Turn to page 235 to find out what happened.

To desire the same things and to reject the same things, constitutes true friendship.

—Sallust,
Catilina. Chapter 20, Section 4.

The Missing Item
(Issue 85)

A junior officer was preparing for an upcoming inspection. One item on the inspection checklist could not be located—an obscure spare part for an essentially discontinued piece of equipment.

A search of all spaces did not turn up the missing part, with supply reporting a shipping time of one year or greater. If the part could not be located, the JO felt it would be an admission to the CO of the JO's inability to accomplish even the simplest of tasks and missions.

What do you do?

It is important that JOs realize that their seniors were once JOs themselves. A JO should not jump to conclusions as to how a senior might react in finding out that a subordinate was unable to solve a particular problem.

When all legitimate avenues have been explored in an attempt to accomplish a mission, the subordinate should then go to the senior and advise what has been attempted and display the results. At this point the senior will take charge and either come up with a workable plan or change the mission.

In any case, it is a rare senior who will hold a subordinate responsible for failing to complete a task when the junior has given the senior notification of the difficulty in sufficient time to allow the senior to work a solution or change the objective.

After mentally exhausting all possible avenues, the JO should consult others, including the senior enlisted (who, incidentally, have usually been in the service longer than the JO). Their experience and expertise may suggest a solution the officer had not previously thought of.

Turn to page 236 to find out what happened.

I seek the truth, whereby no man was ever harmed.

—Marcus Aurelius,
Meditations, Book vi, Scene 21.

To Fail Oneself
(Issue 86)

You were an officer candidate who worked hard to develop both academic knowledge and professional skills. You were accepted into the Nuclear Power Program, and now that you have been commissioned, you have been asked to answer a few administrative questions before you go to your first submarine.

In your earlier academic schooling you did smoke pot on two occasions, and the form you have to fill out upon completing nuclear power schooling asks you to indicate whether you have ever used marijuana. You are very sure that if you say no you will be able to continue with your career. If you admit to smoking pot, it might result in punishment or the end of your career.

What do you do?

The reader might want to consult the article written by Admiral Arleigh Burke that appears in Appendix A for some insights into approaching the subject of integrity. The opening section is particularly applicable.

One of the many lessons to be learned in life is that one can never go back and retrace one's steps. *The past, even though we are the only ones who know it, is with us forever.* While a junior officer has difficulty imagining being 40, and 50 doesn't exist, and 60 is an age at when you will be in the ground, the reality of life due to medical developments is that many junior officers will live to at least 90!

If nothing is said, the officer may be able to continue with a career, but even if four-star status is achieved the officer will have thirty to forty years to live with himself after retirement. Being an officer is something to be proud of, but if you have a "secret" in your past that clouds your career, you won't be able to forget it, and that will dim the accomplishments of your life in your eyes.

If the officer owns up to the mistake, the consequences may be military career ending but will not mean the end of a successful life. Many industry and government executives mistakenly smoked pot in their youth but even their admission has not stopped them from holding some of the highest positions in our society. The fact that they have owned up to what they did removes from them a tremendous burden of guilt for the rest of their lives.

Turn to page 237 to find out what happened.

Training
(Issue 87)

A fellow officer who worked in the Training Department would routinely add a certain percentage of hours to the command's required report to improve the unit's standing among other units. The unit consequently stood out as better than they actually were.

This individual figured the better the numbers submitted for the report, the better the chances of the unit receiving recognition in the form of an award in that particular area, for achieving a standard of performance higher than the other units.

You, a JO, have just been assigned to take over the position occupied by the aforementioned fellow officer.

What do you do?

You consider that even if you don't continue the practice of inflating numbers, your unit might win the prize.

You know the reporting officer in the second-place unit, and are absolutely positive that they report the numbers correctly. If you continue the improper reporting practice it is likely that your unit will win, and you know all members of your command are now working extremely hard to stay on top and win the award.

When you took over your position, no one said anything about fudging the figures, but the climate within the command was highly competitive and the CO strived to excel in every area. Awards of any type definitely served as outside recognition for the unit's hard work. The command pursued many such awards to establish its image, or perception, as the best unit around.

Since the unit has been operating well you realize that if you don't continue to report inflated marks, the entire command's self-confidence will be affected. A possible subsequent investigation of what went wrong would hurt not only the other officer but the CO as well.

As you consider what to do, it comes to your attention that several other units are also falsifying their data. Therefore, it is possible that your unit deserves to be first in any case. Upon further reflection you realize that the officer you relieved was not actually trying to please anyone; just thinking that since everyone was doing it, why not also do it?

Turn to page 238 to find out what happened.

Travel Claim
(Issue 88)

You are an officer assigned to travel to a distant city on official business. The city is also considered a vacation spot, so you think it would be nice to take your spouse along.

You know that government reimbursement can only be made for your travel, but you don't have enough money saved to pay for your spouse's transportation.

<u>What do you do?</u>

During a career of service, no matter how long or short, an officer will always be able to think of a variety of approaches to solving a problem. The challenge is not coming up with a means to achieving the solution to a problem. Rather it is how can a solution be accomplished in a legal and ethical manner that will not send a negative message to others and will set an example of how future operations should be conducted.

If it is important enough for the spouse to fly along—and there will, in fact, be time for them to take liberty together—then maybe it is important enough to apply for a loan from a credit union or simply charge the trip to a credit card and then pay for the trip over the ensuing months.

Officers are expected to be not only good problem solvers but problem preventers as well. It is probable that this is not the last trip that the officer will be required to make, so it might make sense to start saving for the next opportunity and to express regrets to the spouse that the officer will be going alone this time.

Turn to page 239 to find out what happened.

The measure of a man's real character is what he would do if he knew he never would be found out.

—Lord Thomas Babington Macaulay

TRAVEL CLAIM

Use It Or Lose It
(Issue 89)

In addition to regular flight duties, an 0-3 was assigned to an overseas base as the squadron's assistant officer-in-charge. When the squadron deployed to aid a friendly nation in support of American interests in the area, the local government agreed to provide free fuel to U.S. military aircraft as a sign of their willingness to contribute to the overall United Nations effort. This was an above-board legal and ethical practice arranged between the U.S. State Department and the friendly nation.

As background information, it is noted that a squadron is authorized x dollars per quarter to conduct operations, and is required to spend down to $0 without going over in any quarter.

In general, the non-spending of all one's fuel allocation is an indication that one, in fact, can operate with less and thus will be funded for less in the future. The issue centers around taking free fuel, thus saving the American taxpayer money, while in so doing cutting future fuel allocations at a time when you no longer have access to the free fuel for your other overseas base operations.

What do you do?

Based on estimated costs-per-hour (CPH), funding dollars are translated into flight hours. For example: if authorized $491,400, with a CPH of $756, that would mean 650 hours of flight could be scheduled ($491,400 divided by $756). In this instance, there simply were not enough hours in the day for the planes to burn up the total allocation for the entire squadron, because of the free fuel that some of the planes were receiving.

The OIC tried to reach an understanding with higher headquarters to allow the squadron to take free gas, in accordance with American negotiated policy, while at the same time avoiding future cutbacks in allocated fuel resources. But, the OIC was unsuccessful, and was prepared to tell the crew in the friendly nation to stop taking free gas and fly their missions on American fuel.

At this point the assistant OIC pointed out to the OIC that if the free gas were not taken, someone might well call the fraud, waste, and abuse hotline because it seemed absurd to turn away free money (fuel) because of a management problem that should have been taken care of at theater level by reprogramming some of the flight hour money to other squadrons who needed it. Then if or when the free gas situation ended, the squadron's allocation would be continued as if it had, in fact used up all of its normal gas allocation.

This concept of spreading the wealth can be hindered at each command level because of the fear of losing level funding in next year's authorization. Management of funds, in this case, was further complicated by only allocating funds in quarterly increments and not allowing any funds to be carried forward into the next quarter. One possible solution is to allow a carry forward through the first three quarters, with floors established greater than zero. Then, in the fourth quarter, when circumstances have resulted in a squadron having excess funds, reprogram that money to those squadrons that need it without penalty. If it is determined that poor management was the cause of excess funding, then fire the manager, but don't jeopardize the mission of the command by allocating less funding next year.

Turn to page 240 to find out what happened.

Good riding at two anchors, men have told, for if one fail, the tother may hold.

—John Heywood,
Proverbs, Part ii, Chapter 9.

The Accomplice
(Issue 90)

You are an 0-3 fleet squadron senior landing signal officer and pilot training officer. Your CO believes that pilots who are aggressive, competent, intelligent, and spend most of their time being concerned about aviation are most likely to become career aviators.

One of the command's junior pilots has not done well on carrier landings and is not extremely aggressive in the performance of ground assignments. You feel this pilot is slightly below average as a pilot and officer. The pilot has started to show the signs of a fatigued aviator who brings problems to work, including new home, new spouse, and predeployment concerns. This stressload has begun to manifest itself in flawed flying performance.

You feel this pilot can be saved if timely help is provided. The CO feels that additional pressure at work will serve to increase the pilot's stressload and therefore result in the pilot's ultimate removal or withdrawal from aviation duties. The CO asks you to collect data and prepare documentation that will permit removal of the pilot from flying status so that another pilot may be brought into the unit and be in place by deployment time.

What do you do?

As the LSO you are in a position to block the CO's wishes. Furthermore, the CO respects your opinion enough that if you opine that additional training versus dismissal may prove a better option, the CO is likely to concur and retain the aviator.

You recognize that the pilot's performance is below average and you doubt that better than average will ever be attained. You feel that standards are in place to defeat average performance, although average is acceptable. In your opinion this pilot is worth millions of dollars to the Navy but does not meet the CO's standard as to what constitutes a career aviator.

The CO increased the workload on the pilot, who slowly began to fall apart. A Field Evaluation Naval Aviation Board was convened and the board's composition, chosen by the CO, subscribed to the thinking of the CO. The CO chose you to sit on the board, you feel, because of the ability of the other board members to influence you.

Turn to page 241 to find out what happened.

The Friend
(Issue 91)

You are a single officer and long-term friend of a junior officer whom you've known from earlier tours. The JO comes to you to discuss marital problems. After talking to the JO you agree, as a friend, to also talk to the JO's spouse on a one-on-one basis.

In approaching the one-on-one meeting you recognize how attractive, safe, and aggressive the spouse might be if given any encouragement. During the talk the JO's spouse comes on in an extremely strong sexual fashion.

What do you do?

Earlier tours shared by you and the JO fostered a relationship of trust and confidence that allowed you as the senior to keep things at arm's length.

Although the spouse's attitude and confidence that the act of intimacy would help all involved, you realize that even a one-night stand, if discovered, would be the kiss of death to an otherwise successful career. On the other hand, you do recognize some honest feelings toward the JO's spouse. You even consider helping the spouse to get a divorce so you can realize earlier desires.

You feel, though, that the trust and confidence previously developed with the JO is important to maintain, as well as the general tradition of helping a military family survive.

Turn to page 242 to find out what happened.

Something between a hindrance and a help.

—Wordsworth,
Michael, Line 189.

Cheat
(Issue 92)

A newly commissioned 0-1 reported to a first duty station and was a solid performer, full of esprit de corps. The 0-1 rapidly finished qualifications for promotion eligibility to 0-2. Single at the time of commissioning, the 0-1 was engaged to a civilian within the first year of active duty and both pursued graduate degrees at a nearby university.

Upon promotion to 0-2, the officer received an on-base transfer and was married. The graduate courses continued. When it came time to submit a thesis, the officer agonized over the expense of reproducing the thesis proposals and drafts for thesis board members. The agonizing was likely the result of being brought up in a frugal household. There was a government duplicating machine at the office, and although the 0-2 had recently heard the command legal officer speak on DOD standards of conduct and conflicts of interest, the officer reasoned that thesis reproduction could be done on the office copier during working hours. After all, the officer reasoned, the service encourages continued schooling for its officers.

Since the spouse was enrolled in a similar graduate program, the 0-2 wondered if it wouldn't be consistent with the military's policy of taking care of its service families to copy the spouse's thesis documents as well. The 0-2 also wondered whether this wouldn't be a good example for the enlisted in the office who would be impressed with the educational self-improvement example set by the officer and spouse.

What should the officer do?

While as officers we work long hours and are on call twenty-four hours per day, we are not entitled to all government resources, even if doing so will save personal funds.

There will be times when decisions about what is ethical or not are made in the context of the general ethical climate of the command. But that may be a big mistake if there is an indifferent attitude within the organization. Officers are generally held to a strict standard of conduct, and the fact that others might not be meeting that standard is not an acceptable excuse for sinking to a lower level.

To what extent should the 0-2 try to please seniors in the command versus personal commitments? On the one, officers should always try to please their senior if that means that they try to do their very best to accomplish assignments by the senior. On the other hand, this striving for excellence assumes the task being pursued is legal and ethical.

Turn to page 243 to find out what happened.

The Flight Jacket
(Issue 93)

During their first schooling, aviators are issued leather flight jackets that should last their flying careers. Upon arrival at their squadron they are issued an additional flight jacket—made of nylon treated with NOMEX, a flame retardant—designed to last about three years.

As long as aviators have a flying status, they keep the NOMEX jacket and, if it has not worn out, take it with them to their next flying billet. Once they enter a billet that is not a flying status, they are supposed to return the NOMEX jacket to supply.

In time, an aviator received orders to go to a non-flying billet. The aviator heard from a friend that if the NOMEX jacket was reported as lost, an aviator could keep the jacket and only have to pay a modest replacement cost to supply.

The aviator had become accustomed to wearing the NOMEX jacket, which fit very well, and wondered whether it should be reported as lost. Reasoning that by paying the government and then using the jacket again when returning to flying status (without further cost to the government), everyone might be best served if the NOMEX was reported as missing.

What should the pilot do?

The aviator really wanted the NOMEX, but was uneasy about reporting the jacket lost when in fact it was not. On the one hand, if supply were told that the officer just wanted the NOMEX, they might say no. If the jacket were merely declared lost, and paid for, it wouldn't be overt stealing. One must remember, however, that an officer is trusted to always tell the truth.

In thinking about the matter the officer realized that no one would know of the compromise of integrity if the NOMEX jacket were kept. The action, at most, might result in a guilty conscience. By returning the jacket to supply, the officer would not be recognized for doing the right thing. The officer was cognizant, though, that returning the NOMEX to supply would provide psychic income for having done the right thing.

Turn to page 244 to find out what happened.

The Investigation
(Issue 94)

A junior officer was accused of numerous liaisons with enlisted personnel by letters of complaint from several spouses. The complaint surprised no one as the JO was openly seen drinking and dancing with many enlisted during the previous year.

You are the investigating officer. One of the command's chief petty officers tells you in confidence of having had relations with the JO as had most of the personnel named in the letters of complaint.

After completing all interviews, you prepare a draft report. Your senior makes changes in that report, which, in effect, whitewashes the issue. Your senior suggests that you formalize the changes and submit the finalized report.

What do you do?

As you review the suggested changes, you find that statements were changed and statements of a damning nature disappeared. In addition, many of the witnesses tell you that they had been threatened with disciplinary action if results of the investigation were commented upon.

The clear intent of your senior is to smooth things over because it was easier to go that route than it would be to face the questions that would be asked if the JO were to go to Mast and then be administratively separated.

Additionally, so many CPOs and senior petty officers were involved that your senior felt that the shock to the command of ending all their careers would be more detrimental to the service than was warranted by the actions of one JO.

As the investigating officer you have to consider both the desires of your senior and the responsibility your official duties place upon you. Your career may well be on the line, for your senior will have the ability to put a negative endorsement on your report and is likely to reflect displeasure in your FITREP.

Turn to page 245 to find out what happened.

The Computer
(Issue 95)

An officer allowed a junior enlisted to buy and finance the purchase of the officer's home computer. The financial terms covered an extended period of time during which the enlisted was to make monthly payments on the computer to the officer.

What could possibly be wrong?

As an officer, you are permitted a one-time sale within certain limits. Officers should never become friends with enlisted, however, because a familiarity might form that could result in a clouding of the officer's judgment. Objectivity, as a result, may be lost.

An officer needs to be aware of the standards of conduct and follow them. Officers would be well advised to seek the guidance of other senior members of their command or discuss the situation with a legal officer, especially when it involves dealing with an enlisted member of the armed forces.

It is intuitively obvious that some actions by an officer may be either illegal or unethical, though this is not that clear in all cases. Thus, you need to seek advice.

Turn to page 246 to find out what happened.

The officer should wear his uniform as the judge his ermine, without a stain.
> —Rear Admiral John A. Dahlgren, USN,
> *On the night of his death, 12 July 1870.*

Speaking Up
(Issue 96)

On cruise a junior pilot who had previously been involved in a Class "A" mishap was designated as the copilot for the commanding officer. The CO was known for being a hot-dog pilot who, on flights with other officers, had exceeded NATOPS altitude as well as radius-of-turn and angle-of-dive limits.

The two pilots took off and as the aircraft ascended, the CO let the copilot know that the capabilities of the aircraft and the skill required of its pilot would shortly be demonstrated to the junior pilot. The copilot knew exactly what was going to take place.

What should the copilot do?

By not speaking out, the copilot would give tacit approval of what the CO was going to do and thus the senior officer might even feel a license and possibly an obligation to show-off to all the junior pilots.

Having already experienced a severe mishap, the copilot was very uncomfortable with this situation and concerned that if the CO was told about the JO's reservations, the latter would be perceived as weak and timid, not a "warrior."

On the other hand, the CO has never pressured the JOs into hot-dogging it. If the copilot speaks up at the time, the CO may not put the aircraft into an inappropriate attitude. If the JO does not speak up, the CO has no indication of the copilot's feelings and may well consider the silence as tacit approval of the upcoming flight pattern.

Turn to page 246 to find out what happened.

One manner of consent is, when a man is still and telleth not.

—John Wycliffe,
Selected Works, iii, 349.

Locality Pay
(Issue 97)

A senior officer reported to a ship as the supply officer. The officer had previously been stationed in Washington, D.C. The officer's family decided to remain in D.C. while the senior was on sea duty. The officer's housing (VHA) certificate was turned in with the indication that pay should be based on owning a home in the District of Columbia, which is illegal.

An ensign disbursing officer onboard the ship was told by the senior to pay the VHA rate based on the dependents' location in Washington rather than the location of the ship. The VHA rate for the ship's home port location was significantly lower than the Washington rate.

The 0-1 knew that the supply officer was a screamer and had heard that some junior officers had been fired for failing to do as the senior asked. The disbursing officer started paying the senior the Washington, D.C. VHA rate.

You, another ensign, have been assigned to the ship as part of a normal rotation and have taken over duties as disbursing officer. The senior officer tells you to continue paying the Washington, D.C. VHA rate. You, as did the previous ensign, know that the senior was not entitled to the payment, but are afraid of what the senior might do to you if the payment is not continued.

What do you do?

The disbursing officer is both ethically and financially bound to make only legal payments. The first disbursing officer should never have started the improper level of payment.

It is clear that both disbursing officers felt threatened by the senior. Because the senior was known as such a tyrant and was believed to have ruined the careers of some junior officers, the first ensign did as told, even when it was wrong.

When a senior officer puts pressure on a junior to do something less than ethical, it is not improbable that the junior will go along with it. During all officer indoctrination programs, a junior officer is taught to respect seniors, to learn from them, and to emulate them.

Junior officers enter active service with high ideals, but some will be told "this is the way we do it in this unit." Some junior officers may go along with this on the assumption that the end justifies the means. In this case the end may simply be keeping out of trouble with the senior officer.

Turn to page 247 to find out what happened.

The Car Cover
(Issue 98)

You are the officer-in-charge of a group of Parachute Riggers in a medium-size unit when you learn that one of your PRs was called into the CO's office and presented with a torn car cover, made from a parachute, and asked to have it repaired.

Due to the age of the material, every attempt to fix one tear develops two new ones. You keep an eye on how the job is going, and when the PR determines the car cover cannot be repaired, you tell the PR to return it to the CO, albeit with more tears than when the job was started.

You learn from the PR that the CO became furious and accused the enlisted of "ruining" the car cover. The CO demanded that the PR make a new car cover out of material used to make helmet bags and oxygen mask covers. More importantly, the PR was to use off-duty time to perform this task.

What do you do?

You realize that it wasn't the fault of the PR that the old car cover was irreparable. Recognizing that the CO is in charge, you tell the PR to finish the job.

You have some qualms about what has happened and wonder how the CO had a car cover made from a parachute in the first place. As you think more about the matter, you wonder about the propriety of making a private car cover out of government material.

After awhile the CO asks you how the job is going and you let him know that the PR wasn't too happy about the task and grumbled to you about being forced to do a job that was not in the PR's position description.

Turn to page 248 to find out what happened.

Leaders are the custodians of a nation's ideals, of the beliefs it cherishes, of its permanent hopes, of the faith which makes a nation out of a mere aggregation of individuals.

—Walter Lippmann

Thoughts On Ethics in Military Leadership

by

Admiral Leon A. Edney, USN

(*Note:* Admiral Edney's career includes 340 combat missions, more than 1,000 carrier landings, a Master's degree from Harvard, service as a White House Fellow, Commandant of the Brigade of Midshipmen, Chief of Naval Personnel, Vice Chief of Naval Operations, NATO Supreme Allied Commander Atlantic, and Commander in Chief U.S. Atlantic Command.)

- - - - - - -

I was pleased when my old friend and distinguished U.S. Naval Academy professor, Dr. Karel Montor, asked me to contribute some thoughts for a book dedicated to inculcating today's and the future's junior officers with the importance of ethics in military leadership. Whenever one reflects on the need for ethics within the military profession, as executed by those who lead the American soldier, sailor, airman, marine and coast guardsman in the duty of defending our national security interests, I believe it is helpful to reflect on the roots of our nation.

Over 200 years ago, in the 18th century, it was the thoughts of our founding fathers represented by Washington, Jefferson, Adams, and Hamilton that framed the ideas of a government of the people, for the people, and by the people. These thoughts formed the foundation of a constitutional democracy that started with the words:

"We, the people of the United States, in order to form a more perfect union, establish justice, insure domestic tranquillity, provide for the common defense, promote the general welfare, and secure the blessings of liberty to ourselves and our posterity, do ordain and establish this Constitution for the United States of America."

The founding fathers were concerned about the heavy hand of government in the lives of the average citizen. Led by the urging of James Madison, the first Congress under the new constitution introduced a Bill of Rights that was ratified December 15th, 1791, and guaranteed the ordinary citizen certain inalienable rights.

Thus our country was founded on the commitment to live with a government process that recognized and valued the rights and privileges of the individual citizen. Each individual was to have freedom of choice as well as a voice and participation in the governing process. These two documents have had the most profound and lasting impact of any governing articles ever written. These rights are protected under the law and the U. S. armed forces exist to protect this way of life from any external or internal threat. While these ideals have withstood the test of time, in each following century, the underlying principles of freedom have been tested by the darker side of human nature. When this happens, free men and women everywhere must stand up to this element. To meet this responsibility for American security interest is the noble calling of the U. S. military. For those who choose to meet this calling, the value of your life's work equals the value of freedom. You should feel good about your chosen profession.

Those who do make this commitment take a solemn oath of office to defend this country and the high ideals and principles upon which it was founded. The officer corps is entrusted with the leadership responsibilities of this nation's most valuable asset, our youth. This places a special burden on every member of the officer corps, to always be worthy of the special privilege in the eyes of those you lead and the public at large. As you develop your leadership traits in the junior officer ranks, I encourage you to focus on two essential ingredients of successful leadership: integrity and ethics.

Rank does not confer privileges; it entails responsibilities. Young Americans under your direction will place you, at once, on a special pedestal of trust and confidence, as will most of the American public. They will expect unfailing professional performance and integrity from each of you. As military leaders, you need to consistently display that match between words and deeds, between behavior and professed values, that we call personal integrity. There can be no compromising on this issue in a profession where the ultimate that you can demand of people is that they lay their life on the line in the execution of your orders.

When all is said and done, leadership must have a moral base, a set of ethical values, to keep us true to the high ideals of our forebears who provided us with the cherished inheritance of freedom. The integrity of an officer's word, signature, commitment to truth, and what is right must be natural, involved, and rise to the forefront of any decision or issue. There can be no double standards. Leadership by example must come from the top; it must be consistently of the highest standards; and it must be visible for all to see. "Do as I say and not as I do" won't hack it in the fleet.

The challenge of military leadership is measured in individual and unit readiness to execute the mission assigned. The ultimate test is readiness to engage in combat and win. Winning in combat is built on teamwork. You must develop the mental, physical, and disciplined toughness in your training and daily operations to explore the outer limits of your fighting capabilities. Winning is built on high standards and adhering to those standards. Winning is built on rules, or doctrine, that depend on each member of the team complying with established procedures. There are rules in every walk of life. Failure to comply with established rules in the profession of bearing arms can cost your life or, even worse, someone else's life.

There is sometimes a misconception by a few junior officers that to win in combat requires throwing all the rules away; "anything goes." This false argument leads some to believe their work is outside the norms and rules of society. Left unchallenged, this same attitude is sometimes reflected in the individuals' off-duty activities. Nothing could be further from the truth. Adherence to rules is extremely important to military good order and discipline as well as the execution of tactics in the heat of combat. Combat toughness depends on knowledge of your own force's capabilities stretched to perform at the outer limits of superior performance, the intimate knowledge of your enemies' capabilities, and a team effort that emphasizes coordinated tactics, which allows a fluid response to the tactical situation. Some rules are deviated from and even broken in the urgency of combat situations. Whenever the rules that are broken involve ethics or actions that are wrong under the rules of international warfare, however, accountability is held based on what was expected and right under the circumstances.

Notice that in listing the qualities that enable winning in combat, no mention was made of vulgar language, grossing people out, sexual harassment, group demeaning attitudes towards minorities, macho images, and false bravado. The idea that these elements are part of the equation that enables us to explore the outer edge is unacceptable. We don't rely and never have relied on these characteristics to generate a winning effort in combat or any other endeavor. America and its armed forces have always stood on the side of right and human decency. You do not throw these core values away in the process of defending them.

My advice concerning rules is to keep them simple and understandable. Do not try to write a rule for every situation and cover all possible exceptions. Leave the decision making of good leadership to provide the right interpretation to clearly stated guidance. There is one rule you should always adhere to, and that is the Golden Rule: "Do unto others as you would have them do unto you." This does not mean that you seek popularity, or adopt a go-along to get-along attitude. It does mean that you ensure that the dignity and feelings of those placed under your authority are part of your leadership concerns.

In the military profession, you will work hard and play hard. When observed in either endeavor, by anyone, you must reflect the institution's core values of respect for decency, human dignity, morality, and doing what is right—in or out of uniform, on or off duty. Some individuals have the mistaken opinion that you can do things away from home or when lost in the anonymity of a crowd that you would not do at home or if identified as an individual. The fact is, core values remain constant no matter where you are. If anything, when you are away from home they are more important because you are representing your country and loved ones as ambassadors of good will. A good test of any activity you choose to participate in is, would it stand the light of day? Would you feel comfortable if your seniors, your parents, your spouse, or your loved ones were watching your activities? If the answer is no, it is a good idea not to participate in the activity. Most questionable off-duty actions would not be done if put to this simple test. I also believe that good men and women have a conscience that warns them when they are about to cross the line from right to wrong. The true test of integrity is doing what is right when no one is watching. You know, and that is all that is required to do what is right.

Whenever an individual or collective breakdown in our core values is observed, immediate corrective action must be taken. Any number of courses of action are available, and the best one will depend on the circumstances at the time. What is never acceptable is the toleration of observed wrong actions or the acceptance of an environment that allows such action to occur. To allow this would be a fundamental breakdown in the integrity of the leadership responsibilities and trust placed in the acceptance of your oath of office. Above all else, military leadership is a commitment to seek out responsibility, to understand and accept accountability, to care, to get involved, to motivate, and to improve. A leader's task is to get the job done the first time. Mistakes will happen and can be corrected, usually with a positive learning curve. To cover up mistakes and responsibility cannot be tolerated. Thus, your leadership traits must demonstrate, above all else, a commitment to integrity and ethics.

Throughout your careers you will face tough decisions, difficult questions, and moral dilemmas that may not resemble any textbook case you have ever studied. You will have to make choices in a world where absolutes are often replaced by degrees of right or wrong, and where tough decisions are the rule, not the exception. Reliance on your core values will enable you to always do what is right. Guided by these principles, and with your inherent abilities, you have my faith and confidence that this nation's defense will be in good hands. Good luck and may God bless you in this extremely important endeavor.

- - - - - - -

(Admiral Edney's personal awards and decorations include the Defense Distinguished Service Medal, the Navy Distinguished Service Medal with gold star, the Legion of Merit with two gold stars, Distinguished Flying Cross with four gold stars, Bronze Star medal, Meritorious Service Medal with gold star, Air Medal with gold numeral 8 and bronze numeral 30, Navy Commendation Medal with Combat V, and the Republic of Vietnam Gallantry Cross with gold star, as well as various campaign and unit awards. He has accumulated more than 5,600 flight hours.)

Tailhook '91
(Issue 99)

Several lieutenants in a branch of carrier aviation they felt was looked down upon, ridiculed, disregarded, and treated with disdain attended Tailhook '91 with the thought that their presence might improve the image of the community.

Although none of them were actually involved in the infamous "gauntlet," they were in a room nearby and could see and hear much of what went on. In considering what to do they reasoned that trying to stop the gauntlet would further reinforce the negative opinions they felt existed concerning their community.

As they considered what to do they were influenced by a few of the women going through the gauntlet more than once. Various courses of action could have been taken, but the final decision was to do nothing and hope that things wouldn't get out of control.

Why was a do-nothing approach taken?

In thinking about what to do the LTs first thought about trying to get the individuals involved in the gauntlet to stop. This was rejected due to the feeling that this was a tradition, and that gang mentality coupled with alcohol made this option unworkable. Second, they suggested getting hotel security to intervene, but they were already there and did nothing as well.

Their third choice was to find a flag officer to try to stop the gauntlet, but none were around, and it seemed to these LTs that some mid-grade officers who were there were content to let it ride.

By doing nothing the LTs felt that the short-term view of their community as okay would be realized. Those LTs in favor of stopping or trying to stop the gauntlet pointed out that by intervening, many of the women would not be manhandled. Further, they would be stopping something that was obviously wrong.

Those LTs who didn't want to get involved argued that: (1) they would be further ostracized as a community; (2) they were severely outnumbered (ten to one) in the hall; (3) they didn't want to be branded as snitches who ruined the fun of others because they were newcomers to the convention and "who are we to tell them how to run their party?"; and (4) if senior officers wanted it stopped, they would do so, for it seemed to the LTs that no one else viewed the situation as being abnormal.

Turn to page 249 for ethical decision considerations.

The Classified Inventory
(Issue 100)

An officer monitored two individuals conducting a classified material inventory. Later that same day a document from that inventory could not be found. A search located the document in a two-person controlled safe that had been opened once since the inventory, but no material had been placed in it.

The officer doing the monitor was the department head of the individuals conducting the inventory. The department head was responsible for ensuring that the inventories and monitors were performed.

What might have gone wrong?

The monitoring officer had the basic responsibility to set the right example for juniors by ensuring a complete and accurate inventory. The handling of classified material is a sensitive issue. It is interesting to note that a proper monitor, and thus proper inventory, takes only minutes.

In addition to this duty the department head had other "paper" responsibilities, and was required to initial the monitor check-off sheet to ensure the inventory requirements had been met.

No one but the monitor and persons doing the inventory is likely to find out if an improper inventory was done. The officer is trusted to conduct the inventory correctly. There is not enough money to pay to have a team watch every officer to make sure that they do their job correctly.

Turn to page 251 to find out what happened.

To be persuasive, we must be believable;
To be believable, we must be credible;
To be credible, we must be truthful.

—Edward R. Murrow

The Dinner
(Issue 101)

You are the 0-2 government representative on a rather large private industry construction project being done for the military. You have maintained an outstanding rapport with the firm's senior management.

As a result of the contractor's completing the project, on time and within budget, they are having a dinner at a local restaurant to reward the company's employees for their hard work.

A week before the dinner you receive an invitation from one of the company's senior management officials who lets you know the time and place. The company notes that they would be honored if you would attend.

What do you do?

You consider the successful operation of the project and the probability that the government will go back to this same contractor for future work. In this regard you are concerned that refusing to attend might degrade future relationships between the government and this contractor.

You are aware of the government's standards of conduct rules but recognize that you are only invited to a dinner, and not a trip to Bermuda. Further, you have received orders for a distant assignment and thus know there will be no further contact between you and this company. You rationalize that your attendance cannot possibly result in your throwing business their way.

Turn to page 252 to find out what happened.

There may be justification, or even a definite need, to restate in strong and clear terms those principles of conduct which retain an unchallengeable relevance to the necessity of the military profession and to which the officer corps will be expected to conform regardless of behavioral practices elsewhere.

—General Maxwell Taylor

THE DINNER

The NATOPS Test
(Issue 102)

You are a junior officer holding the position of Naval Aviation Training and Procedures Standardization (NATOPS) Officer. You have been given the task by your commanding officer of taking an annual NATOPS test for a senior officer. As you consider what to do, you go through soul-searching, apprehension, and fear of reprisal if you do not comply with the CO's wishes. The ethical climate in the command can be summed up by one phrase made by the CO to all officers: "A little apple polishing goes a long way."

The test is a required part of the annual currency qualifications in naval aviation. Each person is required by NATOPS to take both an open- and closed-book test once annually to remain current in that specific type of aircraft.

NATOPS says that each person must complete their own test. This also ensures that each individual has the requisite book knowledge to understand the aircraft and its systems. It is a Navy order and a matter of flight safety. Everyone is bound by this order regardless of rank.

You know the CO is most eager to please higher authority. If you, as NATOPS officer, do not complete the ordered task, the CO will most likely relieve you, punish you with a poor fitness report, assign you to another job, and then get another JO to take the NATOPS job. That new officer would be faced with the same choices as you.

What do you do?

As previously stated, the taking of the test for someone else is against the rules and therefore unethical. The NATOPS officer has the legal right and responsibility to refuse to be a party to falsifying the test.

But the JO perceived that officers in higher pay grades felt the rules did not apply to them and decided to ignore the rules and advice of their subordinate officers. They pressured and coerced junior officers into complying with their wishes.

The JO feels limited in recourse because of being in a deployed status and because those involved are in the JO's direct chain-of-command. The JO considers that getting in trouble with the CO will probably cause reassignment and quite possibly jeopardize a promising career, as a result of a negative comment on the JO's FITREP. On the other hand, taking a stand will result in a good feeling because the right path was being followed.

The NATOPS officer was very troubled and talked to many friends and peers. Everyone felt that the JO should not take the test, but everyone also knew what the punishment might be for not obeying the CO's wishes.

The NATOPS officer talked with an immediate boss, who then talked to the CO. The word came back loud and clear that the CO expected orders to be carried out—that was the bottom line; end of discussion.

Turn to page 253 to find out what happened.

I prefer to do right and get no thanks, rather than to do wrong and get no punishment.

—Marcus Cato,
Plutarch, Lives: Marcus Cato, Chapter 8, Section 9.

Repair Parts
(Issue 103)

On a new assignment you find yourself in charge of an activity responsible for the supply and maintenance of parts for military equipment. Working with a contractor who supplies parts not available from government supply, it does not take you long to realize that something is drastically wrong.

It appears that invoices for parts from the contractor are extremely overpriced and that repairs were being requested for and paid on parts that were not broken. A review of pricing within the contract shows that the contractor was, in fact, being reimbursed at the bid price, which seemed exorbitant. You also notice that a few parts on the price list seemed extremely low.

About this time, rumors began to surface that the contractor was having some of its maintenance personnel change as many parts as possible, even when it was not called for. It appeared that the incentive for the contractor was to increase profits by increasing business.

Realizing that you are new in the command and that senior personnel had been involved in awarding the original contract, you decide to investigate the situation and then report the results to your CO, if warranted.

Your investigation determines that (1) the government is being overcharged for some parts; (2) the contractor was purchasing nonfunctional repair parts at reduced prices and then charging the government new part prices (which were also severely inflated), as well as charging the government to have them repaired; and (3) the contractor had sent parts off to a subcontractor to be repaired when they were not broken. The subcontractor would then send them back at no cost to the contractor, who would charge the government full bid price for their repair.

You brief your CO, who fully supports your wanting to have the matter investigated. The contracting shop is not interested in getting involved, however, and the investigative agency is also not interested because a past similar investigation had gotten the military into hot water for the bad press it eventually caused.

What do you do?

You decide that something has to be done to correct this illegal and unethical activity. You are able to convince your CO, whose support you admire, that the matter should be pursued. You call the investigating agency and after some "verbal pushing," convince them to conduct an investigation. Once they begin, they pursue the matter fiercely.

In addition to what the supply and maintenance officer found out, the agency also learned that there had been improprieties in the way the contracts were let and that the contractors were not, in fact, the low bidders, as required in this particular procurement. The agency was able to solve the mystery of the low bid prices: Instead of using all bid prices for award, only a random selected number of items were utilized. Oddly enough, these were the same prices that were the lower-than-usual bids by the contractor.

As the investigating agency predicted, the next few months were indeed rough for them, as well as for the S&MO who had earned a reputation at headquarters as a troublemaker. The S&MO had also aroused the enmity of the contracting agency who had supported their own contracting officer's efforts. The S&MO caught a great deal of grief and sometimes feared for his career, which was indirectly threatened by some of those with whom business had to be conducted during the investigation.

Turn to page 254 to find out what happened.

We know that there are chiselers. At the bottom of every case of criticism and obstruction we have found some selfish interest, some private axe to grind.
—Franklin D. Roosevelt,
Radio Address, 22 October 1933.

Civilian Attire
(Issue 104)

You are a junior officer who observes two enlisted personnel on liberty status wearing inappropriate civilian attire. The command routinely inspects liberty parties for proper civilian attire.

What do you do?

You realize that the two enlisted have not seen you. By your inaction you will avoid evoking the enmity of the enlisted in the unit.

There is also the question of which rules should be enforced and which shouldn't. What message is sent to the troops by not enforcing some of the rules? If you do speak to the enlisted directly, will you be accused of improper actions, since these two individuals are not in your direct chain-of-command?

Further, if you take any action, will you be reflecting negatively on those who inspect the enlisted before they go on liberty? What is the distance from the base? What are the time factors of when an officer should take action on infractions of the rules?

You wonder whether your senior will see it reflecting negatively on you for becoming a rule enforcer during liberty hours.

Turn to page 254 to find out what happened.

The keenest pangs the wretched find
Are rapture to the dreary void,
The leafless desert of the mind,
The waste of feelings unemployed.

—Byron,
The Giaour, Line 957.

The Prank
(Issue 105)

Two newly winged 0-2s, with orders to their squadrons, were asked to participate in a prank.

In general, their training command displayed the highest ethical standards. In this instance, however, while the individuals were not coerced into performing the prank, they were certainly not discouraged by their seniors who were 0-3 staff instructor pilots. The subject of the prank was to be the chief of staff of the jet training command. The prank, in honor of the training squadron's outgoing CO, was to take place at the change of command ceremony.

The squadron CO was a superb officer and had earned the absolute respect and loyalty of the squadron. The C of S was considered by the 0-3s to be less than an outstanding officer. While nothing was ever done or said in public, the squadron perceived personality differences and a genuine dislike between the CO and the C of S.

A few days before the change of command, several squadron pilots temporarily removed (that is, stole) a large picture of the chief of staff from the Officer's Club. On the day of the change of command, as the two 0-2s arrived, they were approached by 0-3 staff instructor pilots. They were asked, not forced, to consider performing the following task: Retrieve the C of S's picture from its hiding place, take it to the O'Club, bolt it in a toilet stall in the men's room, and hang a sign on the door of the stall which would announce that the only appropriate place for the C of S was in the toilet. This was the first that either of the 0-2s had heard of the picture or the intended prank.

What should the 0-2s do?

The 0-2s considered doing the task (1) to gain peer acceptance from the 0-3 instructor pilots; (2) to poke fun at an unpopular officer; (3) to show support indirectly to the CO, whom they considered an outstanding, well-respected, and well-liked officer; and (4) to get out of standing at attention for one entire hour during the change of command ceremony and be first in line for the beer at the reception.

While some might classify this as harmless fun, the facts are that the 0-2s (1) had possession of stolen property; (2) were UA from a mandatory command function; (3) were improperly at the O'Club during

154   THE PRANK

nonbusiness hours; and (4) were disparaging the C of S, who was both senior to the 0-2s and in their chain-of-command.

The 0-2s had four possible courses of action: (1) decline to participate and inform the instructor pilots that what was being proposed was unethical and that the 0-2s were going to report their actions to the proper authorities; (2) decline to participate and tell the instructors that they (the 0-2s) believed the act was unethical, but then keep quiet; (3) decline to participate and say nothing about the ethics of the prank to the instructor pilots, and forget they had ever heard of the prank; and (4) elect to participate.

Turn to page 255 to find out what happened.

Tact in audacity is knowing how far you can go without going too far.

—Jean Cocteau,
Le Rappel a l'ordre, 1926.

The Stories
(Issue 106)

A maintenance crew consisting of 18 men and 2 women has earned a reputation for flawless work. Five of the men have reputations as "lady killers," and they always share their exploits from the previous evening with everyone at the shop while on break.

The women do not ask the men to stop telling their stories, though they always looked disgusted by the time the men had finished recounting their adventures.

You, as a JO, are placed in charge of the maintenance crew, and after witnessing the first session of storytelling, you see the disgusted look on the faces of the women and consider the disregard the men are showing toward the women.

What do you do?

In considering what should be done you recognize that if you step in and stop the storytelling, you may also adversely affect the quality of the work that is being done.

On the other hand, you recognize that if you stop the harassment of the women, their production may increase in both quantity and quality. In addition, by removing some of the irritants between male and female members, the overall quality of the work may further improve. The possibility also exists that the men haven't really considered the feelings of the women and when their inappropriate behavior is pointed out to them, they may both apologize and work harder themselves to make the unit stronger.

On the other hand, by drawing attention to the storytelling, the men may become alienated from the women, who they would reason were the cause of their troubles; the overall production quantity and quality might go down. In fact, the women might not want anything changed because some form of ostracism might result.

A basic question that has to be addressed is to what extent is the telling of stories wrong, if it is only done during break periods? Is it unethical for individuals to enjoy their breaks?

Turn to page 257 to find out what happened.

156

Selecting Candidates
(Issue 107)

The command had just undergone a division inspector investigation of perceived racial prejudice. Afterward, the Marine battalion commander called his subordinate commanders in and told them, "off the record," that during the upcoming screening for a select program, special consideration would be given to minorities. All of the subordinates thought this undermined the purpose of the program, which was to select the best qualified person regardless of race or ethnic background.

The subordinate commanders perceived the off-the-record instructions as an attempt to counteract the effects of the recent discrimination investigation.

<u>As one of the subordinate commanders, what do you do</u>?

Such special consideration might have had an adverse impact on the entire command, and in some cases, it might hurt those who were not selected, even though they were better qualified.

The question becomes, do subordinate commanders elect to do what is ethically correct, or out of loyalty to their commander, do they do his bidding and quite possibly embarrass the command through mission failure?

A further consideration had to do with whether selecting less-qualified Marines would increase the backlash among better-qualified Marines, and thus have an even greater adverse effect on the unit than the original investigation.

On the other hand, the substitution of qualified for best qualified would open the selection process to all Marines. In the long run, as a result of special training and assignment, this might well remove the perceived racial differences between Marines. This program would have to be carried out in such a way that it did not damage morale. (There is no basis for believing that Marines perform differently when compared on the basis of race or ethnic origin.)

Should the commanders do what they think is right and make their nominations, leaving it to the CO to overrule them if he wanted? The big question is how does one solve such a moral and political dilemma?

<u>Turn to page 258 to find out what happened</u>.

The Legal Officer
(Issue 108)

This issue involves the conflicting duties and obligations of a judge advocate as to how to preserve a client's past secrets/intentions gained from one relationship while serving a subsequent client whose interests are antithetical to client number 1. On occasion, the type and timing of an attorney-client relationship can adversely affect one's ability to totally serve the needs of another client.

As a legal assistance department head you have been consulted by an OINC of a branch medical clinic regarding a professional and personal dilemma. The OINC advises of having transferred an enlisted to another branch clinic to avoid the OINC's further violation of military fraternization policy, with an enlisted of the opposite sex.

The OINC and the enlisted continued to meet one another, however, and commenced cohabitation in a location distant from their workplaces. The OINC plans to marry after the enlisted's obligated service is completed. The OINC, who wants to stay in the service, sought legal advice regarding this course of action. As the OINC's counsel, you advised the officer regarding the obligation and duty to comply with the law, particularly being an OINC whose obligation was to set the example. While the OINC acknowledges the obligation, it is clear that the officer is going to continue the relationship.

Responsible for preserving the secrets of your client, you are unfortunately later transferred to a military hospital, where some months later the unit assumed command of all of the branch clinics, including that of the OINC. Because of your duty to preserve the secrets of your client (the OINC) you cannot reveal the identity nor details of your former client's possibly continuing violation of military policy. Nor can you commence action against the OINC for what might not be a present violation of military policy. In the meantime, the service has tightened its policy regarding fraternization.

By checking, you determine that the OINC is now married and that the enlisted spouse is not a part of your organization. Your position as command judge advocate is to enforce military fraternization policy within your command. In this case you realize that criminal, disciplinary, and administrative action are permissible options.

What do you do?

You determine that the OINC is being very discreet and that no one is complaining. You advise your CO that you are aware of a possible fraternization incident, but, because of attorney-client privilege, you are unable to further identify the client or provide details which you have gained through previous discussions with the OINC.

You advise the CO that you doubt whether you can provide advice or assistance should other information not gained from your interview become available. The CO states that should the event/relationship become public, that advice would have to be sought from someone in order to take appropriate action.

In cases of conflicting loyalties, considered thought can sometimes resolve insurmountable competing allegiances. In this instance it appears that client confidentiality is at odds with military obligations.

Turn to page 258 to find out what happened.

It is difficulties which show what men are.

—Epictetus,
Discourses. Book i, Chapter 24.

Safety
(Issue 109)

A first class petty officer standing a supervisory watch performed troubleshooting maintenance on a submarine component without authorization from the duty officer. In addition, he did not ensure appropriate safety precautions were taken.

The petty officer performing the maintenance was both competent and highly skilled. The actions taken saved an entire day of troubleshooting by circumventing significant plant manipulations that included a requirement to deenergize the equipment.

You are a junior officer, not in the chain-of-command, who observes the maintenance and realize that a fine job was done, no one was injured, and there was no adverse effect on the plant, though proper procedures were not followed.

What do you do?

Safety is always a paramount consideration. Even if no one was injured, such work procedures, if encouraged, increase the probability of fatal injury.

It is impossible for the duty officer in charge of a space to maintain control, or even a knowledge of plant conditions, if unauthorized work occurs.

Reporting the petty officer will serve to enforce the standards of safety and work control and to deter unauthorized maintenance in the future. On the other hand, reporting the petty officer might discourage independent action and aggressive problem solving by a team of highly competent enlisted.

Turn to page 259 to find out what happened.

He is safe from danger who is on guard even when safe.

—Publilius Syrus,
Sententioe. No. 127.

SAFETY

The Haircut
(Issue 110)

You are a newly qualified ensign standing your first officer of the day watch on the quarter deck. Only a few days earlier the ship's executive officer put the word out that all hands leaving the ship must be in proper uniform or civilian attire.

Obediently, you send back several junior crew members who try to cross the quarterdeck with improper haircuts and shaves. Several hours later, after all junior crew who are going ashore have left, a highly respected and hardworking chief approaches who is obviously in need of a haircut.

What do you do?

Several members of the crew are working on deck and all eyes are on you. You realize the chief is leaving late on liberty, having been helping one of the new personnel learn their assignment. The chief would have been within rights to simply leave earlier, but helping new people is one of many strengths of this senior petty officer.

Haircuts are a minor part of the ship's mission, and since liberty hours will soon be over, you consider talking to the chief, explaining you are carrying out the XO's orders. While you are letting him go this time, you "trust that appearance standards will be met in the future."

Turn to page 260 to find out what happened.

What is shown by example, men think they may justly do.

—Cicero,
Epistoloe ad Atticum, Book iv, Episode 3.

Integrity and the Nuclear Officer

by

Commander William P. McBride, USN

(*Editor's note:* The following are the basic points made to all personnel in the nuclear power program. Their re-reading by officers from time to time will help reinforce the reasons for the requirement for 100 percent ethically practicing procedures and following rules. The temptation to avoid doing so is strong when compliance means many extra hours of efforts, but the rewards are greater: avoidance of a nuclear disaster!)

Why worry about nuclear safety? The consequences of a reactor accident are global. The effects of a large quantity of particulate and electromagnetic radiation released to the outside could potentially hurt many people, close off a wide area of land, poison food sources, to name just a few of the problems.

Why bother with nuclear power? Nuclear reactors are long-lived power sources that require no oxygen. They are a good choice for vessels such as submarines and carriers. They are not the only choice, nor the perfect choice, but they are the optimum choice, especially in a tactical sense. To enjoy the benefits of nuclear power, operators need to be dedicated to safety above all else.

Do some organizations operate reactors with other priorities? The results of nuclear power operated without safety being the primary concern are evident all around us.

Three Mile Island showed what happened when expediting maintenance became more important than safety.

Washington Public Power System showed what happened when business managers planned the construction of a reactor with money and ease of construction being more important than safety.

In California, full understanding of the effects of the fault lines are not considered when locating some units.

In New York and New England, the slow development of evacuation plans greatly hampers the safe start-up of some units.

Of course, Chernobyl illustrates the potential damage that can result when safety is not the top priority.

Even in the Navy, two reactors (Thresher and Scorpion) lie uncontrolled on the ocean's bottom. Even though the problems here were platform in nature vice reactor, it doesn't alter the final outcome of the cores.

How is safety ensured? Safety is the top priority, period. No discussion is allowed. Plans will be thoroughly scrutinized; procedures will be thoroughly tested; equipment will be thoroughly inspected and religiously maintained; operators will be qualified to a high standard and periodically retested.

How can safety be undermined? The perfect design with the most complete procedures is worthless if the operators cannot be trusted. If operators fail to report a condition, if their logs are incomplete or wrong, if they lie to cover up a mistake . . . any action such as these carries the potential of undermining the entire program.

Are honest mistakes allowed? An operator may not receive a medal for a mistake, but if the error is quickly and honestly reported, it can be addressed and corrected. Procedures attempt to prevent the honest mistake. Valve positions, red tags, and inspections all require second and third checkers in an attempt to prevent the honest mistake. Valve status boards, equipment logs and records also help. Even the design and placement of switches and equipment attempt to overcome the honest error.

Do you have integrity? Consider how you live in everyday life. You swear to defend the laws and Constitution of the United States, but do you then break the law by driving over the posted speed limit? Do you lobby to change the law, or do you simply break it, assuming that (1) the law is inconvenient, (2) you won't get caught, or (3) everyone does it? Laws are changed when concerned people make an honest, forthright effort to correct what they consider an inequity.

Do you consider yourself an honest person who wouldn't steal? Look at your desk at home; is it filled with government pens and paper? At what dollar value do you consider stealing to no longer be stealing but rather a privilege? Where did you get the idea that stealing anything is a privilege accorded anyone?

Underage drinking is a crime and everyone knows it. How can one be trusted to properly obey all reactor regulations when one can't be trusted to obey a simple drinking-age law?

Rationalizing is an attempt to justify irrational behavior. If you are in a situation that you must justify to yourself or others, chances are good that you have lost your integrity and are now relying on situational ethics. In this case, there is no right or wrong, but rather what is appropriate for the situation. Stealing is wrong... except in such-and-such a case. Lying is wrong... except when speaking to so-and-so.

Integrity lost can be recovered, but it is very difficult. One lie can brand you a liar no matter how many "atta-boys" you have to your name. And once branded a liar, you'll find it very difficult to regain the trust of others. It takes a long time of very trustworthy behavior.

Synonyms: integrity, honor, trust, good ethics, honest, moral
Antonyms: liar, untrustworthy, dishonest, immoral

In running the reactor the *primary* concern will be safety. As a part of this, every nuclear operator will be expected to behave with integrity. If one indicates in any way that they are not to be trusted, they will be removed from the nuclear power program. This is not considered a disciplinary procedure; it is an administrative procedure designed solely to ensure reactor safety.

One of my duties while serving as executive officer was screening Captain's Mast (nonjudicial punishment). A certain percentage of these cases involved integrity issues. The person who cheated on a test or the person who lied about the time spent studying was, in addition to whatever else was awarded as punishment, dropped from the program.

Once, while I was serving in the engineering department of a surface combatant, we were preparing for a big engineering inspection. As part of the inspection, logs and records are reviewed for the preceding year. One record documented tests completed prior to the start-up of the plant. It was more than 100 pages long. As each step was completed, the "doer" and the "checker" were supposed to initial the form. On one of these forms dated more than eight months earlier, a single initial was found missing on a simple step deep into the 100-page procedure.

When word reached the chief engineer that a problem had been discovered, a request was made to see the form. When the form arrived at the chief engineer's desk, the missing initial had been filled in.

The leading petty officer of the division immediately admitted to filling in the missing initial, with the following rationale:

(1) This procedure applied to a start-up done months ago and so the form had no real meaning now.

(2) It was obvious that the step had been performed, only a slip-up had been made by the person failing to initial the form.

(3) Why take an inspection "hit" on something that is so easy to "correct"?

The petty officer was removed from duties and from the nuclear power program, never really understanding that by his compromising a signature once, no one would ever really be able to trust those initials again. Although attempts to explain were tried, the petty officer did not understand that "passing the inspection" does not authorize any behavior beyond the rules. This petty officer would rather have the passing grade than honor. The petty officer did not understand that there is a proper way to correct any situation. In this case, the internal audit found the error, and the operator who made the mistake was counseled and retrained. But the proper way was "too hard." It was easier to hide or cover up the error. Nuclear power requires integrity from all who work with it in order to ensure that safety remains the top priority.

The Valve
(Issue 111)

During a submarine shipyard overhaul testing program, a valve was found out of position in the engine room. The shipyard procedure required for this event is to stop all work and inform the shipyard, the engineer, and the commanding officer.

A critique is held, corrective action taken, and a resolution is issued for the record prior to resuming work. This process normally takes one shift or more. In this instance, the engineering duty officer decided to reposition the valve without informing the shipyard, as the cause was known and it didn't affect the engineering plant.

Subsequently, a second valve was found out of position in the area, prompting the EDO to become concerned with conditions in the plant, though it was known that this matter could also be easily corrected.

<u>What do you do?</u>

The EDO realized that if the second valve is reported, then the first valve situation should also be reported. Not reporting the first valve lessened the importance and severity of the concern over the second valve.

On the other hand, reporting the first valve condition would mean immediate censure of the EDO. There was no provision for the EDO to correct the first valve problem without notification of others.

The EDO realized that if only the second valve were reported that much time would be lost due to an insignificant problem with a known cause and an easy method of correction.

The possible courses of action were: (1) to report the second valve out of position immediately; (2) to correct both out-of-position valves (and any subsequent ones) without reporting them; (3) to report the affair after the second valve was corrected; or (4) to report the second valve out of position immediately and report the first valve as well.

<u>Turn to page 261 to find out what happened</u>.

Standing Watch
(Issue 112)

You are an 0-2 standing watch and expecting the relieving officer to show up. After an hour past watch relief, you recognize that for an unknown reason, your relief is not only late but may fail to show at all.

Standard procedure in your unit is to notify the command duty officer, but doing so will result in the missing officer being reprimanded and all of your peers knowing that you were the one who blew the whistle on the tardiness.

What do you do?

On the one hand you have a duty as an officer to report events that are out of the ordinary, and the failure of an officer to show up for watch fits that bill. It may well be that the late officer has had an accident. By not reporting the lateness, you will be in trouble for not having followed standard operating procedures.

On the other hand, by reporting the late officer you know that other junior officers will shun you for not keeping the faith with a fellow officer. They may also become annoyed with you, and when you make the slightest slip, they'll report you to your senior, thus creating an untenable environment in which to work and serve with these other officers.

Turn to page 262 to find out what happened.

When duty comes a-knocking at your gate, welcome him in; for if you bid him wait, he will depart only to come once more and bring seven other duties to your door.

—Edwin Markham,
Duty.

Specifications
(Issue 113)

You are an officer who has noticed an out-of-specification reading on a piece of equipment for which your work center is responsible. The normal procedure is to report such incidents to the commanding officer so that records might indicate a trend in either equipment failure or quality of work center output.

By reporting the problem, however, you realize the work center might be perceived as being unable to properly maintain equipment and your reputation for professional competence to run the work center might be affected.

What do you do?

The officer felt that the work center had been doing good work and thus was concerned that reporting the out-of-spec equipment reading would earn the displeasure of the CO. Further, the officer felt that the equipment reading would eventually correct itself, consequently it wasn't worth spending time trying to fix a piece of equipment that was probably operating properly.

The officer did consider that the equipment might, in fact, not be operating correctly and that the out-of-spec condition would be eventually noticed. Failure to report the condition might earn the displeasure of the commanding officer, who could perceive the officer to be untrustworthy.

Also considered was the possibility that if the problem was not reported and corrected, the cost of repair would eventually be higher in time and money compared to correcting the problem when it was discovered.

Turn to page 263 to find out what happened.

The one permanent emotion of the inferior man is fear—fear of the unknown, the complex, the inexplicable. What he wants beyond everything else is safety.
> —H. L. Mencken,
> *Prejudices. Series ii, Page 75.*

Discipline
(Issue 114)

A junior petty officer had been placing inappropriate notes on a chief petty officer's car, without self-identification, while it was parked in base housing. The junior petty officer had practiced this form of harassment because he felt the chief had taken advantage of higher rank to improperly park on property assigned to the lower-ranked enlisted.

You are the junior officer in charge of both individuals and carry out an investigation that ascertains that the junior petty officer was actually wrong. In considering what to do, you have to take into account that what you decide will affect not only the junior enlisted but also the spouse and family.

With wages already low, and considering the effect bad marks in the service record might have on the junior's career, you have to come to a decision as to the best approach to take.

What do you do?

Sympathy for the family of the junior petty officer does have a place in making just and appropriate decisions and recommendations. The Navy "family" includes the spouse and children as well.

On the other hand, sympathy needs to be balanced against the effect of non-punishment of disrespect toward a senior member of our enlisted troops.

A commissioned officer should remember that no matter how junior, they are responsible to maintain order and discipline. If the incident is kept quiet, and no disciplinary action is taken, it will have the effect of saying to the junior petty officer that rules only selectively apply. Furthermore, the lack of action by the JO would undermine the position of the chief. In essence, the officer would be saying that less than total respect is okay when dealing with one of the unit's senior enlisted individuals.

Turn to page 263 to find out what happened.

First-Time Use
(Issue 115)

An E-8 with sixteen years of active service tested positive for use of cocaine in a random urinalysis screening. The enlisted was disciplined at nonjudicial punishment (NJP) and an administrative discharge board was convened.

Board members were an 0-4, 0-2, and an 0-1. The E-8 offered no explanation and adamantly denied drug use, saying "It must have been in my food or drink, as I have never used drugs!" Zero tolerance and mandatory discharge processing is military policy.

An investigation indicated that the urinalysis was sound. It was the E-8's sample, and the level of cocaine was consistent with use. The government's counsel asked for Other Than Honorable separation.

You are the 0-2 on the board. How do you vote?

The board must decide if misconduct due to drug abuse has been committed. If not, should the E-8 be retained or separated? If separated, what characterization of discharge is warranted? Each officer must work independently based upon the evidence at the board. Conversations with other than board officers, mandates of the CO, and personal stereotypes must be avoided.

The records indicate that the E-8 is a 4.0 individual who had been recommended for promotion to E-9. There has been no prior misconduct and no history of abuse. The enlisted is married with two children, and the E-8 is the only source of family income.

While the chain-of-command testified to the E-8's performance as being outstanding, and the drug abuse was said to be uncharacteristic and unbelievable, there is no question by all testifying officers that drug abuse cannot be tolerated.

The defense counsel asks for a finding of no misconduct; if separation is recommended, then it should be an Honorable Discharge.

Turn to page 264 to find out what happened.

You are the officer of the day (OOD) on a submarine. You are approached by one of the enlisted for permission to pump sanitaries overboard. This evolution involves the safety of the ship and requires permission from the commanding officer.

You are aware of standing orders by the CO, who is in the rack, but you don't want to awaken that officer. You feel certain that the CO would agree to the dumping since it is the midwatch of the day before your return to port, and the evolution needs to be completed within the next eight hours.

<u>What do you do?</u>

On the one hand is consideration of whether the standing orders of the CO should, for good reason, be disobeyed. In so doing the officer needed to consider the effect on the crew, who would know that the OOD was assuming authority not so delegated.

The question is whether it is up to the OOD to make the determination, considering the current situation, or whether securing the permission of the CO is a necessary requirement. On the other hand, the OOD felt that the CO, as the busiest person on the submarine, needed the rest and thus the OOD was merely showing loyalty to a senior by anticipating the approval that the CO would have given if awakened and asked.

<u>Turn to page 265 to find out what happened</u>.

Boldness, without the rules of propriety, becomes insubordination.

—Confucius,
Analects, circa 500 B. C.

Counseling
(Issue 117)

A leading petty officer failed to accomplish tasks on time, did not show any sense of responsibility to seniors, and failed to do the best for the division.

The PO's division officer had an extremely busy schedule and considered transferring the PO to another command or effecting an administrative discharge for the enlisted, as a solution to the problem.

What should be done?

Transferring the PO to another command would immediately solve the problem and allow the officer to spend more time taking care of duties and the crew. With loyalty to ship first, shipmate second, and self third, the officer has to consider the best use of time; what for example, would not be attended to if too much time were spent counseling the deficient PO?

While arranging for an administrative discharge would take more time than transferring the individual, and could be more appropriate, the easy solution to the problem was a tempting alternative.

Turn to page 266 to find out what happened.

When all is done, the help of good counsel is that which setteth business straight.

—Francis Bacon

The Notepapers
(Issue 118)

As a newly commissioned officer in the U.S. Navy, an ensign quickly realizes that it becomes imperative to attain warfare qualifications to remain competitive for promotion. Throughout Surface Warfare Officers School, students review many classified publications involving various threat parameters, procedures, and equipment capabilities.

This information, along with other class requirements, serves to facilitate a student's ability to have the SWO Personal Qualifications Standards booklets filled out and signed off at the first command after school graduation. The booklets have to be completely signed off through validation at school or by a qualified SWO before a board is convened on the ship to conduct an oral examination. This case starts with the importance of SWO qualification during first tour of duty in order to select for SWO Department Head School, signifying the upward mobility of the young officer toward eventual command at sea.

During various courses of instruction at SWO basic school, students take classified notes, which stay within the confines of the school, thus maintaining security of the information and allowing students to study for tests. Upon school completion and graduation, the students' classified notes are sent, using standard security procedures, to the officer's ship or station for further study and review as they pursue completion of their PQS booklet.

In this case the ensign decided that the notes were so important to future ability to attain SWO qualification, that security arrangements were bypassed. The officer carried the classified notes to the first command to ensure that they did not get lost using the standard procedure for classified document transmission. Knowing that questions would be asked about security arrangements, the ensign decided to keep the notes at home (with other professional papers) where the officer felt that they would be secure and an explanation would not have to be made about their location.

In the ensuing years the officer moved six or seven times, allowing the moving company to move the notes along with other professional books. Some years later, and now an 0-4, the officer came across the notes from years ago.

<u>What should be done</u>?

The 0-4 has basically three paths to follow: (1) turn the information into burn bags, risking getting caught somehow; or (2) burn the information without anyone else's knowledge; or (3) keep the notes.

This officer had become very successful after the basic course, qualifying as a SWO in the shortest possible time-frame and selected to Department Head School well in advance of peers. As an 0-4 the officer is now faced with a dilemma.

While most of the systems and equipments were no longer in use, the 0-4 had a decision to make involving the hard right choice or the easy wrong one. We must also consider that if the situation is made known, a career may be ended and the military service would lose a highly competent officer for a mistake made years ago. The 0-4 realized that the security of the United States may not have depended on action being taken, with the overwhelming concern centered around the ability to compete against other hard charging officers.

Turn to page 267 to find out what happened.

I hope I shall always possess firmness and virtue enough to maintain what I consider the most enviable of all titles, the character of an "Honest Man."

—George Washington,
Moral Maxims.

Sleeping on Watch
(Issue 119)

You are the engineering duty officer (EDO) on a nuclear submarine. You have worked hard for many years to obtain this position of responsibility and authority. The watch standers working for you have also worked hard for many years and are professionals in all aspects.

A new commanding officer recently reported to your ship. You are impressed with your CO's abilities and sense of fairness, and you are enthusiastic about supporting the CO's policies. The CO has stated unequivocally that sleeping on watch is unacceptable and that all offenders will be processed for administrative separation from the Navy.

On a shutdown nuclear submarine in port, typically the only watch stander in maneuvering is the shutdown reactor operator (SRO). The EDO's work will be mostly in maneuvering, with coming and going allowed as necessary. The SRO is a senior experienced enlisted electrician. The current SRO was very helpful in the long and arduous process of your qualification. The SRO has always been willing to answer questions, help you research answers, and generally has bent over backwards to help you learn your new job. As the SRO's division officer, you know that the other members of the division look to the SRO for answers, both professional and personal. On days off, the SRO often comes to work to help others or accomplish necessary work. The SRO has spent more time at sea than you have in the Navy.

It is 0500, and you have been on watch for twenty hours, with only two hours of sleep. The SRO has had roughly the same amount of rest. The reason you have had so little sleep is that you have been coordinating complex propulsion plant testing. You and your watch standers have aggressively and successfully conducted this testing. You just got off the phone with the chief engineer, who has congratulated you on doing a good job during the night. You pass the good word on to your watch standers.

You are filling out the turnover sheet for the oncoming EDO, who is scheduled to show up in a couple of hours. While writing, your eyes shut and your pen draws across the paper. No one else saw you, and it only lasted several seconds.

You complete filling out your paperwork and decide to stand up and get a cup of coffee. While standing up you knock a book off the shelf which hits the floor with a loud bang. You notice that the

SRO—with chin on chest, eyes shut, and limp arms and legs—did not move at the sound.

<u>What do you do</u>?

You wake the SRO and the two of you go to get coffee. In thinking about whether to report yourself and/or the SRO to the CO for sleeping on watch, you know you want to support command policy, maintain your personal integrity, and possibly identify a policy that leads to sleeping on watch.

On the other hand, you consider the possible damage (possibly the end) to your career, damage (possibly the end) to the SRO's career, which would influence the morale of the electrical division and disrupt the entire crew by removing two key watch standers from the watch bill.

If you report yourself and the SRO for sleeping on watch, you cannot know ahead of time what the results will be. You expect, at a minimum, that the CO will hold Mast for each of you. It is possible that you and the SRO will be administratively separated from the Navy. But it is also possible, especially in view of your honest and forthright admission, that the CO will be lenient.

<u>Turn to page 268 to find out what happened</u>.

Divine Providence has granted this gift to man, that those things which are honest are also the most advantageous.

—Quintillian,
De Institutione Oratoria, Book i, Chapter 12, Section 19.

Passing Inspection
(Issue 120)

Prior to an inspection, particularly an OPPE (Operational Propulsion Plant Exam), the stress level in the engineering department always begins to rise. It is during this period—usually a week or less away from the start of the inspection—that one might realize that a page entry in someone's service record is not there as required. By then it is too late to qualify someone properly and correctly in that needed billet. Thus, the temptation is for the engineering division officer to qualify that one individual by just typing *qual* in the service record; that is, not making the person do the actual PQS for the watch station.

While this may solve the initial problem of passing the inspection—assuming that the newly qualified person is not tested—it does not help when a real problem or situation arises that requires this person to know the job; for example, a fire party. The stress that may be placed on a junior officer is not to make sure everything is done properly, but that everything is in the proper order. This problem, unfortunately, is not just an engineering problem; it has been known to happen prior to other significant inspections in other departments on other ships.

The task at hand in this case is to either gundeck the *quals* for certain individuals or to take a failing grade on a major engineering exam. As the ensign in this case, your senior, tells you "Just fix it so we pass, or . . ."

What do you do?

One of the problems, of course, with the gundeck approach is that there are not qualified "qualified" personnel standing a particular watch station. Also, personnel lose motivation and respect for seniors due to this unethical way of dealing with the problem.

If the situation is handled in an ethical manner, the ship will fail its inspection. Along the same lines, however, if the junior and senior officers had been doing their jobs properly from the start, there never would have been a problem. We live in a real world and things do slip through the cracks.

Why this happens is relatively easy to explain. With advancement and screening boards becoming harder and harder in each cycle, the pressure is on to excel. One negative mark may ruin a career. An officer may wonder whether it pays to be honest and ethical in the decision-making process.

Turn to page 269 to find out what happened.

PASSING INSPECTION

The Fall
(Issue 121)

An ensign, who had graduated from the Naval Academy, was accepted for Flight Training and was scheduled to arrive in Pensacola after a summer of leave. In a stopover at his home, he joined some of his high school buddies for beer at a local night spot. Leaving the club after too much beer, he fell, hitting the back of his head on a concrete step losing consciousness.

When he came to, he was in a local hospital undergoing testing by a neurologist. The test disclosed that the reason he had been unconscious for a little over an hour was a small contusion on a frontal lobe of the brain caused by the jolting the brain received in the fall. He also had no smell or taste due to movement of the brain stem as a result of the fall.

By the time he reported to Pensacola, he had recovered totally and felt ready to start flight training. All that remained was the completion of a questionnaire concerning head injuries. Reading through Navy Air physical qualifications he learned that: (1) a head injury which results in loss of consciousness for less than fifteen minutes is not disqualifying; (2) a head injury which results in loss of consciousness of greater than fifteen minutes, but less than two hours is disqualifying for at least two years; and (3) a head injury which results in loss of consciousness for more than two hours is permanently disqualifying.

How should he answer the questionnaire?

The ensign had always wanted to fly and now his dream was within reach. By the time he reported to Pensacola, he had recovered his sense of smell and taste and the advice of everyone he talked to was the same. As long as he was okay, he should not disclose the injury. After all, if there was anything really wrong, the EEG physical, to be taken at Pensacola, would disclose it anyway. With Navy Air getting more and more competitive and slots being reduced as the military was downsized, his chances of continuing his Navy Air career would be slim- to-none if he reported the fall. Even the neurologist who had cared for him agreed that the two-year rule seemed unduly bureaucratic and unbending, and that EEGs were not significantly advanced that they could detect that a fall had taken place.

An exam, taken by a private physician, indicated that his eyes and overall physical condition were perfect.

The ensign knew that if the Navy learned of his injury, he could be disqualified for at least two years. He felt great. There were no marks or other indications of the injury. There was no apparent way the Navy would find out unless he offered the information. He anguished over the need to tell. On the one hand it was the basic, honest thing to do; on the other hand, it seemed so unfair since he was fully recovered and felt as good as he ever had. Should he really let his lifelong dream go, even though he believed he was in excellent health.

When he reported into Pensacola one of the first things he had to do was fill out the questionnaire which asked: "Have you ever suffered any head injury? If so, describe below."

Turn to page 270 to find out what happened.

Honest men fear neither the light nor the dark.

—Thomas Fuller,
Gnomologia, No. 3696.

THE FALL

ISSUE 1 - COMPUTERS

<u>What happened</u>: (Issue 1 from page 12) During the "hotline" investigation it was determined that leave was taken to conduct personal business, as opposed to family affairs. The officer was discharged and required to pay the value of the "personal" services he had received; that is, computer and telephone usage.

ISSUE 2 - TRAVEL ORDERS

<u>What happened</u>: (Issue 2 from page 14) Desperate, and unwilling to ask for help (but thinking he was owed air transportation), the officer forged a set of flight authorization TDY orders. He was caught when the clerk at the terminal tried to issue him a commercial ticket on the fraudulent orders. Trying to get *priority* as a courier was unethical as well. How simple it would have been for the officer to pay for his own commercial airline ticket.

The officer's criminal actions caught everyone in the command by surprise. He was arrested at the military terminal by security personnel and subsequently was convicted in a court-martial.

Here again we see an individual going wrong because he not only didn't trust the organization for which he worked, he also failed to discuss the matter with peers or seniors. He similarly failed to take advantage of the presence of both command JAG and chaplain officers. He also could have purchased a commercial ticket to fly to CONUS!

We should do the right thing because it is the proper thing to do, not because of fear of being caught. Officers and subordinates alike must understand the rule of law and obey the rules.

ISSUE 3 - COMMAND READINESS

<u>What happened</u>: (Issue 3 from page 16) As a result of various individuals not ensuring that they knew what was to be done and how to do it correctly, there was a mishap and the crew chief and aircraft were lost at sea. (In addition to everything else, the chief was inadequately restrained in his harness before the crash due to failure to follow NATOPS cabin procedures.)

In any military organization the commanding officer is ultimately responsible, though subordinate personnel have varying degrees of responsibility depending on their assignments.

SOLUTIONS   181

For subordinates not to be fully prepared is both an unethical action on their part and a display of disloyalty to their senior, whose objectives they should be trying to meet.

It is important for all levels of the chain-of-command to realize that their mistakes affect not only themselves and the mission but are also a reflection on their seniors. The NATOPS rules are a guide developed from previous mishaps; not following their guidance is as much an ethical failure as knowingly not showing up for a deployment.

ISSUE 4 - THE PARTY

What happened: (Issue 4 from page 18) Both the senior and the subordinate lived to regret their mutual lack of communication.

When a subordinate thinks something is wrong, then it is the responsibility of the junior to ensure that the senior is fully apprised in a timely fashion as to what has gone on. It is, of course, also the responsibility of the senior to listen, with the junior applying as much bravery and directness in talking to a senior as they are expected to show in dealing with an enemy.

ISSUE 5 - SOFTWARE

What happened: (Issue 5 from page 20) The JO decided to go forward and suggest alternative software to be used in the system. The JO was the duty expert for the system even though only the assistant project officer.

In the meantime, the contractor continued to work on software development. The JO kept pointing out "bugs" in the proposed software package the contractor was going to deliver.

The JO did find some alternate software packages that had proven results and were owned by the government.

The JO was ordered to "cease and desist" all further attempts to determine if additional off-the-shelf software for the computer system existed. The JO was told that the research undertaken was disruptive to the contractor.

The contractor went ahead with their software package development which cost the government an inordinate amount of money. The JO was removed from the project and given a lukewarm fitness report. As a result, selection to the next higher rank was not achieved.

The JO, however, never questioned the decision to go forward because of loyalty, integrity, honesty, and the importance of accomplishing the mission. This particular story does not have a happy ending, but we in the military must always opt for the ethical and proper course of action.

As evidenced by this case, there is more than one form of combat; this JO showed the courage that we expect of all officers of all ranks. Fortunately, this is an isolated story. If the officer corps in general will remember the principles by which this JO lived, they will be able to emulate the many fine deeds done by officers in and out of combat.

"Do the right thing, even if it means dying like a dog without the esteem of anybody you value knowing what it cost you."

Admiral James B. Stockdale
"The World of Epictetus"

ISSUE 6 - RESCUE MISSION

<u>What happened</u>: (Issue 6 from page 21) The squadron commander took no action to have the falsified report changed. The officer thought that by not initiating any action to reverse the falsified report he was doing the right thing and supporting his senior.

The mistake here was confusing loyalty to a person with loyalty to the truth in particular and the service in general. An officer's word must be relied on if we are to operate in the fast-paced operations customarily involved with military units.

We can rationalize that we don't know all the facts, that others have the big picture, and that the chain-of-command is in charge, all of which is usually correct. Actually, one does not have to question the chain-of-command in an issue of this sort, for no officer is obliged to obey an illegal order, and the falsification of an officer's report is illegal.

The mission was undertaken and failed, and many years later the squadron commander still regretted that he took the easy way out. It might have cost him his career to do the right thing. His record shows many times his willingness to risk his life for his country, yet, in this case, he was *not* willing to risk his career for his country.

If the task force commander sent the false report to throw off a listening enemy, at a minimum the squadron commander should have

SOLUTIONS   183 filed a "memo to record" stating that the report was filed over his objections, with a copy to the unit's CO and the task force commander noting that what had been sent was not what had been reported, though there may have been good reasons for doing so.

If you are immoral, without a conscience, then doing wrong will cause you neither ulcers nor worry. If you do know right from wrong, however, then not doing the right thing will be with you as long as you live.

ISSUE 7 - DEALING WITH A VENDOR

What happened: (Issue 7 from page 22) Upon finding out about the gift, the commissary officer advised the civilian that the matter was under investigation, and that the employee had the right to remain silent, to have union representation, if desired, and to choose an attorney. The officer pointed out to the civilian that government employees are not allowed to accept gratuities, this provision being spelled out in Standards of Conduct regulations.

The officer further pointed out that it was the civilian's position as a purchasing agent that brought about the gift and thus the appearance that he was using his position for personal gain, making him suspect. It was a "hotline" complaint against the civilian that brought the matter to a head in the first place.

While there was not loss to the government, the appearance of wrongdoing did exist and thus the matter was investigated. The baby food was returned.

While the officer knew the Standards of Conduct regulations, such had not been emphasized to subordinates. The incident might have been avoided if annual training had been done as required, the lack of which raised questions about the officer's competence.

ISSUE 8 - COMPONENT PARTS

What happened: (Issue 8 from page 23) In this case there was no violation. As it turned out, one of the component parts was urgently needed before the others.

It is not enough to be a good problem solver. While the investigation cleared the contracting officer of wrongdoing, it still took needed time away from other activities.

The extra time it takes to inform all concerned as to what is being done is far less than the time needed, after the "hotline" complaint has been filed, to clear the matter up.

The point also needs to be made that many "hotline" complaints could be avoided if the so-called "whistleblower" had taken time to ask the chain-of-command. Those who perceive some "impropriety" are obliged to tell their chain-of-command instead of immediately picking up the "Hotline." Simply asking might well result in a satisfactory explanation and save everyone time and effort.

Every action by an officer should be the result of prior planning, education, and training. Just as a pilot thinks about and practices combat maneuvers—considering what the enemy might do—so must an officer consider how others will view the action and its results.

ISSUE 9 - TRAINING SUPERVISION

What happened: (Issue 9 from page 24) While maneuvering his aircraft vertically, the pilot stalled the aircraft (experiencing negative and near zero "G" flight conditions) and failed to apply proper recovery techniques. The pilot was seriously hurt and the aircraft was lost.

During the mishap investigation it was determined that the pilot had not had enough flight and practice hours in this particular aircraft, nor had he had *any* stall training in it. The squadron had also failed to monitor the pilot's proficiency training, and they had not received any indication from his previous command that he had completed stall training as required.

By the time the mishap investigation was completed, it was clear that the pilot should not have been assigned this particular mission and that complete training records were needed before he was assigned any mission. If this complete training record had been known, someone else would have been assigned the mission.

Every risk that can be imagined and trained for should be included in a pilot's training program to ensure the greatest possibility of successful mission completion. This mishap could have been avoided if the CO had been a little more willing to risk hurting the feelings of the pilot by not allowing him to fly until his training record was fully known.

Courage on the part of a CO means not only the courage to take on missions but also the courage to make sure that personnel are not permitted to fly missions they aren't ready for (especially in peacetime).

While being courageous is not synonymous with being ethical, having the courage to do the right thing is acting ethically.

ISSUE 10 - SUBMARINE INVENTORY

What happened: (Issue 10 from page 26) After long deliberation, the lieutenant determined that the only viable option was to consult with the squadron supply officer. After discussing the matter with him in his office, the squadron supply officer immediately briefed the commodore.

After learning about the dilemma, the commodore called the lieutenant's CO and ordered him to ensure that a full inventory of all subsistence items be conducted prior to the relief's arrival, as was required by Navy regulations.

Although it was the most difficult decision that the lieutenant had to make thus far in his career, he still felt certain that it was the proper one. He had been forced into the uncomfortable position of having to put his commanding officer on report with his boss.

As a direct result of his decision, the lieutenant received an extensive lecture on the chain-of-command, and an already strained professional relationship was virtually destroyed. In addition, his detaching fitness report was negatively affected. (*Editor's note:* With the help of the commodore this FITREP can be thrown out: that is, expunged from the record by appealing to the Board of Review and Corrections.)

Even so, the lieutenant is proud of the decision that he made that challenged both his personal and professional code of ethics, and when telling the editors of this book this story, he commented, "I can go to bed at night knowing that I did not compromise either my personal or my professional ethical standards."

(*Editor's note:* The lieutenant did have a fourth alternative, and that was to ask his CO to go with him when he went up the chain-of-command. Although that wouldn't have made the CO very happy, he probably would have allowed the inventory to go ahead, and would not have felt that the lieutenant was jumping the chain-of-command.)

We are prepared to give our lives for our country, let us be equally prepared to give our careers. No military officers will ever have a problem securing a position in the civilian sector, especially if they are people who act ethically.

ISSUE 11 - THE "EXPERIENCED" OFFICER

What happened: (Issue 11 from page 27) Before an officer accepts a commission, it is important he/she understands the *values* which bound expected behavior as an officer. Since values can and do change over time, leaders must unambiguously inform all officers of changes in values. Officers must then either accept these changes or resign their commissions.

While this volume addresses the reality that officers accept service values and ethics when they accept a commission, it must not be forgotten that what officers do signals the enlisted members' acceptance of service values as well. Their ethics are just as important as an officer's, and thus officers need to set the example and be aware that ensuring enlisted compliance of our standards are equally important as their own behavior.

A formal investigation was launched and LCDR F. was relieved of his command for cause. The relief determination was based on perception, fact, and an accumulation of marginal behavior reports.

In addition to the failures of LCDR F., it is also noted that *he* was failed by seniors, peers, and subordinates who took no action nor counseled him during his enlisted and early officer days. Others apparently paid all of their attention to F.'s getting the job done and little attention to how he did it. The military is an ever-changing world, and it is incumbent on all of us to help our fellow servicemen make the transition—or suggest that the person resign. If, when he was enlisted, an officer had spoken with Jack F. and when he was an officer a senior had not overlooked his actions for so long—they might have contributed to the development of an all-around good officer, instead of the one we now write about.

Undoubtedly, through BMC F.'s negative example, several other promising career military personnel learned how not to act, with consequent negative results; that is, BMC F. unwittingly took a few others "down with him."

ISSUE 12 - MAINTENANCE SUPERVISION

What happened: (Issue 12 from page 28) An investigation into the mishap (including the activities of the mishap victim for 72 hours prior to the incident) found that the dead crewman had a .127 blood alcohol level at the time he died. Further discussions with other members of the ground crew revealed that both the dead crewman and others had made it a habit of having a "little" to drink before the day shift began.

If this were the first time that any of the ground crew had a drink before starting their daily duties, and their personnel records showed that they had never had an alcohol incident, then we can say that the maintenance officer could not be held liable for so unexpected and illegal an act.

Further analysis revealed that in fact, the maintenance officer did have some responsibility in the matter, for as indicated above and according to subsequent testimony of other base personnel, this particular maintenance crew had a well-known habit of consuming alcohol before the start of their shift. A secondary level of responsibility lay with those who knew something wrong was going on and did nothing about it. As Edmund Burke said centuries ago: All that is necessary for the forces of evil to win is for enough good people to do nothing in the face of wrongdoing.

In this situation, failure to observe was coupled with failure to monitor the results of training. It is not enough for the officer to meet requisite standards; there is also the obligation to ensure that subordinates comply. Special trust and confidence is placed in all officers, as evidenced by the scope of the operations over which they are in charge.

The ethical issue here is that the officer did not ensure that all personnel were adequately training and obeying military regulations. Possibly, the officer was simply lazy and failed to walk around and observe personnel. A leader has this moral responsibility, and if it had been taken, this unfortunate incident might have been avoided.

ISSUE 13 - FUND RAISING

What happened: (Issue 13 from page 30) After the ride had been auctioned to a bidder for several hundred dollars, someone in town filed a "hotline" complaint that special treatment was being given to someone for a fee that could not be taken advantage of by the average taxpayer.

This violation of the Standards of Conduct was viewed as ill-advised by the Service Chief who felt that the CO, by virtue of rank and years of experience, should have known better.

The CO was directed to return the money. As the money had been spent by the time the ruling came down, restitution was made from the CO's own pocket.

SOLUTIONS

ISSUE 14 - QUARTERS COMPETITION

What happened: (Issue 14 from page 31) The lineal listing of who is awaiting quarters is generally known, as is the date when an officer comes on post and is eligible for quarters.

In this case, one of the other officers, waiting for quarters, realized that the flag aide had been assigned quarters ahead of him even though he had been assigned to the base longer.

This resulted in a "hotline" complaint, as the aggrieved officer was aware that military housing regulations require officers of the same rank to compete on an equal basis for quarters.

Officers are responsible to know the limits of their authority and have an obligation not to take advantage of situations in which they might find themselves. In this case, upon realizing that influence must have been used, the flag should have reversed the quarters assignment arrangement. While loyalty was owed to the subordinate aide, even greater loyalty was owed to the law and to the rest of the officer community.

ISSUE 15 - ELECTING TO AVOID DISASTER

What happened: (Issue 15 from page 32) Actually, it was the junior officer pilot who was at fault because he failed to complete a cockpit "fit check" to ensure he could reach all equipment, controls, switches, and emergency egress devices.

When the emergency occurred, all attention became focused on the lack of "fit." The pilot and crew failed to recognize that they were in a situation that didn't require them to eject.

The ethical error here was the failure of the pilot to follow appropriate preflight checks, including having a cockpit "fit" completed. Being ethical implies that one takes every opportunity to ensure that one does the right thing. One of those right things is being totally familiar with not only NATOPS but any and all special requirements for flying each and every aircraft one enters.

This aircraft loss was a result of an officer not taking the time to ensure he could, in fact, fly the aircraft under all conditions, including those involved in an emergency. "What-if" type thinking is important when preparing to do any job. Say to yourself, "if this happens, what will I do?" and "if that happens, what will I do?" In addition, an officer should check with available enlisted personnel and officers to verify that things are being done correctly. All of this may seem to be carrying the subject of ethics too far, yet the loss of life and aircraft that will be avoided will be well worth the extra effort.

ISSUE 16 - REQUEST FOR TRANSFER

What happened: (Issue 16 from page 33) The OIC's first step was to document all incidents that might relate to differences of opinion with the XO. The next step was to approach the XO with a formal written complaint that was addressed to the Bureau of Personnel through the chain-of-command. Through this process the OIC demonstrated moral courage by directly confronting the issue (the XO) and thus precluded any further unethical behavior or reprisals. By facing the issue squarely, the OIC obtained the support of the unit CO and transfer orders were issued with department head credit.

ISSUE 17 - GOVERNMENT EQUIPMENT AND SERVICES

What happened: (Issue 17 from page 34) As soon as a loyal member of the command pointed out to the commanding officer that the help being given his civilian friend was improper, all such activities ceased.

The interrelationship between a base and the civilian community is close, and sometimes it is difficult to separate that which is done in a sense of improving community relationships and that which involves prohibited activities. It is best before entering into any arrangement with those not involved in military operations to check with the local Judge Advocate, who can advise about the legality of operations being considered.

Generally speaking, those services provided to specific individuals in a community and not available to all, need the JAG's blessing to ensure legal and ethical actions are taken.

ISSUE 18 - MOTIVATION ISN'T EVERYTHING

What happened: (Issue 18 from page 35) The pilot exceeded his ability and experience, for he had insufficient familiarization training and failed to recognize an approaching stall. Fortunately, the pilot was able to eject, but a very expensive aircraft was destroyed.

The CO could have done more by checking with the personnel mentioned in the case. The signs were there: a pilot who had other things on his mind. If the CO, who was probably extremely busy, had followed up his hunch that the pilot might not be fully prepared, then the lack of refresher training and inexperience would have shown up and the pilot would not have been allowed to fly. Ethics is not an abstract subject but rather goes to the very core of our actions.

Not losing the pilot was important, but it is interesting to reflect that the loss of this one aircraft equals half of the operating budget of the entire U.S. Naval Academy for one year.

ISSUE 19 - OVERPAYMENT

What happened: (Issue 19 from page 36) A nonpunitive letter of caution was issued to the officer by the CO because he felt timely steps to make repayment had not been taken, as could be expected of an officer.

Actually, two mistakes were made: first, was not stopping the flow of unauthorized funds, something that could have been done by notifying the disbursing officer; and second, the funds were not promptly repaid.

It was a poor excuse that there were other, higher priority matters to take care of.

Personnel officers also have a responsibility to ensure expeditious processing of travel claims so that hardships for military members do not result.

ISSUE 20 - THE DRUG TEST

What happened: (Issue 20 from page 37) No matter how good a performer, tolerating this behavior is a bad precedent to establish.

Action must be taken. Perhaps not a discharge, because you only have his word (maybe he just wants to quit the Navy because of an upcoming deployment), but certainly counseling and removal from personal reliability programs would be in order.

The appropriate action is not always taken, and in this instance it wasn't. The division officer let it go by, though he did counsel the sailor, who has been a good solid performer since then, without any reported or evidenced problem with drugs.

This case simultaneously challenged both the ethics and compassion of the division officer. We would maintain that the officer made a bad decision because he did not have the authority to decide not to report the E-5; he did not have the authority to decide that the Navy's zero-tolerance policy did not apply in this case; and he endangered his crew, because the E-5 had demonstrated weakness under stress.

The division officer should have reported the E-5 for further investigation, which might have determined that this wasn't the first usage, and second, that one-time use of cocaine has been shown to be addictive, so a disaster was tentatively waiting to happen. While reporting the E-5 should have been done, it would also have been appropriate to testify on his behalf as to his performance.

The point is that officers must support the rules, for by not doing so, they also send a message that each member of the armed forces has the right, at times, to decide which rules are to be obeyed and which are not. A division officer's inaction can adversely affect the morale of his division. Most members of the military do not want to serve alongside an individual who is irresponsible and unreliable. Such an individual is "an accident waiting to happen," plus a morale buster.

ISSUE 21 - STRESS AT THE BINGO POINT

What happened: (Issue 21 from page 38) The mentally overloaded pilot crashed into the sea, losing both the aircraft and his life. This was a mishap waiting to happen, for the record clearly showed that the pilot had had difficulty (sensory overload) under high-tasking conditions.

The military is a complex world in which to operate. It is especially dangerous for those who cannot perform at the required tempo and performance level. This was a "real-time" situation; it was the responsibility of the CO to send the pilot to the beach, and afterwards to review how the matter was allowed to happen in the first place.

Relieving someone of their lifelong ambition is not easy, but that is one of the responsibilities that goes along with command. The pilot should have been grounded. Problem avoidance, where possible, is better than problem solving, which may not be possible.

There were others, including both the training and operations officers, who knew this pilot had difficulty under high-tasking conditions, but they said nothing because they saw themselves as friends trying to help out another service person. Unfortunately, they failed the pilot because they didn't speak up other than offering reassuring words of comfort.

SOLUTIONS

ISSUE 22 - THE CHRISTMAS GIFT

What happened: (Issue 22 from page 39) The attitude of the command's leadership was always to do the right thing. The command was also pragmatic in its approach, allowing for the traditions and local culture in its overseas location. Given this background, the officer was confident that all parties could be satisfied while keeping to the spirit of the ethics contained in the "Standards of Conduct."

The officer's experience had also taught him that only when someone tried to "go it alone" or hide an incident did that individual suffer. He elevated the issue to its proper level in the organization and let the legal experts help him resolve it. The legal counsel determined that it was proper not to return the gift, but rather to have the officer anonymously donate its contents to the command's Christmas party.

This way the professional relationship between the government and the contractor was maintained and the appearance of contractor influence on government affairs was negated. In matters such as these, it is always well to contact the military legal counsel who will know what is proper to do, thus saving embarrassment to the individual officer as well as to the U. S. Government.

ISSUE 23 - DRINKING CONTEST

What happened: (Issue 23 from page 40) The officers had not asked for permission to operate the bar during their off-duty hours and thus were censured for that dereliction and admonished for their poor judgment in not stopping the drinking contest.

An officer's career progression is not based so much on other past achievements as the judgment of seniors about the ability to perform at more demanding levels in the future and the ability to use ever-increasing good judgment in handling new situations.

When officers use poor judgment at lower levels, their record will reflect that, and further rank progression will become less and less likely as those officers try to move up the promotion ladder.

ISSUE 24 - RESPONDING TO AN EMERGENCY

What happened: (Issue 24 from page 41) One aircraft destroyed and one crew fatality.

You will note that the word accident is not used, for that would imply that something happened over which no one had control nor could previous planning have prevented the crash and loss of life. This was a mishap because it could have been prevented, if all concerned had done their job.

Command responsibility not only concerns itself with doing one's own job but also, more importantly, making sure that subordinates know how to do theirs. Thinking is the key: if the pilot's senior had thought about what might go wrong, rather than having the positive attitude that nothing could go wrong, the pilot and aircraft would have been saved.

The message here is that officers are responsible for far more than what may be written down. An officer must engage in "what if" thinking about all that he and others do. It is not enough, after something goes wrong to tell a senior that if you had thought about it a little more, you could have predicted the outcome. Take the time to think about all that you are involved in *ahead of time*. It probably will make a difference.

ISSUE 25 - BILLET ASSIGNMENTS

What happened: (Issue 25 from page 47) Recognizing the imbalance of previous crew assignments and the need for the Navy to have a balanced force, and assuming that both of the new people were trainable, the XO assigned the minority crew member to operations and the non-minority to supply.

This sent a clear message that segregation was over, and assignments would henceforth be made on the basis of merit in the case of equally qualified personnel, that every effort would be taken to ensure the obtaining of a homogeneous crew.

Additionally, the XO met with the operations officer and all division officers to point out his expectations of their working out harmoniously and fairly the integration of these two seamen into their sections.

ISSUE 26 - OFFICIAL TRAVEL

What happened: (Issue 26 from page 48) John Paul Jones, ethical father of the American Navy, admonished all hands to not only do what is right but to avoid situations that might give the appearance of wrong.

SOLUTIONS

It is wrong to adjust a flight plan to accommodate the wishes of another military person who wishes to participate in a personal endeavor. Every military activity involves both risk and cost, but that risk is justified by the needs of the service. By adjusting operational plans for personal needs, we encounter risk taking for nongovernmental purposes—a risk that is not accorded other members of the taxpaying public.

In this case, because the officer used military aircraft for his own private needs, a nonpunitive letter of caution was issued that reflected his poor judgment, which adversely affected the officer's career.

ISSUE 27 - BRIEFED ALTITUDE

What happened: (Issue 27 from page 49) Complacency is generally considered to be the most common downfall of experienced aviators. In this instance the rule—not flying below the specified minimum altitude—was violated, with disastrous results: loss of the aircraft and both pilots.

Minimums exist for safety reasons, as learned through the experiences of other pilots. Loss of situational awareness, complacency, indolence, and poor judgment all conspired to make this a fatal mishap. It appears that an overall lack of self-discipline was the primary cause of the mishap, though the installed low-altitude alarm system may not have been loud enough for the pilots to hear.

ISSUE 28 - SYSTEMS ACCEPTANCE

What happened: (Issue 28 from page 50) The project engineer reasoned that the 0-6 would not be directing him to sign an acceptance form if, in fact, the system wasn't ready for military delivery.

He also knew that it was wrong to impugn the integrity of his senior, since he may not have known all of the facts. (It might even have been a test of his own integrity to see what he would do under such pressure.)

Instead of signing the acceptance document, as he had been directed, the project engineer mailed the unsigned acceptance document and his report, along with a letter of recommendations, to the 0-6 for the latter's signature.

The project engineer's career was not hurt by his actions, and the 0-6 directed the contractor to fix all discrepancies before he accepted the system.

ISSUE 29 - THE CANTEEN CORKS

What happened: (Issue 29 from page 51) Knowing that his battalion and his company were due for inspection, our company commander went to his contemporaries in other battalions and persuaded them to lend him their canteens with corks for his company's use during the inspection. He promised to return them afterward.

On the day of the inspection the CG found that, in fact, the CO did have all the canteen corks he was supposed to. The CG surprised the company commander with the question: "You borrowed them in anticipation of my inspection, did you not?" The latter admitted that he had.

The CG said further, "When I am inspecting, I am not just inspecting an individual unit, I am inspecting the entire division. If you willfully cover up the ineptness of the supply system, you are not demonstrating loyalty. As a matter of fact, your cover-up reflects worse on yourself than would the lack of canteen corks. I know the problems in the supply system and realize that a lack of canteen corks does not reflect unfavorably on you or your unit. I know, however, that your attempt to grandstand and look good personally reflects adversely on your professionalism and professional loyalty. You knowingly or unknowingly could have contributed to my making a bad decision based on faulty information that you supplied."

The CG further said to the company commander: "You have a great future in front of you, perhaps. But I don't think it is in the Marine Corps." The company commander later resigned. The words of the commanding general spread among the other commanders like wildfire. A valuable lesson was demonstrated and communicated to the leadership of the Marine division.

There is no such thing as a legitimate lie to one's self, one's senior, or one's country. That is one concept you embrace when you accept a commission.

ISSUE 30 - INTER-AIRCRAFT COMMUNICATIONS

What happened: (Issue 30 from page 52) An after-accident investigation report revealed that NATOPS emergency procedures had not been discussed before the flight.

Further, the investigation determined that weight and balance were improperly calculated and cargo was not properly secured which resulted in cargo shifting in flight. The aircraft control was thus adversely affected by the shift in the center of gravity. Findings also concluded that communication and cockpit coordination between cargo air control and the two aircraft were inadequate.

ISSUE 31 - SHORTAGE OF FUNDS

What happened: (Issue 31 from page 53) The senior enlisted chose the easy path and altered personnel documents to cause a dependency allotment to be issued, which netted him an extra $10,000 over time.

The trusted senior enlisted was not immediately found out, resulting in collection of this sizeable amount before detection during a routine audit.

As a result, the senior enlisted was fined the amount taken, reduced in grade and separated from the service. Although retirement pay was received, entering into civilian life took place earlier than planned. The pension received was considerably less than that received from a 30-year career as an E-9 would expect as a result of good performance.

ISSUE 32 - FRATERNIZATION

What happened: (Issue 32 from page 54) If nothing is done, morale will eventually be severely affected, as other personnel wonder why they aren't accorded the same exception to the rules. An infraction of this nature, left unprosecuted, will send a message to the enlisted and officers alike that Navy policies are subject to "specialized" interpretation by those in authority and will not be adhered to in every instance.

Recognizing the need for evenhanded treatment of the troops, the CO initiated an investigation, collected data, and subsequently reprimanded both individuals.

This sent a message throughout the command that the Navy was serious about its policy on fraternization and further, that all ranks were expected to obey the rules. A quick and decisive approach to this matter sent the message that illegal actions on the part of anyone would not be tolerated.

The proper way to handle this matter in the first place would have been for the XO to immediately bring the romance to the attention of his commanding officer and, in addition, to seek the counsel of the base JAG officer. The best approach would have been for the ensign to be transferred to another base, certainly not to be kept at the same base without the specific approval of the base commander.

ISSUE 33 - AIR SHOW

What happened: (Issue 33 from page 55) The aircraft was destroyed, though no one was hurt.

The after-accident investigation determined that the mishap pilot had been experience "burn out" (motivational exhaustion) and was not current in annual flight time, number of approaches, landings, and aircraft qualification requirements.

As to how the NATOPS evaluator could have retained his qualifications without being current, the answer goes to the heart of the need for and use of trust in the military service. We depend on it. The selection of an evaluator is based on the individual's past performance and his or her demonstration of integrity and the acceptance of responsibility, including maintaining currency.

In this case the evaluator took advantage of the system. While the CO of a squadron is provided on a monthly basis with the state of each individual's meeting NATOPS requirement, the senior evaluator is expected to make sure that no one flies who is deficient. In addition, this was a failure on the part of both the operations and training officers for not checking all their records to ensure that only pilots who are "current" are allowed to fly.

From their first crew coordination classes, pilots know that flying when NATOPS requirements have not been met will surely lead to the end of one's flying days, and in some cases dismissal from the service.

Notwithstanding these points the mishap would have been avoided if the copilot had spoken up as to his reservations about the steepness of the approach. Officers have an ethical duty to tell their seniors when they think that a mistake is going to be made. It is not easy speaking up to a senior, but loyalty to that senior dictates that kind of feedback. Ethics is not just a philosophical concept that barely enters our lives, it is our daily willingness to seek truth and justice. In the Armed Forces it also saves lives and equipment.

ISSUE 34 - THE GIFT

What happened: (Issue 34 from page 57) Three months later the command Inspector General, acting on a call received through the DOD IG hotline, investigated the case. It appears that a few months after the party—but not because of the party—the contractor fired the company's project manager on this contract for poor performance. The PM concurred with this decision.

After being dismissed, the former contractor's project manager made a call to the DOD IG hotline and gave the account of the incident. The IG brought charges against both the FM and PM officers for coercing a contractor to provide a gratuity, accepting a gratuity, and conduct unbecoming an officer.

The case was dealt with at Admiral's Mast. The two officers voluntarily reimbursed the contractor for the cost of the art work.

Lesson to be learned: As soon as an officer finds that an unethical practice has been going on, immediate steps should be taken to stop the practice and notify the staff judge advocate, through their senior, to determine what remedial steps should be taken. Every civilian and military employee of the Federal Government has access to the military's fraud and abuse hotline, which has been established to catch and prosecute wrongdoers who are not otherwise challenged within their own organization. There are a great many loyal and dedicated civilians and officers working for the military, and if you do something that is unethical, even if legal, you may well find out something that you don't want to know—how the IG hotline system works!

ISSUE 35 - WORKING WITH A CONTRACTOR

What happened: (Issue 35 from page 58) The officer was persuaded by the contractor to accept overnight lodgings without cost to the government, thus enabling the officer to file for and keep housing reimbursement which was illegal.

Meals were also provided by the contractor, without cost to the officer. Additionally, the officer was involved in several extramarital affairs which further damaged his military reputation. The result was that the officer was fined and given a less than honorable discharge.

Our country expects us to meet higher ethical standards than the average person. When we don't, we let our country down and make it much more difficult for others to feel the same trust as they did before such an incident. All of us must make a major effort to protect and defend the good name of the officer corps.

ISSUE 36 - LETTER FROM HOME

What happened: (Issue 36 from page 59) Four fatalities and two aircraft destroyed were the result of an unethical act by one of the copilots, though during its commission no one said anything.

Three ethical violations led to this mishap. First, the copilot made the decision that reading his letter was more important than what the briefer had to say. Second, those at the briefing who saw the copilot did not have the moral courage to insist that he pay attention to the briefing. Third, the copilot had an ethical responsibility to remove himself from the flight schedule when he was so tired that it affected his judgment.

This mishap was avoidable simply by applying ethical doctrine: do what you are supposed to do, pay attention, and if an officer is not prepared to perform a job as spelled out in regulations, then so advise your senior so that someone else can be assigned the task.

ISSUE 37 - EQUAL TREATMENT

What happened: (Issue 37 from page 60) The administrative assistant tactfully approached the CO and voiced his concerns about the unfair treatment of female lieutenants. He raised the issue that the actions already taken were possible grounds for harassment charges against the CO.

This had the benefit of bringing all parties on board together and, as a result of discussing grievances, the male lieutenants stopped the inappropriate treatment of the women officers in particular and the harassment of females in general at the command. The women's lavatory was also reopened.

ISSUE 38 - THE DISBURSING OFFICER

<u>What happened</u>: (Issue 38 from page 62) For the final time, she went through every bill separately (about $400K). The ensign went slowly and stayed calm throughout the entire process, as she was already reconciled to have to report the shortage. Somehow, her safe balanced with her books.

While the problem above was resolved, there are some key points to be made. (1) While the ensign felt that she had let her boss down, she realized that it is much better to identify a potential problem as early as possible in order to avoid the appearance of a cover-up. Even the appearance of a cover-up, in an accountable position, can hurt one's reputation and possibly damage one's career. (2) A good litmus test for your actions is whether you can go home at night and feel good about something you've done or said. (3) The ensign's covering up losses with her own money possibly covered up thefts, as someone else took small amounts of money.

In addition, by covering up for the shortages, the ensign didn't open up her procedures for scrutiny which might have indicated an easily correctable fault. The thing to remember is that those viewing the actions of someone who breaks the rules, will feel that the cover-up is significant, not the amount of the cover-up.

Generally speaking, the military trusts those in it who reciprocate by acting trustworthy. In the final analysis, officers are supposed to obey the rules, file adverse reports on themselves, and owe their allegiance to ship, shipmates, and self—in that order. Trying to look good rather than being good is both unethical and incompatible with being a good officer.

ISSUE 39 - NATOPS CHECK FLIGHT

<u>What happened</u>: (Issue 39 from page 63) This "pilot appreciation" mindset adversely affected flight preparation and aircrew coordination, which led to several judgment errors.

In addition to the unprofessional mindset that was established, the senior pilot allowed the junior pilot to exceed his level of comfort and skill in flying the aircraft. The result was that the aircraft was destroyed and one life was lost. What was forgotten here is that NATOPS requirements have been developed over a long period of time and are based on lessons learned the hard way.

ISSUE 40 - THE FITNESS REPORT

What happened: (Issue 40 from page 65) In this case, the CO chose to cheat the system and got away with it. All five DHs from year group "A" were selected for promotion. Possibly, the lesson learned by the XO was that to take care of DHs, one needs to cheat.

For the service, the five 0-4s selected meant that other, more-qualified officers, whose COs did the right and ethical thing, were not selected. The decision by the CO was wrong from the "big picture" point of view. Although the CO was a hero among the DHs, the quality of future leadership in the higher ranks was negatively affected.

The concept that cheating the system is okay as long as you don't get caught is not acceptable—period.

America is a nation governed by rules and laws. If each of us determines which rules we will obey and which we will not, anarchy will eventually emerge. This is an especially intolerable situation within the military. Other than in time of global wars, the military operates under a reduced manning basis. This means that the *best* officers are required, at every level, to ensure both economical and efficient operation and the ability to handle "flash" incidents around the world. We must have an outstanding cadre on active duty when and if Reserve and Guard units have to be mobilized to take care of larger conflicts.

This CO disregarded the oath taken to support the Constitution and its laws. Taking upon oneself the determination of what rules should be obeyed and which should not is not only illegal, but also in the long run, detrimental to the Armed Forces of the United States. Loyalty to one's subordinates is commendable, but officers owe a greater degree of loyalty to their service and nation. Basically, the CO was too weak to make the proper decision!

ISSUE 41 - TRANSPORTATION

What happened: (Issue 41 from page 66) The senior officer asked the JOs to help his friend move, and they were most willing to do so in appreciation for all the "good deals" granted them by the senior officer. The move was accomplished and the JOs had their night out with the van. Only one thing happened to dampen this affair: it was a hotline complaint by someone in the motorpool who felt it was inappropriate for officers to commandeer a van for their own personal use of having a night on the town. The final finding was that it was more than just inappropriate, it was illegal for both the senior officer and the JOs to use government equipment. The senior officer received a letter of reprimand and was fined; the junior officers received letters of caution.

It was not wrong for the JOs to help move the senior officer's friend if they had done so using non-government equipment. It was wrong, however, for the senior officer to ask them in the first place since his position would make his request seem more like a demand than asking for volunteers. Not to be overlooked is the realization that a senior officer's actions will go a long way in helping strengthen or weaken the JOs' value system *and* their faith and confidence in the senior. It is important that all individuals dealing with government personnel witness maximum integrity by officers.

In this case the senior officer made three mistakes: (1) arranging government transportation for the civilian friend; (2) arranging for the JOs to have government transportation; and (3) asking the JOs for help. It should be noted that the JOs were also responsible for misusing the government van since they, like the CO, could be reasonably expected to know that government equipment cannot be used for private purposes.

The capability of the Armed Forces is such that they will be approached to help in everything from flood relief to collecting Toys for Tots at Christmas. Rules and regulations as to what is and what is not legal are rapidly changing. To avoid even the appearance of wrongdoing, it is important that officers, before undertaking nontraditional operations, check with their base legal officer to ensure that what is being contemplated out of compassion is in fact authorized. If something appears not to be authorized, then asking permission of higher headquarters—assuming time permits—is appropriate.

Because officers have a great deal of influence and power in making things happen, there's all the more reason to ask a JAG officer for advice as to what is and is not legal. Simply operating on the premise that something is okay is not good enough. This type of incident reflects poorly on the military when in fact the military plays an important part in the defense of the nation and is the most trusted element in society.

ISSUE 42 - THE FLIGHT

What happened: (Issue 42 from page 68) While it is probably apparent that the subordinate acted improperly by arranging a flight for the sole purpose of pleasing and helping out the senior, it may not be as obvious that the senior also did something wrong.

A senior wanting transportation is a self-fulfilling prophecy, as subordinates will do everything they can to make it happen. It is the responsibility of the senior to anticipate such action taken by juniors out of loyalty. The senior needs to ask how things came about and, above all, when first taking command, the senior needs to let everyone know that he or she does not want anything to happen that is illegal, unethical, or has the possibility of being misinterpreted.

In this instance the senior was reprimanded and had to pay for the cost of the flight.

ISSUE 43 - THE BUS TO LIBERTY

What happened: (Issue 43 from page 69) The senior officer becomes impatient over the delay in leaving; consequently, you have both families and the driver board the bus.

The trip to and from the family theme park is made without incident and all concerned had a marvelous time. The trip seemed to be a success.

Several weeks later, however, the junior officer who organized the trip was called to give evidence to an investigator from the IG's office who was responding to a hotline call about the extravagant waste of taxpayers' dollars that resulted from such a long bus trip for so few people. The question was also raised as to why two officers and families had to have an enlisted driver spend a day ferrying them around the countryside.

The end result was two officers being admonished for lack of good judgment, an action that probably didn't help their career aspirations.

At all times, when using equipment and supplies purchased by the taxpayer, it is well to consider whether you as a taxpayer would feel the expenditure justified. Would you be pleased to see the story on the evening news or read about it in the paper? If neither of these would be pleasant, then you have the answer: Don't do it. Use common sense, spend the dollars allocated to you wisely.

ISSUE 44 - THE HOTEL

What happened: (Issue 44 from page 70) The officer decided to accept the brother's offer and received the additional discount as the family crossed the country.

One of the motel's staff made a hotline complaint, because he knew that the motel chain would lose money because of the double discount. He was a loyal individual who constantly looked out for what was best for his company.

As officers we will find ourselves often accorded special privileges because of what we have done, are doing, and may do. While officers are individuals and have private lives, they must also recognize that, as with movie stars and other personnel in the public eye, what they do in their private lives is also looked at in a "public" way.

Officers are expected to set a higher example than the average citizen. In this case, what the officer was doing was similar to borrowing someone's "over age 21 ID card" which is both illegal and unethical, an action which reflected negatively on the officer corps. It is unethical for an officer to accept special treatment which others cannot. Second, such acceptance may be taken as a sign that the officer might be willing to throw additional business toward the motel chain. The perception that an officer is receiving or giving special favors is harmful, even if such is not the case.

The final result was that the officer received a letter of caution and the brother was admonished by the motel chain. It is important to remember that once you have fallen for something, it is hard to stand up for anything in the eyes of your seniors, peers, and subordinates.

ISSUE 45 - STANDARDS

What happened: (Issue 45 from page 72) Having thought the matter through, and realizing that his own actions had been cowardly and unethical, the legal officer decided to confront the XO concerning not only the injustice of the present situation but even prior instances to which the legal officer was a party.

Resolved to make amends for past weaknesses, the legal officer prepared a written statement concerning all those events and submitted them to the XO, prepared to see that justice was served even if it meant his own career would be ended.

As a result of the aggressive action by the legal officer, the new ensign was allowed to assume the duties of legal officer. The XO finally realized that he had been too quick to order the administrative separation of minority personnel in previous cases. From that moment forward, due process was restored in that squadron, with attempts made to rehabilitate personnel who had strayed from standards rather than separating them from the Naval Service.

By taking a stand, the legal officer saved his own career. He could now return to the high road and ensure that justice was done in his future dealings.

ISSUE 46 - PAY DAY AT SEA

What happened: (Issue 46 from page 73) If the crew wasn't paid on time, it would reflect negatively on the ASO for not having a contingency plan prior to the ship getting under way. The ASO could envision the supply officer jumping through some major hoops to figure out a way to get into the safe to get to the cash for payday.

At the very least, upon the ship's arrival in Subic the ASO would have been called off leave to conduct payday and produce all the necessary reports, balance the cashbook, etc., as required. In addition, the ASO felt that the CO and supply officer would probably always doubt the character and fortitude of the ASO in difficult circumstances.

The ASO realized that by remaining silent, this would force the others to work something out, but that wasn't the right thing to do. The ASO was concerned for the crew who depended on their paycheck being on time to send home to their families. The ASO's responsibility to *ship-shipmate-self* made it clear that the CO and supply officer had to be reminded that payday was supposed to take place while the ship was transitting to Subic from Hong Kong, at a time when the ASO wasn't scheduled to be on board. Thus, the ASO advised the supply officer, who told the CO.

After giving the dilemma some thought, the CO told the ASO to stay aboard for the transit to the Philippines. The couple was disappointed of course, but the spouse understood and they arranged to meet in Subic. The transit was nasty and the ship stayed just in front of the storm for a couple of days before breaking away and steering clear. After some more leave in Subic, the couple said their goodbyes and the ship continued on its deployment for another four months before returning to home port.

The term "psychic income" applies here, for the ASO realized that the payment of the crew was a responsibility that should not be passed to others. The crew also realized the sacrifice of the ASO and the entire ship showed its appreciation by their very pleasant attitude in the future dealings. A crew is a team that needs all members working for the good of everyone else. The ASO showed, by example, the high regard in which the crew was held; they reciprocated in turn.

ISSUE 47 - THE WEAK LIEUTENANT

What happened: (Issue 47 from page 77) Although there are several competing courses of action, one must understand the fundamental issue at hand. In this case, the integrity, morale, and functioning of the unit were in jeopardy due to the behavior of one of its most important leaders: a commissioned officer. This one individual could not be entrusted with the lives of men in combat, simply because he could not be trusted in daily life.

That is what drove the decision of the new first lieutenant to confront the CO and divulge all the activities of the *weak* lieutenant. The CO was shocked at this revelation and began to call his officers in for personal interviews. All at once, battle lines were drawn as officers hoped to either distance themselves from the event (cowardice), support the weak lieutenant (poor judgment and misplaced loyalty), or to corroborate the accusations made against the *weak* lieutenant (the morally and ethically correct thing to do).

The matter culminated when the CO called all the officers into his stateroom. Verbal accusations were made. Officers nearly resorted to blows, and one individual began to cry when realizing the scope, severity, and ramifications of such behavior amongst officers.

There were painful consequences for this delay in bringing the matter to the attention of the CO. Officers chose not to be in the same room with one another for the remainder of the deployment. Officers began to routinely lock up all their personal belongings at all times, in fear of retribution from the weak lieutenant. The event was well-known throughout the rest of the Marine and Navy personnel aboard other vessels, and the Marine CO suffered as a result of such publicity. Officers requested transfers to other vessels to finish out their deployment, and an environment of suspicion permeated the small group of officers on the ship. The *weak* lieutenant was discharged from active duty.

SOLUTIONS

In reviewing this matter it will be clear that loyalty to shipmates rather than first loyalty to ship caused the matter to continue when it should have been resolved before the new first lieutenant came on board, that is before the unit went on deployment. It is never easy to tackle such matters, but good officers just don't do the kinds of things the *weak* lieutenant did, and the failure of other officers eventually led to the destruction of esprit-de-corps on one of our ships—an avoidable consequence.

ISSUE 48 - CERTIFICATION

What happened: (Issue 48 from page 78) The officer's judgment that no one would be able to detect the error was wrong in that divers recovering the practice mines would have determined what actually happened.

Regardless of detection, your credibility as mission commander and as a naval officer would be compromised if you did not report the incident. By reporting the matter, the lieutenant earned the respect of crew, peers, and seniors alike.

Moral courage is an integral requirement for an officer, and the lieutenant's actions gave the CO the needed assurance that he was well informed and that overall command readiness would be accomplished.

Basically, we should do things because they are the right thing to do. Sometimes a senior may be testing a subordinate to see if he or she will, under pressure, do the wrong thing. Doing things wrong usually catches up with one, as would have been the case if a "new" radar had observed what had happened.

ISSUE 49 - FOOD FOR FRIENDS

What happened: (Issue 49 from page 79) Unbeknownst to you, one of your other neighbors, who is stationed at the same base you are, files a hotline complaint based on your having purchased food at the commissary for your civilian neighbor.

You are confronted by your commanding officer as to whether the charges are true, and upon acknowledging that they are, you receive a letter of caution to desist from the practice of buying commissary supplies for civilian friends even though you were motivated by the best of intentions.

This issue stems from a failure to recognize that there is a distinct difference in the services available to military personnel and civilians. It will probably seem obvious that one could not take one's neighbor child to sick call, and this separation of service also extends to the Post Exchange to buy clothes and other merchandise.

There is nothing wrong in helping drive another's children to school, though when they drive your children, it would be improper for you to fill up the gas tank in their car at the PX. Military personnel help their neighbors in many ways, including the most obvious—defending the nation against attacks by others.

The reason to make this fine distinction is brought home by the very complaint that brought the issue about in the first place. Often, perception governs the thoughts and actions of others, and it is important for the people of this country to hold their military personnel in the highest regard so that they have confidence that their tax monies are spent not only wisely but properly.

The merchants in town know that the military bases sell for less, but they cannot compete and stay in business if more than just military personnel are able to take advantage of these lowered prices. Such pricing is provided as a convenience for and a recognition of the fact that military personnel, on the average, make less money than their civilian counterparts. Military base locations often dictate that family needs be taken care of as efficiently as possible.

ISSUE 50 - ASSIGNMENT OF OFFICERS

What happened: (Issue 50 from page 80) After interviewing each officer, the XO discovered that the female ensign majored in mechanical engineering and sincerely desired to be involved with shipboard propulsion. The male ensign majored in political science and aspired to do graduate work in the public affairs arena.

The XO thus assigned the female ensign to the DCA billet and the male ensign to the administrative billet where he could also begin establishing a public affairs office, which had been sorely lacking.

It was therefore possible to optimize both officers' maximum potential as well as to send a message to the command that assignments are based on merit and expertise. This dispelled previous misconceptions that women are better suited for traditional roles and cannot handle more technical assignments.

ISSUE 51 - TAKE-OFF TIME

What happened: (Issue 51 from page 81) The captain felt the pressure of a much more senior officer giving him orders to change the flight take-off time, and rationalized that although the orders seemed to be illegal, surely a senior officer wouldn't give improper instructions.

The captain then radioed in that the take-off time was to be shown as 0602, and the colonel said thank you.

Two days later the captain received a message from command headquarters to show up and explain the incident in which he had falsified take-off time. From their review of the flight crew logs and his radio message, he appears to have reported the wrong time so that his unit would appear to have been operating perfectly, when in fact they were not.

Upon reporting to command headquarters, the captain was apprised that he was going to lose his flight-examiner status and his right to fly, for he had compromised his integrity by incorrectly reporting the take-off time. The captain explained the radio conversation with the colonel, and the investigating major played the recorded radio conversation, showing that the captain was right in what he said had taken place, but he was wrong in what he did. The colonel was on the IG's staff; the captain had failed the test of acting with integrity.

He realized, after it was too late, that he had succumbed to higher-officer pressure. Rather than standing on principle, he had obeyed an illegal order. The officer corps depends on the complete trust and honesty of its officers—those who stray not only jeopardize the lives of others, but their own careers as well.

ISSUE 52 - THE COMBINATION

What happened: (Issue 52 from page 82) Having both combinations made things easier and faster if the second person couldn't be found. The choices were: (1) to follow the rules, and possibly inconvenience officers with authorized access; or (2) disregard procedures in favor of personal convenience.

The most suitable, and fortunately most common, choice is to endure the inconvenience and obey the rules. These officers decided that the rules didn't apply to them, as they were both honorable individuals. So what was the harm?

This is not a debatable issue; it is betrayal of the special trust and confidence the President and Senate entrusts to each of us when we accept a commission. When an officer does something wrong, it reflects poorly on all officers. It is a negative reflection on those higher in the chain-of-command for not having done a better job of training subordinate officers, and is a negative reflection on fellow officers who may be suspected of having overlooked matters to be "a good guy."

As previously noted, this unacceptable procedure was discovered when one of the officers went into the communications center to retrieve some classified study materials from the security container without the second officer being present. The officer was observed opening both locks, and this was reported to the CO. As a result of this incident, both officers were reprimanded by the wing commander, and greater attention was placed on training officers in CMS procedures.

This incident also resulted in permanent marks in the officers' fitness reports, which shortened their careers. It is important to report that CMS education and training was both improved and made more frequently. It is also important to note that if the command had really been on the ball, the whole subject of security would have been given greater emphasis, and the incident might possibly have been avoided in the first place.

The military runs on trust, otherwise it would have to follow the former Soviet military system, with two chains-of-command, i.e.: one military and the other political, to ensure that military officers performed as they were told.

Your oath requires you to take action when you even suspect something wrong is being done. You should not be both traffic policeman and judge. As an officer you are not only to do the right thing yourself, but report those who do not, so that a thorough and impartial investigation can be made to either lead the individual concerned or have that person removed from the opportunity to do further harm. Complacency, particularly with classified materials, is detrimental to national security. The Walker and Pollard spy cases both bring to mind how failure to react to appearances of impropriety can lead to disaster.

ISSUE 53 - THE PERFORMER

What happened: (Issue 53 from page 83) Sending the PO to CO's Mast sent a strong message to the rest of the work center regarding responsibility and discipline. After Mast it was made clear to the PO that reversal of past performance must take place and work center policies could not be ignored. Unfortunately, further violations and additional UA incidents led to the PO's administrative separation from the service.

If the JO had given the PO another chance, the enlisted may well have learned the lesson and straightened up and salvaged what had been a promising career. On the other hand, if the enlisted's performance had not changed, the morale in the work center would have been seriously damaged. The JO, however, doubted that the PO would have changed and felt that the path taken was the correct and ethical way for *all* concerned.

The JO in this case felt that the attention the PO received for outstanding work was too much for the PO, who apparently decided not to be someone whom others would look up to as a role model. In the final analysis the JO felt that the work center was saved by making the decision to prosecute the PO. In this way the JO felt that twenty individuals had been saved versus the one lost, and in the end the ship was better off.

This would seem to be a fairly clear-cut case without need for further discussion, yet the following is offered for the reader's consideration. It appears in this issue that the JO did everything that could be done and thus met the ethical responsibility required of taking a stand and pursuing action when one thinks it is necessary.

Could something more have been done? The editors would like to suggest that the behavioral change was something that should have been investigated further. That is, an attempt should have been made to look below the surface behavior for the root causes. Failing success with that approach, the PO should have been brought to the attention of a trained Medical Service Corps psychologist. On the other hand, we do not conclude that the JO acted unethically, but we have to consider whether the PO's separation from the service could have been avoided. If skilled counseling had taken place, and the PO helped to realize the reasons for the aberrant behavior, then the PO might have been returned to the ship and continued what had been a promising career, with obvious benefit to the Navy.

We need to be aware in the service that the individual is the basis for all accomplishments. We need to recognize that sometimes we will have to admit to ourselves that greater counseling skills and ability to understand personal performance are needed than what we possess. It then becomes a matter of ethical conduct on our part to admit we can't solve a problem and ask for help.

SOLUTIONS

ISSUE 54 - REPORTING READY STATUS

<u>What happened</u>: (Issue 54 from page 84) Convinced that you would be fighting a losing battle by continued objection to the practice of on-time reporting of readiness, you let the practice continue without further comment.

Several months later, during a joint NATO operation, your fighter wing was called upon for a maximum effort at 0500. It reported, as in the past, that it was fully operational. Although it was a training exercise, the fact that your wing was not able to put sufficient aircraft in the air was a great embarrassment to the Commander, US Forces Europe, who in turn investigated what had happened.

As a result of the investigation, the Wing Commander was relieved as was the Commander for Maintenance. The deputy commander was retained long enough for a new commander and deputy to be appointed and move into place, and then he was allowed to resign—a promising career ended.

One needs to maintain maximum integrity at *all* times. If this hinders one's career, it's best to find this out early and shift professions!

ISSUE 55 - OFF-DUTY EMPLOYMENT

<u>What happened</u>: (Issue 55 from page 85) You recognize that even if there are multiple instances of violations by others at the post, that would certainly not justify the continuance of a known breaking of the rules. You point this out to the major and have a lengthy discussion with him about the "Standards of Conduct," with special reference to his compromising the Army by wearing his uniform when doing business.

Your next step is to talk to the two antique dealers in town to assure them that the Post Commander considers their complaints to be quite serious and needing immediate attention. You point out the major's financial problems and indicate that the Post Commander will tell the major to disassociate himself from the business he has with his wife. You are successful in making the town antique dealers aware of the Post Commander's commitment to doing the right thing.

This personal approach proved to be successful; the town antique dealers agreed to have the major's wife continue to handle all the business arrangements.

The military is very much a part of every community they are collocated with, and since we both are concerned with the welfare of the same nation, we have to work together. The point of this issue is to consider in advance anything and everything that is done by an officer to ensure that it will have only positive effects on the community. If, by the very nature of the military's mission, there may be a negative effect, that must be discussed with the community that will be affected. We must always be sensitive to perceptions others have of us.

ISSUE 56 - GRIEVANCE HEARING

What happened: (Issue 56 from page 87) The JO recognized that the XO was attempting to take the unpopular, but what he believed morally correct, course of action on behalf of the unit—a course of action that might bring him great criticism and possibly destroy his career.

The JO was cognizant that if he supported the XO's allegations, and received an unjust fitness report as a result, he could file a petition and have it removed. This, he knew very well, would be an uphill battle, but he wanted to take the honorable course of action and ensure he never had "second thoughts" in the future when similar situations emerged. He wanted to do what was right.

The JO decided to do what he believed was honorable and right and made a statement on behalf of the XO. The JO reasoned that not to make a statement would be an endorsement of the derogatory aspects of the CO's behavior, and would be taking the easy, weak, and irresponsible approach to Marine Corps leadership issues. After the commanding general reviewed all the preliminary statements, he determined that adequate proof existed to substantiate the executive officer's charges and thus ordered that a formal investigation be initiated.

The CO was found guilty and lost his command. The JO was transferred to another unit within a few months. The JO received a commendatory fitness report and was promoted to major.

ISSUE 57 - FLYING A SCHEDULED MISSION

What happened: (Issue 57 from page 88) The mishap pilot briefed a different training mission without clearing the change through the operations department, the commanding officer's representative.

Upon interrogation, the mishap pilot contended that he was unfamiliar with the full definition of ACM and felt that basic fighter maneuvering, consisting of missile breaks and guns defense, was separate from ACM and thus not subject to the same rule. Had the rules been followed and ACM not flown, the departure and subsequent mishap would not have occurred.

In this instance the mishap pilot's wingman was the flight leader and did not question the mission changes directed by the mishap pilot. There is no question that when an officer perceives that something wrong is done, he has an obligation to question that order even if it is given by a senior. It is also suggested that having a senior flying in a junior supporting role may also need to be reconsidered to ensure that when training dictates this kind of arrangement, the two officers understand the need to reverse their normal senior/subordinate roles.

Since the commanding officer had specifically scheduled a mission for which *everyone* was authorized to fly, and current instructions clearly spell out ACM definitions, maneuvers, and restrictions, it was the responsibility of the flight crew to be fully cognizant of all rules and restrictions as they applied to their aircraft and mission.

The point is simple: rules in the military, especially those pertaining to aircraft, have been developed through the experience gained from the mishaps, injuries, and deaths of hundreds of people. Officers have placed in them a special trust and often are not checked up on. When they fail this trust they fail themselves, their teammates, and their country.

Only under the most rigorous of combat conditions, when an officer has lost all means of contacting seniors, may the officer feel free to change the rules. To have it otherwise removes the advantage our military gains through its training, knowing what everyone is going to do without further having to talk with them over unsecured circuits or having to undertake untrained personnel for evolutions in other than the most desperate of situations.

ISSUE 58 - THE THIEF

What happened: (Issue 58 from page 89) The good friend did not confront the thief with the possibility of that officer's involvement with the other missing items.

Because the thief was such a good friend, the officer didn't want to discover the truth and merely wanted to remember the thief as a good, dear friend, not as a potential thief or kleptomaniac.

After the thief was kicked out of the service, the friend wrote several letters but received replies only from the spouse. Subsequently, the officer was forced to give up on the thief and their friendship.

Failure to confront the thief did not preserve the friendship but it did remove the possibility of determining whether the thefts from fellow officers had also been perpetrated by this same individual.

In effect, what the concerned officer did was to worry about the feelings of a thief over those of fellow officers. Because the matter of the thief was handled so quietly and the officer only seemed to be leaving the unit for another assignment, the officers who remained were left suspecting each other and to this day still feel that they served with an unknown thief. What could have been a great number of friendships were not allowed to flourish because one officer didn't want to face the truth that a longtime friend had been a thief.

It is suggested that the matter should have been discussed with the unit's commanding officer, along with a request that a further investigation of the thief's personal effects—at home and in the unit—be conducted with the hope that it would solve the problem.

ISSUE 59 - HUMOR

What happened: (Issue 59 from page 90) The XO realized that each and every military member is to be treated equally and fairly. This meant that the CO's integrity, as well as that of others, was to be assumed flawless until proven otherwise.

The XO started a full investigation of each side of the story to determine exactly what had happened. His first action was to advise the CO that he felt the need to investigate the matter and report his findings. He indicated that if he was ordered to drop the matter, it would then be necessary to report the matter up the chain-of-command.

Through conversations with the CO, the command master chief, and the command chaplain, along with interviews of other members of the command—both male and female—it was determined that the CO had been engaging in less than perfect conversational behavior with some of the female members of the command, in that he had observed how form fitting their clothes were and that they certainly created an attractive addition to the office. These and other remarks with sexual overtones were disturbing to the females in the office.

When the evidence was presented to the CO, he apologized to the individuals concerned and thanked the XO for getting involved.

It is important that female naval personnel lose neither their confidence in the chain-of-command nor in the Navy. Morale will be detrimentally affected if the female service members are denied the due process of investigation, and both male and female members of a command will become concerned if any member is mistreated.

It took courage for the XO to say something to the CO and carry out the investigation, yet it was the right thing to do. It resulted in a better operating command and a feeling among all personnel that everyone was being held to the same standard.

ISSUE 60 - MISSILE TEST FIRING

What happened: (Issue 60 from page 91) The illegal backdating was never needed because the shot did take place at 1623 on 30 September, seven minutes before range closure!

The fact was that if they had shot on 1 October, many people would have known, including 9 officers and 45 civilians, who would have had to be trusted to keep it quiet.

Even were only one person to know that something illegal was to be done, that person would have taken the first step toward compromising their own integrity, as Admiral Burke's article in Appendix A points out.

Again, the message is one of trust, integrity, and ethical behavior. When one person considers doing or does something that is illegal, then it says to all others that they too may unilaterally decide which rules they will break. We are a team operation in the military, and one person or more doing something wrong leaves open the question as to how many other things are also being done wrong, with resultant bad effects on the military.

In swearing our oath to the Constitution of the United States, we are also agreeing to obey its rules as long as we retain that commission.

ISSUE 61 - SUBMARINE PICTURES

What happened: (Issue 61 from page 92) The ensign told the Ship Superintendent he wasn't going to trade shrimp for pictures. He then let his CO know what had occurred, and the CO had a talk with the Ship Superintendent, who had the pictures taken and printed.

This further reinforced, in the mind of the ensign, that the ethical climate of the FBM was good. This is a case of a junior trying to please a senior, but managing to do so without compromising his integrity.

The rest of the command was unaware of the incident, but in this case making the right decision, though it might not have gotten the CO's pictures, was a good thing for the ensign. He made the CO aware of his integrity and the CO appreciated that more than the pictures.

In this case, the ensign maintained his own personal integrity and thus was able to provide the crew with the shrimp that was rightfully theirs. While it was likely that if the ensign had chosen the "easy approach", and had traded shrimp for pictures, no one else would have known, the ensign would have known that his own integrity had been diminished.

This situation shows how, by its actions, the chain-of-command can serve to strengthen the moral and ethical climate and behavior of an organization.

ISSUE 62 - COMMUNICATION

What happened: (Issue 62 from page 93) In the end, the officer candidates who were training with the unit were the ones hurt by the situation. Their interpretation of the standards of proper chain-of-command communications and conduct was confused.

Unfortunately, the CO did nothing, believing it was up to the 0-3 to work out a method of improving the relationship. The fallacy in this approach is that the 0-3 had shown by the poor communications that prevailed in the unit that the JO didn't have the knowledge and/or desire to straighten the situation out.

There is more to being an officer, no matter what the grade, than doing one's own job and ensuring that immediate subordinates do theirs. The position of commanding officer—whether you be an 0-1, 0-4, or 0-7—includes responsibility for everything that happens in the unit from your level down to the lowest rated enlisted in the ranks.

The ethical failure in this case is partially the responsibility of the 0-3 and the E-8 for not trying to work out their differences, but mainly it is a failure on the part of the CO for not intervening and alleviating the lack of communication existing within the command.

The organizational benefit derived from an involved commander of a unit is often underestimated. The CO should have stepped in to encourage and promote better communication by helping the two individuals better understand each other and the importance of their working/ communicating together for the benefit of the organization.

Since both the 0-3 and the E-8 wanted the very best for their unit, but did not know how to go about resolving their differences, the CO should have spent time with these two, which would have benefited the entire unit. The officer candidates who were training with the unit would have also benefited from the CO's involvement as well.

ISSUE 63 - THE JUNIOR OFFICER

What happened: (Issue 63 from page 94) The JO chose the *ethical* approach on the spot by focusing on his future reputation as an officer, his future ability to lead and discipline, and his goal to clean up the act of air crews and the command.

In this case the command *was* cleaned up. Many personnel disliked the "new order" and shunned the officer involved. His CO liked the outcome but gave little open support. The JO was ranked high on his FITREP, however.

It is important to note that as the CO and other personnel changed, the command in question also changed—being and staying more ethical.

The JO saw it through, met his personal goals, and felt he did the right thing for the command and the Department of the Navy and eventually moved on to better assignments.

ISSUE 64 - LACK OF COURAGE

What happened: (Issue 64 from page 96) In time, it was the CO's total disregard and lack of respect for the full weight of his position that led to the demise of command unity. In turn, the operational efficiency of the command suffered.

As for the 0-3, the other officers, and senior enlisted who recognized how wrong things were, they did nothing! The 0-3 transferred during mid-deployment with an intact service record, feeling deep sadness that he and fellow officers had lost sight of what it means to be a leader.

SOLUTIONS

219

This is an example of highly trained, competent officers—educated and trained to put their country, mission, and comrades before their own welfare—failing to take responsible action and to be accountable to their oath of office. They were prepared to sacrifice their lives for their country, but were not prepared to sacrifice their careers for the good of the service and the nation.

These issues were reported to the editors by the people involved, and it is apparent that there is deep regret on the part of some of the officers in this command that they did not have enough moral courage to speak out against the prevailing unprofessionalism that existed in this unit.

This is a sad case to report. Commissioned officers take an oath to uphold the Constitution and what it stands for, and after their basic training should be equipped with the tact and skills necessary to resolve serious unprofessional behavior, as evidenced in this particular command. It is crucial for junior officers to understand the impact such conduct has on the esteem of the commissioned officer. Avenues exist to ensure such conduct—even by a CO—does not go unnoticed. Your legal officer or chaplain is always available. As commissioned officers, you are held to a level of conduct that should be beyond reproach.

ISSUE 65 - EXTRA LABOR & EQUIPMENT

What happened: (Issue 65 from page 97) The 0-4 used the subordinates, who were almost all foreign nationals, for his own personal gain. They cut the lawn at his military quarters, trimmed his shrubs, and worked on his personal car at government expense.

The O-4 was fully aware that he was violating standards of conduct for his own personal gain, but there was no "adult" supervision of his activities. The military's image suffered gravely in the eyes of the foreign nationals who knew the score.

Ultimately, a new CO/XO team arrived and put a stop to the conduct, but by this time serious damage had been done to America's image. Clearly and simply, this is a case of authority and responsibility gained by virtue of one's position being used to reap undeserved personal benefit at government expense.

SOLUTIONS

In the final analysis two wrongs don't make a right. Even when an officer serves in a command that has less than a total ethical way of operating, the officer must be strong and resist the temptations offered so that the service is not disgraced and subordinate personnel are not led astray.

The ultimate cost of this betrayal of confidence placed in the officer damaged the service and earned a reputation, for the officer, which led to no further promotions.

ISSUE 66 - THE COMPETITION

What happened: (Issue 66 from page 102) While the concept of cheating is abhorrent to the military, the requirement to win requires officers to constantly do a reality check on their ethical approach to winning.

In this instance, the A-6 crew violated air competition rules by taking target area photographs. Winning, at any cost, had become the primary goal. Even though they were in a training exercise, the concept of winning consumed both aviators. The rest of the community was outraged at their conduct and the aircrew found it advisable to withdraw from the competition.

As with all the other incidents treated in this book, the consequences of acting unethically outlive the actual situation. These two officers had their service reputations and futures irreparably damaged.

We must do things right, not because we are afraid of being caught, but because we can feel a greater sense of satisfaction knowing we have bested the competition in a fair fight, and we have enough regard for other members of our military that we consider them a team rather than persons we are trying to take advantage of and defeat.

Remember the test of whether something you have done, are doing, or will do is ethical: Are you willing to tell others whose opinion you respect? If you are not prepared to do so (as in the case of these pilots), then it may well not be ethical.

ISSUE 67 - FRATERNIZATION

What happened: (Issue 67 from page 103) Although there was an excellent command master chief and Family Service Center at the home base, the officer failed to seek their help after the initial contact with the enlisted.

The JO offered to share the BOQ room that was assigned and proceeded to help the enlisted talk through problems. Between sharing the room and free time at school, the two developed a mutual emotional attraction.

The JO should have assisted on the spot initially, but then should have sought assistance for the enlisted through proper channels. Instead, their fraternization ended the career of the JO and prevented the enlisted from reenlisting.

As it turned out, the enlisted never received any professional military counseling. Officers are granted special trust and confidence, and a great deal of latitude may be taken without necessary approval by seniors. It is the trust placed in officers that makes it imperative that they carefully think through all of their actions in advance.

The JO forgot that all officers are sometimes judged by the actions of a few. By failing to seek counsel from the local military chaplain and judge advocate, a situation developed that was almost predictable and ended two careers.

An officer should also, as a leader, be aware of all services available for subordinates. Being aware of the professional services the military offers for its members may have helped this JO make a better decision as to appropriate senior-subordinate relationships.

It is emphasized that fraternization can occur on or off base. The commissioned officer must always remain beyond reproach—even when away from home port or one's command. Location of a violation is never an excuse. You are an officer of the Armed Forces of the United States all the time: twenty-four hours a day, seven days a week. You can never escape the responsibility.

ISSUE 68 - THE EXAM

What happened: (Issue 68 from page 104) The officer didn't even try asking for leave, which the command might have approved. The officer/student left town and flew home, taking along classified material to study on the flight. When the student returned, the logs were falsified by stating that studying had taken place all weekend long. Other students had not seen their peer studying in the classroom over the weekend.

The officer's actions were discovered, and that individual was taken to Mast and given an administrative discharge. Because of the falsification of official documents, the officer is no longer in the service.

This officer was trapped from the moment the first rule was broken. The following quote from Appendix A applies:

"Finding no way out, you begin to rationalize, and then you are hooked.

"The important fact is, the officers who travel the path outlined above have misused the very basic quality and characteristic expected of a professional officer, or any other professional for that matter.

"They have compromised their integrity."

In addition to everything else, this officer took the chance that classified material wouldn't be lost on the trip, which could have jeopardized national security and adversely reflected on the entire officer corps. In a future of declining military budgets, it is the responsibility of every officer to ensure that nothing they do provides the basis for further reducing our defense budget.

ISSUE 69 - INFLATED READINESS LEVELS

What happened: (Issue 69 from page 105) The most suitable course of action would have been to follow the required training as per the instructions vs. inflating readiness levels in order to look good.

During the course of meetings between junior and more senior officers, a great deal of conflict was generated between the O-3 aviator, assigned to a Fleet Maritime Patrol Squadron, and the O-4 Training and Operations department heads.

Sadly, we report that the pressure was too much; while the JO should have insisted upon sticking to the specific requirements governed by instructions, such was not the case.

There is every likelihood that the seniors would have felt pressured to do it right if the JO had insisted. Again, we have the instance of an officer willing to die for the nation but not willing to lose a career to fight for doing what is right and appropriate.

ISSUE 70 - SOUVENIRS

What happened: (Issue 70 from page 106) When service personnel return from overseas, whether on ships or aircraft, they have to complete a customs form upon their reentry to the United States.

This requirement to file a customs form applies whether one is returning from deployment, post "war," permanent change of station, etc. You are *not* allowed to import certain items and others, if declared, result in paying customs fees. It behooves military personnel upon their return from overseas deployment to check the latest customs regulations to ensure that they are in compliance.

Military members are also required to pay customs fees for a number of articles, though the great number of places that can be found to hide "gifts" makes it impossible for customs agents to search everywhere. This, at times, among some service personnel, results in an attitude of: "Well, just don't write it down." "They will never know."

Another dodge is to have a crew member who has not used up his duty-free quota declare items for someone who is over the limit. An officer who so helps his buddy is also acting unethically. An easy test of what is right or wrong when coming through customs, is to ask yourself whether there is anything you are doing that you don't want the customs agent to know about, and to further double check yourself by telling the agent *everything* you *are* doing.

This syndrome of only obeying the rules for which someone may be caught can affect all ranks—as many as think it doesn't "really" matter. As seniors take these illegal liberties, they infect their subordinates as well as peers with the idea that you have only broken a rule if you get caught.

In this case an honest member of the military knew what others were doing, reported the matter to customs agents, and when all the presents had been passed out at the homecoming reunion, customs agents appeared and arrested those who had perpetrated the fraud against their fellow Americans. As can be imagined, this was detrimental to the careers of the guilty officers and enlisted personnel.

ISSUE 71 - VIDEO HARASSMENT

What happened: (Issue 71 from page 107) The lieutenant realized that the authority entrusted to him as a naval officer demanded that justice be obtained. He submitted a formal grievance through the chain-of-command.

The video was destroyed, the individuals who made up the skit were censured, and the XO was given a letter of reprimand.

If we as American military officers do not embrace the responsibilities and accept the challenges of stifling discrimination within our workplaces, decreased morale and animosity between the races will be perpetuated.

High morale and mission accomplishment can only be achieved in an environment of equality and fairness. Established policies and procedures dealing with equal opportunity must be enforced and adhered to in order to obtain equal treatment within the Armed Forces.

You must do the right thing, even if it brings you under fire from those senior to you in the chain-of-command. Each of us is prepared to die for our country, let's make sure we are also prepared to live for it, even if it means sacrificing our career in pursuit of encouraging growth within our military.

ISSUE 72 - THE LONE RANGER

What happened: (Issue 72 from page 108) The JO refused to falsify records and was subsequently taken off the list for "good" orders.

The command, due to the refusal to cooperate, had to fly numerous sorties to achieve qualifications that normally would have taken one flight. By not allowing a senior officer to influence the decision, nor the command's acceptance of less-than-honest qualifications, the JO helped the command to ultimately attain legitimate qualifications.

This is yet another example of a resolute JO sticking to time-honored naval principles that subsequently caused a squadron to honestly meet qualifications. Certainly everyone wanted the squadron to look good, as did our JO—but the JO wanted it to be achieved honestly.

Edmund Burke said two centuries ago, "For evil to triumph all that is necessary is for enough good men to do nothing." An officer takes an oath to defend the Constitution and thereby swears to uphold the laws of this country. This, in turn, includes obeying the rules.

This officer made the correct ethical decision despite all the pressures of peers and seniors to do otherwise. Officers are always expected to do the right thing, and thinking through possible future questionable ethical practices will help ensure that you make the proper decision when the situation arises.

Officers should be selfless in their service to our nation. At times, this may anger others who may not be as principled. The right decision was easy for this particular JO because he knew by taking a stand that the squadron would be much better prepared in the future to successfully carry out their mission.

Whenever an officer does something wrong, others will know about it. Thus, the first step in building a climate of distrust and falsification has been taken. In the military we sometimes do things to make our boss look good; in fact, if by our labor we can accomplish that, so much the better. But when there is no substance to achievement it reflects unfavorably on the unit and the CO—the very person you might have been trying to help. Every CO is expected to know what is going on within the unit and is thus held accountable for all that is bad as well as being rewarded for all that is good.

There is a concept known as "psychic income," which implies that while we may not receive real dollars for doing our best, we will have the knowledge, when we do right, that we did make a difference.

ISSUE 73 - THE PARKING PASS

What happened: (Issue 73 from page 109) As a result of counseling by fellow officers, the officer who had made the realistic fake pass decided not to use it to secure a better parking spot.

This is a case of other officers not standing idly by while a friend did something foolish. They risked an argument and possible disruption of friendship to ensure that their fellow officer and comrade did not commit an unethical act.

At the time, the ethical climate was such that a number of personnel were engaged in improper activities without repercussion from the command. It was therefore particularly appropriate, and all the more significant, that these other officers spoke up.

The officer's ethical base was improved by this incident, but another, weaker officer—seeing how easy it was to make a fake pass—did so and was caught. During interrogation, that officer implicated the officer from whom the idea had originated.

The "caught" officer was heavily disciplined and the instigator of the entire affair was censured. Both officers lost the trust of their peers and seniors because they didn't have the ethical underpinnings to understand that the pranks of college life have no place in the officer community. By not having destroyed *all* copies of the fake pass, the officer made it possible for the friend to be caught and was lucky that the copy carried was never identified.

The forging of a pass is stealing, and when it appears that a friend doesn't understand this, all officers have an obligation to explain and educate that officer why such things aren't done. Anyone who thinks of ship-shipmate-self in that order will never bring discredit to other members of the command, for their own or anyone else's gain.

Most colleges have some form of honor code/concept whose purpose is to train and regulate the conduct of everyone at the school. Lying in the military to fellow officers, enlisted, or government officials is never permissible. As you read this statement, do yourself a favor and don't try to find an exception. It may lead to either your dismissal, that of a friend, disgrace to the military, or all three.

ISSUE 74 - MARIJUANA

<u>What happened</u>: (Issue 74 from page 110) The non-pot smoking JO did not really know what to do and excused himself from the rest of the evening's activities. The next day the concerned JO consulted a more senior JO who notified the chain-of-command. The problem was taken out of the JO's hands and an investigation ensued. The results were that all three pot-smoking JOs careers were ended: one received a dishonorable discharge; the other two were awarded less-than-honorable discharges.

The wardroom was in an uproar for many months. Some officers felt that trust and friendship had been violated, while others were outraged that illegal drugs were being used by officers. There were no legal ramifications for the JO who had shown concern, but there was sadness at the loss of friendships. The situation had an effect on the feeling of pride the JO had in the unit, since some of the officers, by their actions, showed their displeasure with him.

Doing the hard, right rather than the easy, wrong thing, or taking no action at all, is never easy. But it is a hallmark of our country's expectations of its officer corps.

Reasonable officers may disagree as to actions to be taken, but all officers, in swearing allegiance to the Constitution, agree to uphold the laws of our nation. Drug use has caused deaths in our military, and quite frankly, "friends" are not the kind of people who do illegal acts and expect their companions to overlook what they have done. Friends do not paint friends into a corner where the only legal action is to do what this JO had to do.

These three officers tried to take advantage of their friend. It is obvious that they felt the innocent JO would either join in or say nothing. For them to have felt that way means that they also felt the JO wasn't really a professional officer. It is the professionalism of officers that binds us all together; without that, we merely have a job. JOs, who want to build self pride and advance in their profession, will act as they would expect seniors to act, thus establishing by their actions their readiness for advancement.

Illegal actions by a commissioned officer, at any level, are intolerable. The citizens place their trust in the efficiency and allegiance of the military to obey existing laws and regulations. Violation of that trust is hypocritical and exceedingly unprofessional. Officers need to remind themselves of the criticality of this allegiance to law and order. (For further discussion of this point, see Plato's essay on "Guardians of the Republic.")

ISSUE 75 - DESIGNATION

<u>What happened</u>: (Issue 75 from page 111) While some of the unqualified officers benefited by these lax standards, the remainder of the squadron felt that morale, training, and readiness were compromised.

The message is clear: do not qualify any individual who does not fully meet the standards and expectations of the position. Individuals who cannot legitimately qualify will be channeled into a military career more suited to their abilities.

The majority of personnel in the squadron lacked the confidence that these "special" individuals were fully qualified to assume their designated duties. As a result, many of the aircrews requested not to fly with the "special" people during both training and operational tasks. This probably had an *adverse* impact on flight/crew scheduling, as well as operational performance, thus further affecting squadron operational readiness.

It is not easy to take a stand on an issue when you first join a unit. Yet, if you do not take a stand when you view or read of unprofessional conduct or possible unethical behavior, you quickly become a part of the problem rather than a mere observer.

ISSUE 76 - KEEPING EVERYONE HAPPY

<u>What happened</u>: (Issue 76 from page 112) The problem is that the CO didn't want to displease anyone, nor did he fully understand the new ACIP law.

Although the XO objected to not obeying the law, the CO managed to convince the appropriate department head at BUPERS to go along for the ride.

This is an example of where doing wrong seemingly works out well for those who have something to gain. This is merely a momentary advantage, however, for those who live above the law eventually are caught up by the legal system and punished.

The officer corps runs on trust, and further assumes that the playing field for everyone is level. These kinds of "deals" become known, and the resentment they build does far more to hurt the Naval Service than does the illegal action described to help morale. In fact, those who understand when something improper is done for them also resent their benefactor.

In this case the XO still regrets the action of the CO and BUPERS. It should be noted that the XO failed his own ethical responsibility to pursue the matter and will bide his time until he is in a position to do something about the inequities described. This is somewhat similar to the time when then-Commander Elmo Zumwalt was ordered to assign black officers to recruiting duty so as to ruin their careers. The day came when Admiral Zumwalt was able to reverse this policy; hopefully our XO will someday be able to exercise his command and ensure that such illegal acts are not practiced.

ISSUE 77 - THE COMPLAINT

What happened: (Issue 77 from page 113) The officer decided that although the enlisted was not an immediate subordinate there was a call for help. An officer's overall responsibility is not merely limited to those areas for which they are accountable.

Officers, by their oath, swear allegiance to the Constitution and the upholding of the laws of the land. Harassment is not only illegal, it is wrong. By doing nothing, the officer would be saying to the enlisted that *they* were wrong. At the very least, it would appear that the officer did not think it important enough to act upon.

We expect loyalty from all enlisted personnel, and thus all officers must concern themselves with all enlisted crew members. The officer has to do something, the only question is what?

The officer reasoned that doing nothing would not make the problem go away, and it might reappear in a way far more embarrassing to the command. Although talking to the accused officer might stop the action or ascertain that nothing had happened, it would not stop the enlisted from further complaining to others—including the IG.

SOLUTIONS

The officer reported the incident up the chain-of-command; an investigation was initiated. The enlisted, as well as others who know about the incident, felt that the command was concerned about its people, for as General Order 21 of the Navy states: When the Navy shows an interest in its people, its people will show an interest in the Navy.

In this case, the accused officer was found to have ill-considered some actions, and the CO determined that a warning was in order. Consequently, that action stopped harassment across the board. Just as importantly (assuming no other instances of alleged harassment took place in the future), the accused officer was saved from a possibly more intense investigation in the future.

Officers are human beings; they can make mistakes. It is up to their peers to care enough about their fellow officers to take action, for doing so may save a career rather than end one. It might have turned out that the complaint would not have been found to be justified, but it was the right thing to allow the chain to investigate. Being an officer will sometimes require that actions be taken that are not universally agreed with, but that is one of the things for which we are being paid.

ISSUE 78 - STANDARDS

What happened: (Issue 78 from page 114) The officer who had overheard the direction to pass the student, no matter what, decided it wouldn't be politically correct to point out to the CO the negative effect this action might have on all other students and pilots who would certainly know what had been done since they were aware of how many previous flight failures had occurred without dropping the individual from the program.

The instructor complied with the direction from the CO. Three months later, after the original class had graduated, wings were presented to the student.

It is not possible to know whether if the officer had spoken up, or not, the CO's mind would have changed, but the officer did fail the senior by not saying something. We expect our seniors to look out for us and must remember that that is a reciprocal requirement. We have to look out for them as well.

Whether telling a senior of a blunder or raising a question as to why a particular action was taken, we as officers do not have the option to say nothing to our seniors if we think they are making a mistake. They depend on our speaking up. While it might turn out that the senior

230   SOLUTIONS

officer holds a grudge for the junior's speaking up, officers should feel free, in private, to let their seniors know what they think.

If, after hearing an explanation, you still disagree with an action taken, then you can request an audience with your senior's boss, making sure that your own senior is with you so as to be able to state the other side of the issue.

It might be well, at times, to re-read Admiral Burke's comments on integrity, Appendix A, for one should never assume that one's boss is doing something wrong just because the action may differ from that which you yourself would take.

It is important to point out that there was one other person who ethically failed in this situation—the student pilot who accepted the special treatment. There is nothing wrong with offering or receiving a helping hand because it makes the service a better place. But in this instance we are talking about a person who knew by what happened to other students that sufficient failures meant failing out of the program. The "failed" student who passed accepted special treatment not offered to *anyone* else and thus was an accomplice to this ethical duplicity. If the "failed" student hadn't accepted the special treatment, then neither the CO nor the instructor would have acted unethically. Accepting unethical help from another is just another way of being unethical oneself.

ISSUE 79 - TRAINING

What happened: (Issue 79 from page 115) You are not sure whether the commanding officer knows what is going on in the unit, but you reason that that doesn't really matter for you to know that something wrong is being done. Your loyalty to your CO, unit, and country prescribes that as an officer you not tolerate a falsification of records.

You recognize that speaking up may well alienate your fellow officers, but your ultimate loyalty isn't to them. It is to the country, doing the job you have sworn to do to the best of your ability.

We train so that we will always be ready even though we may not be called into action for years. Our country depends on us to be ready—not merely ready on paper but ready to perform our mission as requirements say we must.

The JO decided that from that day forward all training was going to be done completely and as prescribed. The first step was to take the falsified report and return it with a short note to the officer responsible, indicating what sections of the training had not been accomplished. The

JO let the officers know that the assumption was being made that the missing training would be done before the next week's schedule, and that the JO was going to monitor training from that day forward.

The JO kept very busy for the next month monitoring all training. The word quickly spread that from that day forward all training had to be done correctly or there would probably be consequences. None of the officers who had allowed their units to shirk in their training responsibilities wanted the matter brought to the attention of the CO, and thus one JO was able to make a difference.

No matter what your rank, you can make a difference if you remember your position/job is to be a professional, not just someone trying to have a long peaceful career. All COs depend on their officers to ensure that requirements are met. We have an ethical obligation to meet that expectation or resign our commission; there is no middle road.

ISSUE 80 - LOST DOCUMENTS

What happened: (Issue 80 from page 116) The time pressure, combined with the pressures of a possible outside investigation, resulted in the individual's decision to solicit another officer to falsify the destruction record.

Although the officer was considered by all friends as trustworthy, and they had strong feelings that the material had indeed been destroyed, the officer could not get anyone else to falsify the statement as a witness. They felt that their integrity would be compromised by consorting in such a plot.

Due to the resistance of others, the individual realized that integrity was being compromised by asking for someone to countersign the paperwork. Finally, the officer came to the realization that without a destruction record, the consequences of telling the truth would have to be suffered.

The final decision was made and no one's integrity was compromised, though undoubtedly the officer's service reputation was harmed by having asked fellow officers to compromise their integrity. The material was eventually found. The officer had brought it up for the destruction as part of a larger pile of material. While the other material was being destroyed, the papers in question fell off the table behind some equipment and went unnoticed. When the rest of the pile was destroyed, it was assumed that the material in question was part of that pile. As it was not destroyed, however, no record of destruction was made.

In reporting this case the author noted that: "The final truthful and ethical decision to admit that the destruction record existed prevented any legal troubles when the truth was found out."

(*Editorial note:* While this issue was reported as the achievement, ultimately, of ethical conduct, we have to observe that the willingness of an officer to compromise the integrity of another and self indicates a rather weak individual who didn't commit a crime only because no one else would cooperate. It certainly raises the question how many times before this incident and subsequent to it would this officer be willing to take unethical actions for self-protection. It is suggested that other officers, knowing of the attempt at deception, should have reported it to the security officer for investigation, for only in that way could they be sure that the officer hadn't been involved in similar incidents. An individual who is prevented from completing a crime due to circumstances is hardly an officer worthy of wearing the uniform of the Armed Forces of the United States.)

ISSUE 81 - COWARDICE

What happened: (Issue 81 from page 117) All members of the squadron bit their tongues and said nothing. They not only despised the XO, however, but themselves as well for their cowardice.

The squadron went from winning two battle "Es" in a row to having poor morale and poor performance. The JO was facing a tough decision.

The chain-of-command is important to the military. When one of its members is overtly violating the UCMJ, however, then it is appropriate for the JO to talk directly to the CO.

Loyalty to the CO demands that that person be given the first opportunity to do something that has an effect on the entire unit. Certainly the CO has the right to know first before the matter is taken out of the unit.

Officers without self-respect will not do their very best, as this issue shows. Some of us may lose our lives in defense of our nation; but losing our careers, by doing something right, will be overcome. Time and again in reviewing such matters with career officers, one finds that those who fail to take action normally don't make it to higher command. They are generally looked down upon, and they themselves bear the guilt for the rest of their lives.

SOLUTIONS

We should never take action out of jealousy or spite, but we do swear allegiance to the Constitution and our willingness to uphold the rules and laws of our nation. To do less is to unethically accept pay for not doing the entire job required of us.

ISSUE 82 - THE MUNITIONS CASE

What happened: (Issue 82 from page 118) The officer again provided his views to the boss and was then directed to modify the recommendations, because of the governmental agency's pressure to obtain a system for Iraq as it fought with Iran. The officer refused to back off from his position; and his boss rewrote the recommendation and sent it up the chain for approval.

OSD reviewed the senior's recommendations and sent back a letter of disapproval, stating that the munitions package should not be delivered to Iraq. They had essentially the same reasons as had the boss's subordinate in the first place. Thus, the sale of classified technology to Iraq was prevented. In the Gulf War we did not have to face an advanced enemy fighting us with our own technology.

It is important to note that the boss did not take it out on the subordinate officer, for in delaying approval the boss had been saved a lot of trouble, from which the pressuring governmental agency could not have saved him or the pilots who had to fly against Iraq in Operation Desert Storm.

Doing what is right is not always the popular way to go, but it is what is expected of military officers of the Armed Forces of the United States.

ISSUE 83 - CONFIDENTIAL INFORMATION

What happened: (Issue 83 from page 123) The junior officer realized that the ethical thing for the personnel officer to have done was to hold the information confidential and not share it with others.

As mentioned in other issues dealt with within this book, all officers should be aware that as part of their military duties they may be expected to face an enemy and/or death in the meeting of their responsibilities to their service and country. Losing one's career is not a fate worse than death. It is reasonable to expect that officers will take that action consistent with their oath of office to uphold the Constitution and the principles of trust we all share.

Although junior, the officer decided that to do nothing was in effect condoning what the officer was doing. That is, approving the concept that each officer entrusted with information is the sole judge of what they should and should not repeat without anyone else's authorization. In this case, the personnel officer did not have the permission of either the individual talked about or the CO to repeat such information to third parties who did not have a need to know.

The junior officer felt ill at ease in bringing the matter up to the CO. The JO decided, however, that unit morale, cohesion, and performance might be affected if personal information was allowed to be bandied about by the personnel officer to help liven up an Officer's Club party, and therefore raised the issue with the CO.

The CO privately investigated the matter and upon determining that the accusation was true, relieved the personnel officer. In addition, appropriate career-ending remarks were made in the fitness report. While the junior officer was praised by the CO for coming forward, joy was not felt about the other officer's punishment.

When we raise our hand and take the oath of office, we swear to uphold the special trust and confidence placed in all officers. In time, the junior officer emotionally/intellectually realized that the right thing had been done, even though it was not the most pleasant of experiences for anyone involved.

As officers, most of our assignments and service lives are replete with positive experiences as we help our country, our seniors, our peers, and our subordinates in working on various mission assignments. There will be times, however, when the hard, right decision is the necessary path to take versus the easy, wrong decision to do nothing. If you want to be a career officer, you have to act like one and take all the responsibilities and actions expected of commissioned officers.

ISSUE 84 - A FRIEND?

What happened: (Issue 84 from page 124) The friend decided to effect a compromise by counseling the pilot. In that way, he avoided having to turn the pilot in while being able to think that future flights would be safely made.

In effect, what the pilot did was to compromise the trust placed in all officers, to uphold the rules. Further, one might ask what kind of a friend is it who will allow someone to risk a career by flying under the influence of alcohol? Who thinks so little of their service that they will allow others to compromise the rules that have been set down for all to follow? Such action reflects on the entire military.

Rules are the laws by which we live in the Armed Forces, and counseling is only appropriate where there is discretion that can be exercised between two equally legal alternatives. Counseling others with personal problems does not imply one method is right and another wrong. In some commissioning sources, while the officer candidate is learning the system, counseling is permitted as a means of dealing with a minor infraction of the rules, but even there it is not meant as an alternative to reporting a serious breach of military discipline.

The drinking pilot knew that others knew how long it had been between the drinks and flying, yet chose to fly anyway. In effect, saying that "friends" were expected to cover for actions and put their friends ahead of the good of the military service and others who might be affected by the drinking pilot having a mishap. The "friend," by flying, was actually covering for someone who did not reciprocate the friendship.

Remember that our oath, as officers, is not to our friends but to the Constitution; by giving that oath we agree to obey the rules set down by our military leaders. Finally, the concept that one doesn't turn in a friend so that they might not turn you in when you break a rule is contradictory to the principles of accountability, responsibility, and trust placed in all officers. If an officer fails to obey the rules, that officer is saying to all officers that they too can decide which rules they will obey and which they will not. This disrupts order and discipline.

Ending another's career is not a pleasant task, but attending that person's funeral because you failed to care enough for your friend to stop illegal action will not be a pleasant one either. If you are going to be an officer, do it right. Resign your commission if you don't have the fortitude to meet *ALL* of the requirements laid down.

ISSUE 85 - THE MISSING ITEM

What happened: (Issue 85 from page 125) The JO consulted a senior enlisted in the unit who thought that a plan might be worked out with one of the civilians working on the base.

A day later the senior enlisted produced the missing part and the unit passed inspection. Everyone was happy, but military ethics had taken a hit!

The senior enlisted convinced the civilian to trade the missing part for two foul weather jackets. As jacket custodian, the JO provided the jackets and received the part.

The common word for this is cumshaw but in reality it is stealing. Not only does it steal from taxpayers' funds designated for a particular purchase, but it also withholds information from senior personnel, denying them a realistic picture of supply requirements.

Cumshaw is neither officially sanctioned nor is it honest. The officer who reported this matter to the editors opined: "A judgment call was made as to the possible harm from this action versus the ubiquitous mission accomplishment requirement. Mission accomplishment won."

When we are not careful, we tend to mix priorities as to what the mission really is. Some individuals will quickly run through a meeting without allowing comment to ensure that all agenda items are raised. Similarly a home owner having trouble sleeping because of a noisy refrigerator, may think the problem is solved by closing the kitchen door so that the noise won't be heard. Neither of these approaches attack the problem but rather address the symptom.

In this instance, perhaps the checklist should have been changed, but by covering up the matter the JO destined others to have to take the time to inventory a part that no longer may be needed. The JO has also encouraged the enlisted to disregard rules and procedures if it will seem to facilitate accomplishment of what the mission appears to be.

When each of us decides which rules we will and will not obey, we send a strong message to our subordinates that they too should act accordingly. The JO may have won a very small and insignificant battle but contributed to the loss of the supply accountability war by resorting to and accepting unethical conduct.

ISSUE 86 - TO FAIL ONESELF

What happened: (Issue 86 from page 126) A junior officer—either the pot-smoking individual or some who knew about it—reported this incident to the editors, possibly in the hope of conscience clearing and/or giving others food for thought. Included in the report were such interesting sentences as:

(1) "To this day this information has not come out, and (it) could damage the individual's career due to a lack of integrity."

(2)   "An ethical decision would be made by coming clean; however, the career could be ended thus making an ethical conclusion the wrong answer."

This individual knows a mistake was made. If it was the person who did the smoking they knew they lied and if it is someone who knows the person, they know they too failed for not reporting the matter, for officers have a responsibility to report the illegal actions of others.

In thinking about what to do, the officer considered that "due to the factor of time it is best not to divulge info." The officer then went on to write: "Final decision: forget about it."

Everyone makes mistakes during their lives, and we are likely to make more early on than in later life. Those ethical mistakes, however, are etched in our brains and will not go away. They fester, reminding us of our failings. We can hope that we don't make an ethical mistake, but when we do, it would be well to discuss the matter with at least the command chaplain, with whom we may have privileged conversation. Possibly through that counsel we will be helped to understand what is the best course of action. Keep in mind that seniors were also juniors once, so seek their counsel as well. They may surprise you with their understanding.

The reporting officer's "forget about it" response has not really worked for the officer is still bothered by it. Thus, if the ethical decision had been made, their mind would now be clear. No one ever said that being ethical is easy, it's just what is expected by the American people of their military officers.

ISSUE 87 - TRAINING

What happened: (Issue 87 from page 127) The JO continued to falsify the reported data and no one questioned the validity of the report, which was approved through the chain-of-command for submission.

As a result of the data submitted, the unit won the award. In this case it was not a matter of how you played the game, but whether you won or lost. Rather than just reporting the training accomplished, the JO had been caught up in the "win at all costs" syndrome.

As time went on this falsification of data weighed so heavily on the mind of the JO that the matter was reported to the editors of this volume in the hope that others might be dissuaded from doing the same.

Commanding officers at every level must recognize that it is possible for officers to lose sight of the end objective—in this case improving training—and to take upon themselves, without the knowledge of the CO, certain actions that may be unethical but are done in the name of making the CO and the unit look good.

All JOs need to remember that everyone in their own unit, as well as others, trusts them to always do the right thing. We do not have a spy system in the U.S. Armed Forces as was the case with the political officers in the former Soviet Union who made sure that commanding officers did what the state wanted them to do.

An officer who acts improperly may never be caught—other than by conscience. We can tell you from talks with a great many officers that those who did wrong know that they did and are both ashamed of themselves and wish they could turn back the clock.

The reason for not doing something wrong has nothing to do with whether or not you will be caught and has everything to do with a sense of loyalty to other officers, the service, and the nation. Either we all do the best job we can as right as we can, or disruption of order will prevail as each officer tries to outsmart all other competing officers.

We are an honorable profession as pointed out by Admiral Bulkeley, and to each of us falls the task of not only seeing that we are honorable, but that others are as well. In this case the JO, upon assuming the training duties, should have immediately told the CO what was going on and only reported true and correct numbers. A unit can handle the truth of a cheat within their ranks far better than having to face other units after having improperly won a command-wide competition.

ISSUE 88 - TRAVEL CLAIM

What happened: (Issue 88 from page 128) On return to the home command, the officer worked out an ingenious solution to the money problem. By submitting a false claim for reimbursement that attested to the upgrading of accommodations that hadn't taken place, the officer hoped to realize enough additional funds over actual expenditures to help offset the additional cost of having taken the spouse along.

Reimbursement was only authorized for the lower rate, however, so the officer complained to the Personnel Support Detachment about not having been reimbursed for the upgraded accommodations (which in reality didn't take place).

SOLUTIONS

The officer's complaint came to the attention of the chain-of-command, which was flabbergasted at the gall of the officer, yet felt that public embarrassment for the command was not in the best interest of the service. The officer was reprimanded for the fraudulent claim and opted to accept the PSD check for the lesser amount.

(*Editor's note:* The blatant stupidity of the individual probably foreshadows future contributions to be expected of this officer. It is presumed that none of our readers think that the officer's actions were correct, but the case is included as a reminder that there are a few such individuals in the officer corps and the rest of us must be on our guard to ensure that they don't succeed in their corrupt schemes.

The officer corps has earned the highest reputation of any profession in the country, but will only be able to maintain that status if all efforts are taken to rid itself of the type of individual described in this case. These individuals deserve little mercy, for through their irresponsible actions, they bring discredit on the officer corps and run the risk of raising suspicion in the minds of civilians [the taxpaying customers] that there are more such officers in the armed forces.)

As we depend on an established basis of trust and confidence, officers must take action when they see wrongdoing of any kind and with anyone. Usually civilian authorities will not have knowledge of some of these actions.

ISSUE 89 - USE IT OR LOSE IT

What happened: (Issue 89 from page 130) In these days of austere funding and enormous budget deficits, it is imperative that each officer look at ways to improve our management practices and save money. But if one finds a way to save money this year, should it automatically mean that less is needed next year? Theoretically, if an operation remains the same from one year to the next, we should be able to operate with the same budget base adjusted for inflation. On the other hand, if the size or tasking of an organization is increased or decreased, there should be a compensated adjustment.

We probably will always be trying to decrease organization size and funding requirements. As we creatively seek ways to accomplish this difficult task, we may well be burdened with the very real "use it or lose it" philosophy that can exist in an organization if its officers don't take a stand.

The message is that the application of ethical conduct applies to a wide range of military operations. Officers have to think constantly about and act to ensure that the expenditure of the taxpayers' money is accomplished in the most economical and efficient manner, possible while not doing anything that is either illegal or unethical.

Until this attitude becomes part of our overall philosophy, members of the military will have to continue to pose ethical questions to themselves, seniors, peers, and subordinates whenever the "use it or lose it" approach seems to be operating.

(*Editor's note:* By using the above persuasive arguments, the O-3 was able to convince the chain-of-command to reprogram money to the next fiscal period so that free fuel could be accepted. In this way dollars *were* saved because an officer took the time and effort, working within the system, to provide seniors with a workable approach. The chain-of-command will work if given the opportunity to do so.)

ISSUE 90 - THE ACCOMPLICE

What happened: (Issue 90 from page 131) You felt that the pilot's fate was sealed even before the board heard from the first witness. As the senior member of the board, you helped deliver the recommendation desired by the CO.

With the board's conclusions of removal, along with the many other stresses this pilot faced, the individual looked for a way out. The CO offered this in the form of a voluntary withdrawal from aviation. The pilot jumped at the chance; removal from flight status was thus indirectly accomplished by the CO.

The reader may ask, "What is the ethical issue?" The words of the officer who reported this case are poignant and answer the question.

> "I view my ethical failure as my being an accomplice to this entire process. The CO respected my opinion enough that had I made it clear that I would not go along with this course of action, the course would have changed. My force of personality was required to sway the board. My evaluation as the senior LSO was necessary for documentation of performance and my role as PTO ensured no other course of action was pursued.
>
> "I make no excuse for my actions, but I will say that when you see a young officer who is trying very hard

to serve the CO, it is easy to not see the forest for the trees. While being told in 'trusted confidence' what a great pilot, LSO, and officer I was, I did not see clearly that the goals and desires of the CO may have been less professionally motivated than personality oriented. What at that time seemed in the Navy's best interest may not have been. A young officer cannot know what is in the Navy's best interest, but the Navy is never well served by mismanagement of personnel issues."

Editor's note: The experienced CO had the obligation to remove an ineffective pilot from flight status. It is never a pleasant duty to document a subordinate's failure, but the effective running of the service requires that those who may hurt themselves, kill others, or compromise the mission must be removed before they do so. The ethical error was not in the CO doing what was thought best but rather the LSO not having the moral courage to tell the CO of a different opinion. If the LSO felt the individual could be saved, then that case should have been made. This LSO regrets not having taken a stand because of wanting to please the CO. While wanting to please our seniors is a strong motivator for officer actions, it must never be used as an excuse. The LSO failed the CO by not standing up and supporting an alternative approach. Having examined a great many mishap reports it would appear that the CO may have saved the life of the pilot and helped avoid an aviation mishap.

ISSUE 91 - THE FRIEND

What happened: (Issue 91 from page 132) After much discussion and soul-searching, the friend and spouse decided that a one-night stand would neither solve the couple's marital problems nor ease the spouse's craving.

The friend realized the importance of not taking advantage of the situation and getting the JO and spouse to professional help. The friend arranged for the start of formal counseling through the command chaplain, which resulted in the couple moving closer to town and resumption of the spouse's career.

This was not an easy choice for the single officer, but it established that, in fact, the JO had a true friend. The hard right is rarely as initially satisfying as the easy wrong. In addition, the single officer realized the importance of friendship and how important it is in continuing a military career.

Editor's note: The officer who reported this situation made the following salient point: "The decision was right to not betray both the trust and career factors. In this case the rules of what is ethically correct are pretty much common knowledge, which makes the hard choice easier."

ISSUE 92 - CHEAT

<u>What happened</u>: (Issue 92 from page 133) By the time the 0-2 finished degree studies, an interest in investing had developed. The officer was able to remain stateside and was promoted to 0-3.

The officer, who had decided that it was all right for the service family to use the office copier, continued to use it for personal investment purposes. The officer had even earned a real estate agent's licensing during the day, reasoning that the troops would learn from the 0-3's financial acumen. Sometimes the officer went home early leaving some of the officer's work for the senior enlisted, hoping to give seniors the impression that great delegating skills were being utilized.

As classes were full for the overseas rotation preparation, the 0-3 opted for another stateside tour. When the officer was not phoning the local stockbroker, time was taken off during the day to sell real estate. What follows is exactly what happened to this officer and represents the extreme exception. It is only presented to illustrate the classical consequences of an officer's lack of integrity and where it might lead.

As the officer rushed around town to make appointments on time, several speeding tickets were received. Incomplete work and declining office morale resulted from lowered fitness reports. Tensions mounted as the 0-3 tried to meet all commitments; excessive drinking became the norm. This, in turn, was followed by spouse and child abuse and divorce. Unable to meet mounting expenses with a declining income, the 0-3 started to hedge on government travel claims and income taxes, believing all the while that the military and country owed the additional amounts due to travel and service sacrifices.

Finally, to get through the day, he resorted to drugs. With the loss of a driver's license, the 0-3's life seemed to be falling apart. Bottom was hit when the military's investigative service proved the travel claim excesses and the officer was picked up for drug abuse by the command's urinalysis program. The IRS filed felony charges for income tax fraud.

This officer's brief career was terminated by a court-martial, dishonorable discharge, and federal prison sentence. While this is a horrendous case, there are lessons to be learned that would do all of us well to keep in mind.

(1)   Don't cut corners, and don't mix personal with military business.

(2)   By your actions try to give special meaning to the words "special trust and confidence" that are part of our commissioned officer corps' heritage.

(3)   Serve the military, not yourself. As officers, our ethical integrity should be a source of pride for us and an example to others.

ISSUE 93 - THE FLIGHT JACKET

What happened: (Issue 93 from page 134) The officer decided to tell the truth and told supply of wanting to keep the NOMEX jacket. Through this action integrity was maintained, which, once lost, is extremely difficulty to regain. The story did not end here.

Supply allowed the officer to keep the jacket and only required the payment of replacement cost. Thus, the aviator obtained both the jacket and a clear conscience. Unethical action *was* taken in this case, however, by both the officer and supply.

No one has the right to directly buy government equipment by reporting it lost and paying for it. The supply officer did not have authority to take the money for the jacket and the flight officer did not have the authority to keep it and pay for it.

Rules are not something that a few officer can modify to fit their ideas of what is right and wrong, or to be accommodating to one another. In this case the supply officer had to fill out a report of survey to say that either the jacket was lost or unserviceable, and since neither of these situations was the case, fraud against the government took place.

The important message here is that sometimes individual officers may not be aware of what is ethically right or wrong, but they can quickly get good advice by discussing the matter with their legal officer. The aviator who reported this case has a clear conscience feeling that what was done was right. It wasn't. Both officers forgot the limits of their authority. Would they both be willing to publicly announce on TV what they had done? Doubtful. That is another way of determining whether something is ethical or not: Are you ready to tell the world about it? Finally, if it doesn't feel right, don't do it.

ISSUE 94 - THE INVESTIGATION

What happened: (Issue 94 from page 135) The course of action suggested by the senior was diametrically opposed to the mandated one of conducting an unbiased informal investigation of an officer's behavior. The suggested direction of the investigation was not only unethical but also illegal.

The investigating officer chose to acquiesce to the senior's suggested handling of the case, and the senior officer elected to cover up the whole issue. The JO was immediately transferred and a carefully worded report was submitted that stated all allegations were found to be without merit.

The entire command knew of this whitewash, and morale hit rock bottom because the JO and other personnel involved were not held accountable. The investigating officer's senior lost credibility and was ineffective for the remainder of that officer's tour. The JO had to be transferred from the follow-on duty station for the same reason.

A far stronger message would have been sent to the command had the JO and the other personnel involved been dealt with by prescribed standards of investigating allegations. Had such a route been taken, it would have been followed with administrative disciplinary action, if the facts warranted.

The investigating officer's cowardly action sent a strong message to other officers that there was a limit to the risk an officer should take when a career is threatened. If we are to strengthen our ethical climate, we must recognize there is room for improvement. The officer corps has the deserved reputation of being a highly moral and ethical group, and our future growth in this area depends on the education of our junior officers who will be the senior leaders of tomorrow.

As history has shown, a military that stops believing in itself, no longer respects its leaders, and doubts its mission is doomed to defeat when it comes up against an enemy who morally believes in what it is fighting for.

Editor's note: The gender of the officer discussed in this case is not indicated for we desire to make the point in all issues discussed that the handling of unethical conduct by an officer should not be influenced by the sex of the defendant. We will be in transition for some years from an all-male combat force to one that has both men and women. Women have distinguished themselves in combat for as long as our nation has existed, though not in the same numbers as have the men. When we have equal treatment of all personnel—regardless of gender and regardless of activity in which they are involved—then we will have achieved full equality for both sexes in our military.

ISSUE 95 - THE COMPUTER

What happened: (Issue 95 from page 136) The officer violated the standards of conduct because the purchase spanned a long period of time. If the officer wanted to sell the equipment to the enlisted, it should not have been financed by the officer.

Two violations were actually committed. A second, more serious one, had to do with the officer being the enlisted's direct supervisor. Had the officer not had other than a professional relationship with the enlisted, it is probable that the judgment exercised would have been more objective, and action might not have been taken against the officer.

The military standard of ethical conduct required of officers is much higher than for executives in either industry or government. This being the case, every action by an officer that is other than carrying out a prescribed duty should be examined to ensure that an unfavorable circumstance is avoided.

This officer should have considered how it would sound to be selling a computer to a subordinate. Had the officer thought about it, that individual would have realized that others might see the enlisted as possibly being coerced to pay the amount requested by the supervising officer. Going through this thought process in advance, or asking the legal officer for an opinion, would have avoided compromising the standards of conduct, as well as the trouble the officer eventually experienced.

ISSUE 96 - SPEAKING UP

What happened: (Issue 96 from page 137) If a JO is not allowed to confront or does not feel comfortable in confronting a senior officer in the cockpit, a breakdown of crew coordination occurs that could lead to a mishap and possible loss of aircraft and crew.

The JO did not raise concerns, thus failing both officers.

The flying of aircraft is inherently dangerous. In past years some pilots showed their daring and skill through "Flat Hatting," which is maneuvering as close to the ground as possible without hitting it. Unfortunately, this is a "die" rather than "look bad" situation and a number of pilots were killed and their aircraft lost performing these kinds of antics.

Aviation's safety record is improving as these barnstorming antics are eliminated, but their prohibition and saving of lives has been the result of outstanding pilots speaking up and making an issue of safe flying. NATOPS regulations are a reflection of lessons learned at a cost of aircraft and crew losses.

Training a military pilot is a particularly expensive undertaking. The result are JOs who know what is right to do, who are willing to do it, and, most importantly, are willing to not only set the example but also require that others do what is right.

It is not a case of the copilot being timid but simply a matter of knowingly exceeding NATOPS regulations—an invitation to disaster. Although the copilot had already had a mishap, it is apparent that by willingly continuing to fly the pilot is willing to risk life and limb in defense of the U.S.A.

To have the courage to die for one's country is heroic, but not to preserve and live up to its rules is, in fact, cowardice. It implies fear of losing one's career. In the military we do not think it possible to eliminate fear, but it is possible to live with it and that was where the copilot failed the CO, the military, and aviation in general. Someday the CO may have a mishap because of not following NATOPS. This JO might have been able to avoid that if the courage to speak up when viewing wrongdoing was ingrained.

ISSUE 97 - LOCALITY PAY

What happened: (Issue 97 from page 138) Ideally, since they had written regulations on their side, the ensigns should have refused, but they didn't.

At that point, if the senior took the issue up the chain-of-command to order the disbursing officer to make the payment, the XO and CO would have seen that what the senior was trying to do was illegal and would have agreed with the disbursing officer.

If a junior officer has the guts to question a senior officer's actions when appropriate, most likely the ethical option will be accepted by the senior. In this instance, if the disbursing officer would have questioned the legality of the payment, and suggested that they let the XO make the final determination, the senior officer probably would have let the issue drop.

The senior knew the payment was illegal; there was a written instruction making it so. The important point for junior officers to realize about this issue is that the senior would not have risked letting the XO know that something unethical was being pushed as an issue.

As Edmund Burke said long ago: "All that is necessary for the triumph of evil is that enough good men do nothing." The officer corps is constantly on the lookout for unethical behavior. While a few people might engage in it, the principles we live by are against such action. An officer who stands up for what is right will be both recognized and appreciated and have a good career. One should be afraid of following the *wrong* path, not the right one.

ISSUE 98 - THE CAR COVER

What happened: (Issue 98 from page 139) Prior to the project's completion, the CO rescinded the order and the car cover was never completed.

This CO moved up the ranks, becoming an XO of a much larger unit, then chief of staff of a base, and eventually made 0-6. The reader might be asking at this point what the message is. Simply stated, the military is not composed of perfect individuals, and we cannot have confidence that all officers will be trustworthy 100 percent of the time.

The OIC of the parachute riggers failed by (1) not returning the cover to the CO the moment the assignment was received; (2) sending the PR back with the torn cover, thus failing to accept responsibility for the work of a subordinate (that is, the OIC should have taken it back); (3) allowing the PR to make a new car cover; (4) permitting the use of government materials to repair/replace private property; and (5) reporting the grumbling of the subordinate to the CO while not personally speaking up as the OIC.

We don't know how many officers contributed to the CO's learning that commingling of personal property and government property is all right to do. We don't know how many officers taught the CO that it was all right to have enlisted do personal work. But it doesn't take a rocket scientist to figure out that the CO was out of line, and should have done an attitude adjustment long before this incident. The OIC failed miserably to show any courage in dealing with the CO and protecting both enlisted personnel and government resources.

Years ago officers used to put their shoes outside their door in the evening and have enlisted shine them by morning. It was not unusual to have enlisted pack an officer's belongings for a move or have the motor pool fix private automobiles for the officers. While at the time it wasn't called servitude, we recognize today, and for the future, that our enlisted are there to do a job for the unit and nation, not for individual officers. We recognize that the taxpayer expects *every* dollar spent to go for the purpose intended.

Some military dollars are legitimately used to help service personnel through Family Service Centers and other activities. These are not intended, however, to augment an officer's income by competing with off-base merchants.

This book is intended to help JOs in their careers and to let you know that the actions taken by this CO were improper. In the future, all officers will be held accountable for participating in such illegal and unethical activities and future officers will find their careers limited and terminated by such activities. A word to the wise should be sufficient.

ISSUE 99 - TAILHOOK '91

Ethical decision considerations: (Issue 99 from page 146) While the LTs decided that they were not going to participate in the gauntlet, they did agree that their squadron room was going to be a haven for anyone who did not want to participate. While their decision was to do nothing, some of the LTs did try to warn the women about what might happen if they went through the gauntlet.

Their decision to neither try to stop the gauntlet nor to make a serious effort to find a flag officer had extremely long-range implications, including giving a black eye to the Navy in general and naval aviation in particular.

Military history is replete with examples of those who have faced insurmountable odds to save members of their unit and in the process risk their own lives. When Marine Corps Captain John Ripley (a Navy Cross recipient) exposed himself to constant fire for two hours to mine and blow up the bridge at Dong Ha, he knew that if he succeeded 45,000 troops would be saved. When Lieutenant Audey Murphy, U.S. Army (a Medal of Honor recipient) ordered artillery fire on his own position in order to kill the surrounding enemy, he knew that he was endangering his own life for the good of others. When Navy Lieutenant Commander Eugene Fluckey (Medal of Honor recipient) guided his submarine up a thirteen-mile-long river on the surface to destroy an enemy fleet, he knew that they would be under fire on the return, for the river was too shallow to escape submerged. When Dr. Mary Walker (a Medal of Honor awardee) treated the wounded during the Civil War at the Battles of Bull Run, Atlanta, and Chickamauga—and continued doing so during captivity as a POW—she risked her life. Air Force Major Richard Bong, recipient of a Medal of Honor, assigned as a gunnery instructor and neither required nor expected to perform combat duty, voluntarily engaged in repeated combat missions, risking his life. Signalman 1/C Douglas Munro, U.S. Coast Guardsman and Medal of Honor recipient, knowingly gave his life by drawing enemy gunfire and saved the lives of many who otherwise would have perished. These individuals were *trusted* to do what is right and their seniors had the *confidence* they would do what is right.

A few LTs who realized that what was going on was wrong had the capability to preserve the reputation of the entire military from being grievously hurt by a few drunken and self-centered individuals who *really* cared nothing for their country but only their own individual pleasures.

There are many messages to remember from Tailhook '91; possibly the biggest is that it is almost impossible when one fails to act ethically to adequately and completely ascertain the results of that improper action. These LTs had the capability within their grasp to save the careers of many officers and millions of dollars, and there was no chance that they would lose their lives in the effort. They probably were ready to fly into combat and risk death; unfortunately, they were not willing to risk their careers and/or a community bloody nose to stop the action. Their intervention might have caused a fight and a local incident soon forgotten, but their lack of action has resulted in years of struggle to put this behind us.

Tailhook '91 provides the military with an opportunity to view the disastrous results that can occur through unethical action, inaction, and tacit approval of unprofessional conduct. In this case, a few LTs had the opportunity to prevent what came to be one of the most embarrassing moments in U.S. military history. Their inaction brought disgrace to the uniform of all services, and to themselves. As the wife of Command Pilot Michael Smith (USNA '67) said when she presented materials recovered from the *Challenger* disaster to the Naval Academy Brigade of Midshipmen: "One person *can* make a difference. My husband, Michael Smith, did and so can you." If just *one* of these LTs had had the moral fortitude to step forward, organizational embarrassment would have been avoided and many careers would have been saved.

ISSUE 100 - THE CLASSIFIED INVENTORY

<u>What happened</u>: (Issue 100 from page 147) Although it takes only fifteen minutes to do the inventory, the department head conducted the check while doing other paperwork. Consequently, full attention to all details did not occur.

While monitoring of the daily inventories was required by the command, they would happen only occasionally. The program had not been running the way it should.

The answer to what happened is that no one knows because the department head failed to carry out this simplest of assignments in a professional manner. The officer's lax attitude sets a poor example for all subordinates and thus was the weak link in a chain designed to make the unit operate successfully.

Improper monitoring operations set a bad example and are counterproductive to the proper conduct of business. The monitor is meant to find problems, identify causes, and correct them in order to make the system run better.

It isn't enough to understand the theory of ethics and know what the great philosophers have said. Officers are rarely watched in the conduct of their duties; their seniors have too many other requirements for successful completion of their responsibilities.

If you are going to be an officer, then do it right, *every time,* not just when others are watching. The officer corps of the Armed Forces is one of the great strengths of this nation, but if some of our most trusted personnel fail to meet their obligations, then we will eventually have a paper tiger to defend our nation because our leaders will think that our reports are right, when they aren't. Honor and integrity are the hallmarks of our profession. Don't let yourself or others fail to meet those standards, for it hurts us all when individual members of the team decide for themselves whether and to what extent they are going to obey the rules. Failing to act ethically is not a victimless crime. Others, as well as yourself, know what is going on and thus all members of the team are tempted to do less than their best. Your oath as an officer requires more than a perfunctory meeting of standards.

ISSUE 101 - THE DINNER

What happened: (Issue 101 from page 148) The junior officer felt that all that was involved was a friendly dinner with no intention by the contractor to influence the JO.

More, however, was possibly involved than what the JO realized, and so the officer consulted with the XO who raised the question with both the CO and legal counsel.

In discussions, the thought was expressed about the importance of not accepting, or giving the perception of accepting, gratuities from contractors, no matter the amount.

As a result of these talks, everyone concerned agreed that the invitation should be declined, which the 0-2 did in writing, tactfully explaining why and thanking the senior executive from the company for the invitation.

Important to this decision were several realizations.

(1)   The very appearance of the 0-2 at the dinner would give the impression that there was a personal friendship between the officer and company executives.

(2)   While another officer would be taking over the liaison with the contractor, if a new award was made, the perception would be that there was a continuing relationship between the company and the position held by the 0-2.

(3)   The appearance of impropriety must never exist. It may be perceived that the government is favoring one contractor over another. Such perceptions in the past have led to hotline complaints and letters to Congress, and have exacerbated relationships between the military and the locality where work was being done.

(4)   The 0-2 can never be certain that someday, as a more senior officer, assignment back to this area might take place, thus possibly bringing the contractor and the JO back in contact with each other.

A truly honest company will understand, will not be insulted, and will continue to do the best work for the government because of their own self-pride in doing a good job. (That *was* the case with this contractor, as shown by its performance on a subsequent project.)

ISSUE 102 - THE NATOPS TEST

<u>What happened</u>: (Issue 102 from page 150) The bottom line is that the NATOPS officer could follow the rules and pay the consequences for disobeying the CO or obey and know that the rules were being broken as well as the JO's own code of ethics.

While the JO faced compromising personal ethics, there was the knowledge that those above would be pleased. Besides, the senior officer had taken these tests before and the JO knew the senior could do it. It can be further rationalized that the senior officer is much too busy to worry about a little old test.

The NATOPS officer documented conversations with the people involved and put off doing the test for a short time. Eventually the JO filled out the test and delivered it to the senior, leaving the name space blank. This way the senior's choice to use the test by filling in the name would relieve the JO from having participated in the falsification.

The practical result was that the NATOPS officer took the test for the senior officer, for without this help the senior would have failed the test. The JO did, in fact, allow expediency to interfere with ethical judgment.

Ultimately, no one was helped but fortunately no one died. By not having to personally do the test, the senior's cockpit knowledge suffered. When a senior fails to meet a requirement, it sends a message to juniors in the command that their leaders feel they are above the rules and do not have to abide by the same standards as the rest of the officers.

(*Editor's note:* This case is a quick overview of what occurred. The mood and tension felt by those involved is difficult to relate. The JO kept the NATOPS assignment. Several officers protested by refusing to fly with the senior. Everyone that protested was labeled by the CO as a "troublemaker.")

The long-range effect for the NATOPS officer was being held responsible for following an illegal order from the CO. Later that year the senior officer and the CO came under investigation, and both were relieved of command.

Discussions with officers in operational units indicate that increased discussions are being held as to what is and what is not ethical. The Armed Forces of the United States are lifting themselves up by their bootstraps. While there may be dire consequences in the future for those who act ethically, the desire to do so is ever increasing. It behooves the

JOs to comply with the rules so that when they are senior, it can be reported that positive progress continues in the improvement of ethical actions.

ISSUE 103 - REPAIR PARTS

What happened: (Issue 103 from page 152) The S&MO resolved to do what was right, to be professional, and to act with integrity. Still having the backing of the CO, the officer kept pushing for justice.

As a result of the continuing investigation, the contractor was forced to bring their prices into line, which was the reason the investigation had been started in the first place. The S&MO was transferred to another assignment on the base. Since the story had wound up in the papers, investigative reporters approached the officer to go public with the story, but that request was declined.

In the end the officer was not personally hurt. Promoted on time at the end of his tour, the former S&MO received a meritorious service medal. FITREPs were all excellent, and despite the momentary reputation it gave the officer at headquarters, the incident gained the respect of fellow officers within the command and the CO.

As reported by the supply and maintenance officer who related this case: "Most importantly, I felt good about myself; I had maintained my integrity against terrific odds. I felt I did what was right and would probably do it again."

This officer is a prime example of one who was not only willing to be in the military and possibly face death to defend the principles of the Constitution, but was also ready to sacrifice a career should that be necessary to do things right.

As a junior officer you need to know that there are thousands of other officers who make the hard, right decision rather than the easy, wrong one. You will not be alone when you act responsibly, hold yourself and others accountable, and ensure that integrity and ethics are part of every day of your life.

ISSUE 104 - CIVILIAN ATTIRE

What happened: (Issue 104 from page 153) While it is reasonable for any individual to want to be appreciated, it does not follow that officers should have to be liked as a motivation for any action. While we do

254   SOLUTIONS

have to judge at times, we are primarily entrusted with enforcing regulations rather than waiving them.

When an officer enforces only certain rules, the enlisted and/or more junior officers might think they also have the right to make the determination of which rules to obey. When enlisted are off-duty on liberty, they are still subject to the UCMJ, and thus it is the duty for the officer to rectify the situation on the spot—in a polite fashion—and then to report the matter to the enlisted's chain-of-command upon return to the base. The immediate senior of the two enlisted can also talk to them and prevent future occurrences that might not be seen by another officer of the unit.

It is crucial, as professionals, to realize our obligation to enforce rules, behaviors, and attitudes of those who are subordinate to us. A commissioned officer can never escape nor hide from the responsibility vested in their position. Using tact and courtesy, an officer can ensure that respect and discipline exist within the military as a whole.

Since the enlisted may have modified their civilian attire after they left the base, it is not a negative reflection on those who conducted the inspection. Also, the time and distance of applicability for regulations is, for the most part, the same everywhere. For example, a member of the military service is prohibited from becoming drunk anywhere in the world, whether on duty, liberty, or leave.

Junior officers who want to become senior officers will obey the rules themselves, ensure that others do so, and realize that their seniors are confident that their juniors will enforce regulations and trust that moral weakness will not keep them from doing so. Finally, subordinates do not respect seniors who let them break the rules. They may be happy to get away with some action or other, but in being allowed to do so they lose complete confidence in and respect for the senior. They also reason that the senior must be generally loose on rule enforcement because the senior also breaks the rules.

The JO spoke to the two enlisted, emphasizing the points made above. There were no repercussions from the command.

ISSUE 105 - THE PRANK

<u>What happened</u>: (Issue 105 from page 155) Both 0-2s were caught by surprise when asked to participate and had to make a quick decision. They elected to participate because of what they considered positive reasons for doing the task, that is, (1) to gain peer acceptance from the

0-3 instructor pilots; (2) to poke fun at an unpopular officer; (3) to indirectly show support of an outstanding, well-respected, and well-liked CO; and (4) to get out of standing at attention for an hour during the change of command ceremony and be first in line for beer at the reception.

They also considered participating because they thought their chances of getting caught were slim. Additionally, they rationalized that even if caught, they would probably only receive a verbal reprimand and a weekend's duty. After all, they thought, "that is a small price to pay for such a great prank!"

What does all of this say about the 0-2s and 0-3s, their understanding of loyalty, responsibility, integrity, accountability, and any realization of the fact that the C of S of most units has a difficult job? These junior officers were being paid to be officers first and flyers second. Also, what does it say to others who learn about the prank? Furthermore, it demonstrates that anyone can express any opinion about a senior in any way they want, as opposed to having the guts to directly talk to the senior and speak one's mind.

Certainly the prank didn't honor the CO; it showed, rather that the command included a bunch of clowns as members and suggested that the CO tolerated such antics.

The 0-2s considered the prank harmless and elected to participate, without concern for its impropriety and its unethical and illegal nature. The 0-2s lost face with higher-ranking officers but gained face among their peers and immediate seniors. Unlike Tailhook '91, this matter was resolved in-house, without public disclosure of the childish behavior of the officers.

In a small way the 0-2s were trying to please their seniors, but they were also interested in making a statement of their own. They certainly didn't honor their CO, however, by bringing to the forefront any disagreement between the CO and the C of S. Officers who want to honor seniors don't do so by displaying to the world that the senior has failed to teach the juniors what it means to be an officer. This was not the first time that junior officers, by their lack of professionalism, lack of concern for anyone but themselves, and complete disregard for the meaning of their oath of office have embarrassed their commanding officer.

For an officer to do nothing to stop such antics, and worse, to participate, is a complete dishonor to the corps of American military officers.

ISSUE 106 - THE STORIES

<u>What happened</u>: (Issue 106 from page 156) There is the saying "If it ain't broke, don't fix it," but this fails to consider that most systems can be improved, and we have an obligation to look for ways that can produce better performance in the long run.

It may seem that great social changes are taking place, yet it is a longstanding practice of the armed forces to work ahead of the nation to effect positive social change and improve the operation of the military.

Flogging went away at the start of the 20th century. Old timers wondered how discipline could be maintained without occasionally striking the men to remind them who was boss.

Drinking was common on ships of the 19th century and drugs took a hold in the military in the latter part of the 20th century until Admiral Tom Hayward, former CNO, made the dramatic statement "Not on *my* ship, not on *my* watch, not in *my* Navy," and made it stick.

The integration of women in the Armed Forces of the United States is not of recent origin; females ably served throughout the world in both World War I and II, and have since then made a positive contribution to military effectiveness.

In the civilian sector, women have advanced from not having the vote to now holding senior positions in industry and government. The entire treatment of women is gradually changing to one of total equality regarding gender.

It is no more proper to tell jokes that are offensive to women than it is to tell racial/religious jokes or to malign any portion of society, whether it be civilian or military. The fact that the person telling the joke may not understand why it is offensive is immaterial: what is important is that those hearing it also not be offended.

The new officer advised all personnel that the storytelling must stop. He talked to the troops about the need to provide working spaces free of sexual degradation. Had he overlooked the matter and another individual joined the group, who openly objected, the officer would have been hard-pressed to stop a practice that had been allowed to flourish.

When something is wrong, the time to stop it is when you first know about it. Not to do so eventually means you become part of the problem rather than part of the solution. The officer explained the reasons for action taken and noted that the social mores of the armed forces were changing for the better. It was up to all hands to support new policies and strive to achieve a harmonious relationship among all personnel. The JO's support of the new policies was noted as one of total agreement.

ISSUE 107 - SELECTING CANDIDATES

What happened: (Issue 107 from page 157) One of the subordinate commanders asked for further discussions on this subject, and during the meeting, all of the subordinate commanders recommended screening for best qualified versus giving special consideration based on minority status. They asked the CO to reconsider his decision.

The battalion commander opted to listen to his subordinate commanders and then ordered them to screen for the best-qualified Marine for the select program. In the end, the CO realized that selecting the best Marines would enable the organization to do the best job and ultimately cause the command to successfully complete their assigned mission.

It would have been much easier for the subordinate commanders to defy the CO, but that in turn would have destroyed the team concept of the battalion. There are many assignments for qualified military personnel, but in those rare cases where the best person is required, then that person must be selected without regard to race or ethnic background.

It should be noted that all commanders have a responsibility to conduct training in such a way that all personnel have a chance to become outstanding in their performance, and thus be eligible for selection to all programs.

It is also appropriate for every command to continually review its equal opportunity goals, to ensure not only that equal training is provided but also that equal performance is recognized.

ISSUE 108 - THE LEGAL OFFICER

What happened: (Issue 108 from page 159) Throughout this book we have advised consultation with both chaplains and legal officers when in doubt as to what would be an ethical approach to resolving conflicting demands.

The command judge advocate discussed the case with another judge advocate outside the command who, with consent of that officer's CO, agreed that should further action be required, that judge advocate could provide the hospital CO with advice.

When considering action to be taken, if you are concerned about the matter becoming public knowledge, then maybe the case will not withstand the test of ethical propriety.

An easy, quick solution is not often available to determine whether an action is ethical or not, but the importance of so doing must never be forgotten. Officers of the armed forces of the United States have the confidence of the American people to do what is trustworthy. Take the available time to discuss the matter with seniors and peers, as well as seeking out the advice of both the legal officer and the chaplain. The cumulative advice of all of these people can be relied upon, although it is likely that some combination of their input and your values/beliefs will bring you to a practical course of action.

ISSUE 109 - SAFETY

What happened: (Issue 109 from page 160) The typical can-do attitude had prevailed in the division for weeks prior to the incident. The crew had successfully conducted a number of corrective maintenance evolutions in their own way.

While aggressive trouble shooting and independent action are highly commendable, we must look beyond this isolated incident and determine what sort of policy statement is being made by the action chosen. We must remember that our loyalty is to ship-shipmate-self.

If the JO wants, in an effort to get the job done, to promote a policy of little control and reduced concern about safety standards, then complimenting the petty officer and not reporting the incident will surely result in more of the same. JOs are often closer in age to the enlisted than to more senior officers. But it is necessary not to lose the required chain-of-command identification and support of seniors.

In this instance the JO reported the petty officer, and while complimenting the enlisted on the quality of work done, was sure to take the time necessary to explain why there must be control and consideration of safety at all times, and why the duty officer needed to know and authorize all actions taken. To do otherwise is to risk the lives of the entire crew for the sake of a few hours saved.

It was explained to the petty officer that innovation was welcome; in the future, the thing to do when a solution was thought of for a problem was to bring the concept to the duty officer so that it could be considered in light of applicable safety and operating procedures.

In that way all of the enlisted realized that their skill was appreciated, recognized, and needed, yet a future disaster was possibly averted.

In addition to doing their own jobs in the manner prescribed, officers have the responsibility to ensure that their subordinates, including enlisted, do the same.

It is not appropriate to be belligerent when pointing out a mistake to an enlisted. Take the time, rather so that they will understand why something is required to be done in a prescribed fashion. As officers, we must not only act ethically but also ensure that our subordinates know what is ethically required of them—and ensure they follow and meet requirements.

ISSUE 110 - THE HAIRCUT

What happened: (Issue 110 from page 161) This is one of the many times an officer is faced with making the easy wrong decision over the more difficult right one. It would certainly be easier to defer to the senior status of the chief and not embarrass the senior enlisted before juniors. It must be remembered, however, that the chief knew what the rules were, and the decision to appear before the OOD and other enlisted was not that of the OOD, but rather the chief.

All of us in the armed forces want to trust and have confidence in our seniors, yet that loyalty can be broken if juniors see seniors obeying a different standard than that which is prescribed for all personnel.

The chief does, in fact, have certain privileges not enjoyed by those more junior, but they don't exclude meeting ship's appearance standards. The JO should advise the chief to get a haircut in as *discreet* a manner as possible, so as not to undercut the future authority of the chief with the crew.

If the chief is a professional, the order will be carried out without comment. If not, the officer has to insist. The OOD is the direct representative for the commander and will ensure that all orders are obeyed and enforced as if issued by the commander.

In the final analysis, the OOD's upholding the ship's policy for *all* hands prevented establishment of a double standard on the vessel. Another test of ethical conduct met by a junior officer.

ISSUE 111 - THE VALVE

<u>What happened</u>: (Issue 111 from page 167) The EDO called the appropriate personnel and a critique was held. Besides addressing the equipment problem the critique included criticism of the EDO for not having reported the first valve's position.

By the EDO's not disclosing the first valve condition, a chance was taken that if the officer became incapacitated, the replacement EDO would not realize a trend was possibly present when the second EDO came across the problem of the valves.

The failure to report the first valve sent a terrible message to enlisted, who knew the procedure and what should have been done. Leading by example simply means that what you do will be taken as an example for your subordinates to follow.

The correct course would have been to report the first valve incident immediately. No reporting may have seemed to have saved time, but it could have led to bigger problems if there was a widespread occurrence of mispositioned equipment.

Officers are to be trusted, and through this incident the EDO lost credibility. Seniors lose confidence in officers who deliberately fail to follow the rules. It is one thing to do one's best and make a mistake. When that happens, an officer should immediately advise their senior who, having come up through the ranks, will appreciate the honesty and may well excuse the incident as one that couldn't have been avoided, or at least realize that the junior knows how to avoid such incidents in the future.

It is an entirely different matter when an officer chooses not to obey the rules and does not report that he didn't obey them. A senior can never again be sure whether the officer might fail to do his job in the manner specified. In this case the officer did lose the confidence of seniors as to the degree to which trust and confidence could be placed in the officer.

Finally, this officer was willing to jeopardize expensive equipment and an entire crew by failing to report what was a series of engineering installation mistakes. The military runs on trust; if you cannot or will not accept that premise, then for the good of your fellow officers and enlisted you should resign. Enough danger lurks in both training and operational evolutions to suggest that your staying on active duty is a danger to all with whom you come in contact.

Safety procedures are developed as a result of small and large mishaps. No officer has the authority, without discussion with seniors, to set aside any regulation. If you don't agree with a requirement, then discuss that with your immediate senior for resolution and/or consult the legal officer assigned.

ISSUE 112 - STANDING WATCH

What happened: (Issue 112 from page 168) The decision by the 0-2 was to cover for the late officer. Efforts were made to reach the officer, without immediate results. In covering for the missing officer, the 0-2 was more concerned about what others thought than the duty owed the command. Eventually, the officer did show up and relieved the 0-2 so that it was not necessary for the 0-2 to report the missing officer to the CDO.

It should be noted that if more than several hours had gone by before the missing officer showed, the 0-2 intended to report the situation to the CDO. (OPNAV instructions require a report to BUPERS of any officer missing from appointed place of duty for one hour or more. A phone call early on may prevent this from becoming an issue. This is why most watches are scheduled to relieve fifteen minutes early.)

It is not easy being a junior officer, for you are expected to have the honor and integrity of a seasoned adult. It may help you perform your duties by remembering that as a JO, you don't make the rules but you are expected to obey them. If regulations require reporting the lateness of an officer, then two people are hurt when you don't. First is the missing officer, who has failed to learn the importance of meeting responsibilities on time and may eventually lose their career because of repeated dereliction of duty. This could have been prevented if the officer had been called down when the first mistake was made and it wouldn't have been career threatening.

The second person to be hurt when you cover for a friend is you, for the impression given to others is that you can't be trusted to report the simplest of matter, but rather will allow protecting a friend to interfere with doing a job as your seniors expect. If you don't think a regulation is appropriate, then make an appeal for its modification through the chain-of-command. Don't establish a reputation of being someone who makes their own decision as to when and when not to obey the rules.

It may also help the JO to realize that friends do not take advantage of friends by expecting them not to report matters that they are supposed to uphold and enforce.

SOLUTIONS

ISSUE 113 - SPECIFICATIONS

What happened: (Issue 113 from page 169) This would seem to be a relatively straightforward matter; one would expect that an officer who was entrusted with personnel and materiel could be counted upon to exercise the trust and confidence placed in all officers.

The officer's life was not at risk, nor would anyone hold an officer responsible for a piece of equipment going bad that had been properly maintained. That is the very purpose of inspections—to ascertain which equipment has failed before its expected time.

The military services are equipment dependent, and it is critical to know how machinery is operating so that modifications can be made in both current and future produced items.

Unfortunately, the decision was made to try and preserve the image of a properly operating work center by not reporting the out-of-spec reading. The out-of-spec reading was falsifying official documents. Consequently, the work center gained the reputation of hiding problems. The officer's reputation for trustworthiness was lost and the respect of peers, juniors, and seniors was destroyed.

It is sad to recount an event such as this. This particular officer was still immature and hadn't learned to accept responsibility as an adult and officer. The service is no place for the game of hide-and-seek. An officer who tries to see how much information can be withheld is a danger to everyone!

ISSUE 114 - DISCIPLINE

What happened: (Issue 114 from page 170) What makes this an ethical dilemma is the conflict between sympathy for the junior enlisted's family and the duty responsibility of the junior officer.

The junior enlisted should have first approached the chief to politely try to resolve the situation. If that failed, the chain-of-command should have been utilized. In considering the situation, the JO realized that the chain-of-command and respect towards seniors is an essential element if the military is going to be able to meet its mission requirements.

The JO met with the junior enlisted and was careful to disapprove of the actions taken but not the total individual. A drop in marks for military bearing and personal behavior were entered into the junior enlisted's service record.

SOLUTIONS

Through a lengthy discussion, the JO made sure the junior enlisted understood the effect that indecision would have on the entire unit and internal discipline. The junior enlisted was encouraged to apologize to the chief and try to do an even better job than previously, so that this lowered mark would not have a career-ending effect.

Being a total officer implies supporting all aspects of our military organization—not just the earthshaking life-and-death matters. Not only did the JO have to think about the junior enlisted but also about the responsibilities and authority of the chief. A lack of action would have sent a strong message to others in the unit that the chief was really not that important to the organization. The chain-of-command and respect applies within the enlisted ranks as well as within the officer corps. This element of respect for seniors should be adhered to—on or off duty.

ISSUE 115 - FIRST-TIME USE

What happened: (Issue 115 from page 171) The government does not dispute that the E-8 was doing an excellent job and has potential, but any drug abuse is intolerable. The policy, the procedures to obtain assistance, and the repercussions are well-known, especially to an E-8!

Without substantial evidence to the contrary, drug abuse equals Other Than Honorable separation. The chain of custody, collection procedures, and lab work are convincing. The CO and the E-8's chain-of-command reluctantly concur. A finding of misconduct due to drug abuse was entered by a vote of 3 to 0.

As to retention or separation: Drug abuse is not honorable service. Outstanding performance does not excuse or even mitigate drug abuse. What example was this E-8 setting for subordinates and peers? The E-8 knew the consequences, weighed the risk involved, and used cocaine, which equals OTH!

The use of cocaine was considered to be well established. Separation was clearly appropriate, but the type of discharge was an agonizing decision. VA benefits can be forfeited, unemployment is likely, sixteen years of being a professional had to be considered.

OTH was considered to be too severe. The military requires absolute commitment to earn an Honorable Discharge. A message had to be sent to others, yet the E-8's service had to be heavily weighed. It was clear that the family would also suffer for the mistakes of the E-8.

A General Discharge was considered most appropriate, as it penalized the E-8 but left some benefits intact. The message of zero tolerance was clearly delivered to the command. Most duties officers are called upon to perform give great satisfaction, but this type is certainly not one of them, even though we must do it.

This story has been told many times; if you want to avoid having to make the difficult decision these officers did, do not treat drug education lectures lightly. Drug education should not be a once- or twice-a-year evolution, rather, it should be something that you are continually reminding your personnel about. Share with them the medical effects and the legal consequences of drug abuse so that if someday you have to terminate another's career, you will be able to do so knowing that fair warning had been delivered.

ISSUE 116 - SANITARIES

What happened: (Issue 116 from page 172) It is not unusual for a junior, out of a sense of loyalty to a senior to take certain authorities that have not been delegated. In so doing, however, the junior is acting without all the knowledge that the senior would have brought to the same decision process.

In this instance the OOD did authorize the dumping, in direct violation of the CO's orders. However wrong that was, it doesn't compare to what the OOD didn't do, namely, failure to tell the CO of the dumping, not wanting to admit that the CO's direct orders had been disobeyed but feeling that the cover-up was justified since it was in the best interests of the CO.

We have standing orders because no CO can stay awake twenty-four hours a day. It is for that reason that there is an appointed OOD who has been delegated many of the authorities of the CO during the period of watch. Because of the intimate knowledge required with reference to some evolutions, however, a CO may not delegate all authority and by so doing further recognizes that their sleep may have to be interrupted by the OOD. That is one of the responsibilities and sacrifices of command.

The OOD failed to understand that orders are just that—procedures to be followed and obeyed, and only in the case of inability through injury or non-availability or death may a subordinate take over the command prerogatives of the CO.

Officers are granted great discretion in the performance of their duties, and it is assumed that not only will they understand all that they are authorized to do but also all that they are not! The failure to advise the CO that standing orders had been violated was unacceptable and clearly an exercise of poor judgment by the OOD. This was subsequently made part of the OOD's FITREP. When a CO puts an order in the unit's standing orders, the CO must have complete confidence in subordinates to follow same. Officers who will lead must first learn to follow.

ISSUE 117 - COUNSELING

What happened: (Issue 117 from page 173) What makes this an ethical issue, is that the officer made the right decision in deciding that transferring the PO would only saddle someone else with the problem. The special trust and confidence placed in officers includes not passing the buck to someone else.

If an enlisted cannot be helped, then the officer has to consider the possibility that someone with greater experience might be able to accomplish what the officer can't. Consultation with other officers, however, brought agreement that there was no easy solution and that extensive counseling would be needed.

In considering an administrative discharge (which would be quicker and leave more time for the officer to spend with other members of the unit), the realization that such action would waste a tremendous amount of training the Navy had provided motivated the officer to start an extensive counseling program. In time this was successful and saved the Navy a valuable individual as well as adding to the leadership capabilities of the officer.

Not all situations that an officer will encounter present esoteric ethical dilemmas. But it is necessary that for each problem that arises, an officer review the canons of ethics. No matter how small the matter may be, the officer should ensure an ethical approach is taken toward resolution of the difficulty.

We are not paid as much as executives in industry and thus need to look to the concept of psychic income to fill our emotional needs. There is no amount of money that can give one the same thrill as that felt when the counseling of an individual helps the individual, their family, and the service. There is no limit to the number of times per day officers can pay themselves psychic income, it only takes looking around and deciding where to apply one's talents.

Part of an officer's ethical code should include responsibility to the troops. Effective, concerned leadership is tangential to proper ethical conduct!

ISSUE 118 - THE NOTEPAPERS

What happened: (Issue 118 from page 175) After anguishing for many months, the 0-4 decided that since the information was old and outdated, and no matter how slight, risks to a successful career were to be avoided. The officer decided to burn the classified notes, hoping that no one else would know.

While the security of the United States may or may not have depended on whether action was or was not taken, the 0-4's only consideration was what effect actions taken would have on a promising career.

The actions taken were inappropriate and unethical; this officer failed to meet the standards of trust and confidence we all must adhere to. In the highly competitive environment of the career military officer, ethical decisions come into play daily. In an ever-changing world and the country's economic climate, the ladder of success had become very steep. As we move through this period of uncertainty, ethics, morality, integrity, and character will be the hallmark for successful officers who must avoid the temptations that go with success as they march through their military careers.

Officers of the future must be total professionals so that our service and country will not be embarrassed by either our own reporting of what goes on or the reporting of others. The hotline should not be the basis for an officer being ethical but it is well to remember that a number of the issues in this volume were first brought to the attention of the Inspector General because some officers would not take the right action.

In this case, the officer erroneously thought no one else would know of the transgression, and no one would be affected. But the 0-4 knew, and none of us escapes, though it may take the form of psychological and/or physiological (for example, ulcers) punishment. Second, the enlisted who handled classified papers on that first tour suspected the something was wrong since this officer conducted affairs differently from all other newly reporting 0-1s. Thus, the message was clearly sent to the enlisted that some officers make up their own mind which rules to obey and which not to. This set a poor example for the enlisted to follow in taking that same position.

ISSUE 119 - SLEEPING ON WATCH

<u>What happened</u>: (Issue 119 from page 177) The EDO decided not to tell the CO, or anyone else. The EDO was extremely tired and felt that telling the CO in the morning would result in many hours of additional work.

The officer who reported this issue put it this way: "You fear for your career. The SRO is a good watch stander. No one else knows. You feel that even if you do come forward, no changes would be made to allow for more rest."

By the very fact that the officer, who is the subject of this case, reported this matter indicates possession of the knowledge that the path that was followed was ethically wrong though, in the mind of that officer, career saving.

This officer knew about the lost submarines *Thresher* and *Scorpion* and was ready for possible life-risking duty, yet when it came time to act ethically, did not have the courage to do so. As junior officers it will be easy for you to interpret this issue as the fault of the CO for creating such a climate, but it is really an abrogation of the responsibility of the JO.

If we are driving our equipment and our crews past their limits of endurance, then those who know this must speak up. The use of Blue and Gold crews to operate nuclear submarines recognizes that those in charge of the submarine program realize that the equipment is actually more capable of extended operating hours than is its human crew. Safety is, of course, the watch word in all military evolutions, though we are in an inherently dangerous profession. In a peacetime environment, a ship's schedule will usually avoid placing its crew in this situation, particularly when conducting critical and complex testing. But there may be times when this is done to ready the crew for combat.

As previously stated, the EDO was impressed with the CO's abilities and felt that the CO seemed to be a fair individual. Commanding officers *trust* their subordinates to speak up and they show *confidence* in their crews by risking their lives by diving with them. The EDO's career was important, but if each officer fails to report their own human failures, then how will those who design our submarines

SOLUTIONS

know what modifications have to be made so as to accommodate a human crew running an electro-mechanical device that rarely wears out?

If as a junior you speak privately and confidentially to a senior, you can be reasonably certain that the trust you are showing in your senior will be reciprocated. You expect your seniors to place their trust and confidence in you, is it too much to expect you to place your trust and confidence in them?

ISSUE 120 - PASSING INSPECTION

What happened: (Issue 120 from page 178) The ethical way would be to accept the failing grade (which would be difficult) and work on the areas needing improvement. Conversely, the work could be gundecked to achieve a passing inspection grade, but a failing knowledge grade and possible future problems would result.

In this case the officer decided to gundeck the *quals* and the division passed the inspection.

It does not have to be this bleak a picture. Those officers who are looking so hard to beat the system could put that same effort into working with the system and excelling. It will take today's junior officers, working with their more senior officers, to see that this happens. Every junior officer needs to know that doing the right thing will be respected, even if it isn't liked. Your seniors will know that they can count on you if you tell the truth. You will avoid ulcers, even if it means losing your career, by not lying, not cheating, not gundecking, not failing to tell the entire story, and not falsifying records.

There are other ways to approach the problem, such as interim qualification letters. In other words, qualify the sailor on what is known, not on what should be known. This will indicate to the inspecting officer that an honest ship is being dealt with and thus achieve a greater sense of confidence when the officers say that they are prepared in other areas.

America's armed forces are currently the best in the world because of our equipment, training, and commitment of personnel. Other nations, both large and small, are slowly catching up, however, but as long as integrity and ethical behavior—along with acceptance of responsibility and accountability—are our watchwords, we will prevail in future conflicts. It is up to you, the junior officers of today, to make sure we deserve to win.

ISSUE 121 - THE FALL

What happened: (issue 121 from page 180) The officer, realizing a lifelong dream might be shattered, but also having developed a sense of integrity over the years, disclosed the head injury on the report. The matter was submitted to a medical board for decision and the officer had two anxious years while waiting for a final determination to be made.

The medical board was impressed with the truthfulness of the ensign and considering his high level of integrity decided that since the officer had remained symptom free and had passed another EEG, that the officer should be allowed to enter the flight pipeline.

The medical board's decision was influenced by lessons learned over a long period of time. They considered the possibility that the officer might experience further medical problems if allowed to fly under conditions that might increase blackouts due to high G forces sustained during aerial operations.

This was not an easy decision for the board as they had to consider all others who will fly with or in the same air space as the officer.

To not have told the truth would have left the officer always in doubt and fearful that if anyone learned he lied, his career could be ended. The officer corps has no place for individuals who abuse the trust and confidence placed in them.

It is important to understand that if this officer had been turned down and pursued a non-flying career, the very strength of character that resulted in his speaking up would stand him in good stead for the rest of his career and life.

Officers need to realize that their job is to serve the nation first and that their ship, shipmate, and self are important—in that order. While flying, a pilot does not only risk his or her own life but also those of others. We expect a pilot to ground him or herself when not fit to fly. It is an ethical extension of that principle that requires an officer to come forward when anything happens that would cause regulations to be broken or others to be harmed if the truth were not known.

SOLUTIONS

Appendix A

INTEGRITY
by
Admiral Arleigh Burke

The classic treatise on the subject of integrity was written by Admiral Arleigh Burke in a letter to Professor Karel Montor. This treatise was published in the October 1985 issue of *Proceedings* and is produced here in its entirety. Brief definitions cannot do justice to this most important topic. This article, while it does not cover all aspects of integrity, will provide the reader with a good frame of reference for further thought.

"Integrity"

First you find yourself overlooking small infractions that you
would have corrected on the spot in the past.
Soon, you are a participant in these infractions. "After all," you
say, "Everybody's doing it."
All too soon you find yourself trapped: You no longer can stand
on a favorite principle because you have strayed from it.
Finding no way out, you begin to rationalize, and then you are
hooked.
The important fact is, the men who travel the path outlined above
have misused the very basic quality and characteristic
expected of a professional military man, or any other
professional man for that matter;
They have compromised their integrity.

This quotation, from a plaque hanging in the office of the Chief of Staff, Marine Corps Development and Education command, Quantico, Virginia, is remarkable in its simplicity and truthfulness. My old college dictionary defines *integrity* as (1) an unimpaired condition; soundness; (2) adherence to a code of moral, artistic, or other values; (3) the quality or state of being complete or undivided; completeness. As synonyms, it lists *honesty* and *unity*.

These are good definitions, but they are not very exact. They allow a great deal of leeway because the descriptive words may mean different things to different societies, different cultures, and different people. What is integrity for a Japanese may not be so for an Iranian. What is integrity for a cowboy may not be considered integrity by a minister (the disposition of horse thieves, for example). Integrity also varies widely among individuals in the same group. Probably no two individuals have the same ideas about all aspects of integrity. The point is, there exists no absolute definition of integrity.

Since no two people have the same values, how does a person acquire integrity, a code of conduct, a set of standards by which to live? How does a person develop a sense of obligation toward others, whether they make up a civic group, a military service, or a country? Most individuals' standards are learned when they are very young, from family, associates, and other contacts, from reading, and from watching television. It is well to remember, though, that families with high standards have had children who rejected the beliefs of the families and turned out to be first-class scoundrels. The reverse is also true. People with integrity have come from families that have lacked it. Perhaps this does not happen often, but it does happen. The point is that it is impossible to guarantee that any one person will acquire integrity. Development of integrity depends primarily on the individual.

There will be wayward priests, crooked politicians, and wicked naval officers. In a highly moral organization, people who fall below the standard will eventually be recognized and removed from the organization. In an organization of lower standards, they may be punished but still tolerated. In an immoral organization, such as in a criminal family, they will be measured by their contribution to their organization.

Individuals are responsible for their own integrity. They will be influenced by many people and events, but, in the end, their integrity quotient is of their own making. People are responsible for establishing their own standards, and their choices determine the kind of person they will be.

The integrity an individual should look after is his own—not his neighbor's, his subordinate's, his senior's, or his associate's, but his own. You can try to influence people to accept your views, but whether they do or not is up to them. A society or an individual may force rules on others, but no one can ensure that integrity will be inculcated. Only the individual concerned can accomplish that.

The integrity of a society or a group is approximately equal to the lowest common denominator of its people. When the standards are lowered for an individual, the standards of the group or society to which the individual belongs are lowered. Sometimes standards are raised in groups, but more frequently there is a gradual disintegration of standards.

Since the integrity of individuals varies, an organization cannot maintain an absolutely uniform integrity; not even sequestered groups can accomplish this. A general level of integrity can be approximated, but individuals may deviate greatly from the norm, even in organizations that try to keep standards high.

In these days of high-speed teaching methods, young people receive guidance from their families and literally dozens of other groups. They are even given computerized, capsulized advice. Developing individuals observe the people who dole out the plentiful and diverse guidance, and the observations they make influence their acceptance of what is right or wrong, good or bad. The following example is frequently mentioned in regard to education: If merit and capability are not requirements for success in the teaching profession, then young people are likely to judge that merit and capability are not important. Likewise, if developing individuals observe that people with known moral defects, or people who are known to be crooked or liars, are accepted in society without penalty, they might well conclude that integrity is not worth their effort, either.

Still, individuals determine what convictions they want to have and what they want to do about them. They continually adjust what they think is correct, what they want to learn, and how much effort they are willing to devote to each subject. Individuals determine who to like and who to avoid, who to admire and who to emulate, and make decisions about what is important and how to go about self-improvement. Individuals also determine what obligations they are willing to undertake on their own volition.

Since individuals create their own integrity, it follows that integrity is not fixed permanently. Integrity is a variable in one individual, among individuals of the same family and society, and among different societies and cultures. Integrity may be changed throughout life as individuals determine what actions they are willing to take to improve themselves and their integrity. Deciding how much integrity individuals want to develop is one of the most important decisions they make, whether they are conscious of the process or not. The basis of all education is learning to make judgments. This holds true for developing character as well as for becoming expert in any particular field. Individuals' judgments on material matters can be based on what other people have developed, and so can their judgments pertaining to integrity, but the final choices in both areas are made by the individual concerned.

Olympic athletes have devoted nearly all their efforts and time—often their whole lives—to becoming expert in their chosen field. If a person wants to become one of the best gymnasts in the world, that person ought to start training by the age of three—or maybe before. Since many people find that their dreams exceed their natural capabilities, they will make the sound judgment not to continue to try to accomplish the impossible, but to restrict themselves to what they can do well. The lesson must be learned early in life that very few people can ever be number one. This insight is part of learning to make sound judgments.

Individuals who get away with schemes not to mow the lawn do not increase their sense of obligation very much. When individuals decide not to make the efforts necessary to learn arithmetic or calculus, it is not likely that they will be very good in any profession requiring a knowledge of math. The young person who fools around at the piano, not really trying to learn, is making the choice not to be a piano player. If people worked as hard at learning academics and professional knowledge as they do at performing in athletic contests, it is probable that the world would be a better place to live.

It must be understood that a judgment on anything is not irrevocable, although action taken as a result of a judgment, such as hanging the wrong man as a horse thief, frequently has irrevocable consequences. A person with low grades can see the light, for example, and decide to become more proficient in math. If desire is there, most things can be accomplished. It takes more effort, more time, more determination to correct an original wrong judgment—but it can be done. Grandma Moses became a great artist after she decided to try painting later in her life.

Of course, individuals can alter their integrity. Too frequently the alterations are on the side of lowered standards, as has been demonstrated in a number of professions and in government. The crux of this is that individuals make their own integrity by reason of their own decisions, choices, and judgments, and they change their integrity by the same means. At the same time, people should make judgments on other people's integrity gingerly. The many different concepts of integrity held by different individuals, groups, and cultures should be treated with all due respect.

Some of the most vicious wars in history have been fought in the name of religion by societies that had very strong—and very different—convictions concerning integrity. They disagreed on what was right, on their basic mode of implementing what was right, and on their bibles or the equivalents thereof, and thus, each side resolved to force its views on the other side. Both sides were absolutely certain they had the monopoly on integrity, and that the other side had no integrity at all.

The extended upheaval in Lebanon is primarily based on different views of religion: what is right, what is good, and what is the word of God. These differences have been exacerbated by greed, desire for power, and self-interest. The Middle East (like a number of American cities) is full of strong and conflicting views on integrity and full of people who do not seem to have much integrity. Some leaders in the Mideast appear to be scoundrels, liars, selfish in the extreme, and generally without socially redeeming features. It is likely that few people in this country agree with, or understand, their philosophy, and that fewer still would stand for any attempt to force that philosophy on them.

Keeping our own integrity up to par is problem enough. We are responsible for our own conduct; we are not responsible for another's integrity. If we have made the normal number of correct judgments during our lives, we have probably concluded that we should not try to interfere with the religion of others or to determine what is right or wrong for them. We should not interfere unless another group tries to force its views of integrity on us or our organization. Then we must resist, or the other group's efforts will appreciably lower the standards of our organization. In relation to the naval profession, in particular, the following observations are applicable:

— Integrity and motivation are necessary in naval officers, but competence in the profession is also essential.

— Good intentions are most desirable, but nothing can be built or done by good intentions alone—except maybe paving the road to hell. Performance is required. Good intentions may help get performance, but the required end product is performance, not "I meant well."

— Integrity, or lack thereof, is not always discernible. Many people practice successfully to appear to have great integrity, or more than they do have. They can fool many some of the time. But always guard against making a final judgment on another's integrity based only on his own statements or on what appears to be.

— Be wary of self-proclaimed virtue. Do not rely on other people's evaluation of their personal integrity. Perhaps if they had integrity, they would not be their own press agents.

— The marketing of reputations for integrity is a good business. Many leaders have made good livings allowing their reputations to be used to represent organizations with no or poor reputations of their own.

Despite the cynical tone of these observations, most people and a large percentage of naval officers are people of integrity. They are honest; they are reliable; they are professional, and they do have good professional ethics. Have faith in your fellow officers, but be ready if one of them is less valiant, less competent, or less honest than you thought.

All of us can learn from the past. As wise as Moses was, he had difficulty hearing the disagreements of all the people who came before him. The people wanted Moses to settle matters between them and make known to them God's decisions and regulations. His father-in-law, Jethro, observing that Moses was having great difficulty handling the work, suggested:

> Be thou for the people to Godward, that thou mayest bring the causes unto God. And thou shalt teach them ordinances and laws, and shalt show them the way wherein they must walk, and the work that they must do. Moreover thou shalt provide out of all the people able men, such as fear God, men of truth, hating covetousness; and place such over them to be rulers of thousands, and rulers of hundreds, rulers of fifties, and rulers of tens. And let them judge the people at all seasons; and it shall be, that every great matter they shall bring unto thee, but every small matter they shall judge; so shall it be easier for thyself, and they shall bear the burden with thee. If thou shalt do this thing, and God command thee so, then thou shalt be able to endure, and all this people shall also go to their place in peace. (Exodus 18:19-23)

The point is that, when considering weighty matters, an individual can be helped greatly by turning to and relying on others for support, for no one individual has all of the knowledge necessary to be 100 percent correct all of the time.

One question to be considered is, "What should an officer do when he thinks that a senior is lying to the next senior officer in the chain-of-command?" Certainly a junior officer who believes a senior is making a mistake—any serious mistake, not just a mistake with regard to integrity—should inform that senior officer. For example, suppose that the officer of the deck has the conn, and he orders "Come to 080." The junior officer of the deck believes that it is an incorrect order, and he tells the OD right away. The OD rechecks and either corrects the order or tells the junior officer that the order will not be changed and why.

This sort of exchange is common in the Navy. Usually the senior will ask for the junior's opinion as a matter of training, if for no other reason. Seniors do not want to make mistakes, and they appreciate being informed of an error before any damage is done.

Thus, it is a good habit to question suspected errors in normal operations. An officer, however, does not often deliberately lie to a senior.

This example illustrates how important it is for a naval officer to have experience in making judgments. There are, unfortunately, no general guidelines that can be laid down for the contingency of lying. The appropriate reaction to lying depends on circumstances, which are unpredictable. If a junior officer believes that a senior is lying, the junior officer must ask himself questions. Is the junior officer sure that the senior is lying, or is it possible that he is only guessing that the senior is lying? Is it possible that the issue involves a difference of opinion? Could it be a question of interpretation? Finally, does the matter have significance?

The junior must judge whether the lie will have an effect on the organization. If the junior concludes that the senior is lying on a significant matter, and that the senior's integrity is involved, then it is the duty of the officer to tell that senior that the matter will be reported to the next senior in the chain-of-command as well as the reasons why the junior believes the report is necessary. It is particularly important for an officer to confront a senior accused of dishonesty or another breach of integrity, and to advise that officer on the intended course of action, before he besmirches the reputation of that officer.

The decision to accuse is never to be taken lightly. An officer who accuses peers or associates of any kind of wrongdoing knows well, before he utters the first words of accusation, to expect judgments from shipmates and perhaps from larger groups on the appropriateness of the charges made. This is in accordance with the old adage: "Judge not, lest ye be judged."

Therefore, when the junior starts wrestling with his conscience to make the judgment on where his duty lies, he should resist impulsive actions and even consider searching out a second opinion. Friends in the unit will likely take the issue seriously, or at least the more conservative ones will. There may be one or two who have noted the alleged misconduct themselves. I suppose that this sort of a drum-head court martial without the presence of the accused 'would come to a general conclusion, one way or another. Still, the final decision is in the hands of the originator of the charge, and that individual must make the final judgment on what should be done, no matter how much advice was sought and received from others. The decision belongs to the officer—and no one else.

Matters such as these are difficult for a junior officer, a Chief of Naval Operations, or a president. At the Naval Academy, in the year just before they graduate, midshipmen are taught the relationship between duty and honor: "We serve the country first, our seniors second, and ourselves last." The future officers are counseled on honor versus loyalty in the Naval Service, and specific attention is given to the difference between a professional and a careerist. These definitions are given: "A military professional is someone who upholds the highest standards and serves the country with unquestioning loyalty; the professional is not motivated by personal gain. . . . A careerist is someone who serves the country in the best way fit to further his own career." It is noted in this lesson given to our future officers that the careerist is more likely to fall into the zero-mentality syndrome, to be someone who would choose to cover up those things that might draw discredit to his own unit. The professional takes on the issues directly and does not swerve to avoid criticism. These matters are never easy for the officer, but he must take on the issues to fulfill the obligations he holds to country, service, unit, personnel therein, and self.

As a junior officer on a battleship, I was once involved in a delicate situation that I did not handle properly. I recount it here so that others may not need as much time to learn when the proper action should be taken in such a situation. On a Labor Day weekend I had duty as one of three officers of the deck. My relief did not return to the ship on Monday morning to relieve me, so I stood his watches on Monday without reporting anything amiss. When the derelict officer showed up on Tuesday, he told the senior watch officer that he had made arrangements with me to stand his watches before he left for the weekend. That was not true. He simply took the chance that some dope would fill in for him. I did not do anything about that misstatement, either. Within two years that officer was dropped from the rolls of the Navy for a similar offense. Had I reported him the first time, he might have been jolted out of his expectation that there would always be some volunteer who would step in to carry his part of the load.

There is also the question of what to do about a "whistle blower." The answer involves knowing whether the individual has made an honest effort to correct the wrong by using the chain-of-command channels that are available. A clever whistle blower can parlay an error into something that produces publicity and promotion that is not deserved. Recognizing the media's hunger for material to present to the public should cause any person to ask, before he blows the whistle, whether all possible steps have been taken to correct the situation. The Naval Service is an organization made up of people, and people are subject to making mistakes, but it is important for the public to know that efforts are being made to find mistakes and to correct them. It is wise to wait before making a judgment until you know why the usual steps were not taken or why those steps were not successful. It is also wise to listen and not make a premature judgment. Every organization needs good internal checking, internal policing, and internal corrective apparatus, just as every organization needs an external inspector, an external check, and means for external correction.

It is suggested that codes of honor and integrity must not be so rigid that they are beyond the capability of human beings to follow. I believe it should be the personal responsibility of individuals to decide whether to report lying, cheating, and stealing, and that they should do so only after completely scrutinizing their own conscience regarding integrity. When a person steals a pencil, perhaps absent-mindedly picking it up from someone's desk, the observer should have the discretion to judge whether the theft should be reported. A person can dream up many examples and possibilities, most of them minor, when there is no doubt that a theft, a lie, or a cheating incident has occurred. But the incident may have been so inconsequential that an individual of good conscience could interpret it as not significant enough to be reportable.

In summary, we must instill in individuals a sense of personal honor, an obligation to their organization and other groups, a desire to keep their own standards high and to keep the standards of their organization high. This sense of honor gives real meaning to the feeling engendered from belonging to a "Band of Brothers," and to other nostalgic emotions that are essential to a taut, high-standards organization. However, an honorable person should have the option of determining whether to believe that others are honorable and whether to take appropriate action in each case. The appropriate action is not usually reporting the offender to the senior, but confronting the suspected culprit with the charge first. What should be done must be individually decided at every step. A fixed rule that insists that a person never squeals on a classmate, a shipmate, or a buddy is just as wrong as a rule that says that everything that could be construed as lying, stealing, or cheating should be reported to a senior.

APPENDIX A   279

Likewise, it is also important to comment on the issue of "pleasing the boss." "Greasers"—those who play up to their bosses strictly for personal gain—do not last very long in the service, because their method of operating is discovered and disliked, and they are discharged. But also keep in mind that bosses are pleased to have confidence in the competence of their subordinates, and that there are few subordinates in any profession who do not want to please their bosses. Bosses have been put in positions of responsibility and authority because their bosses think the individuals know what they are doing—and what their subordinates, in turn, should do. What pleases the boss is usually getting done what should be done. It is proper that all officers of the Naval Service should want a reputation for contributing to the improvement of their service. There is nothing wrong with that. Every unit's effectiveness is determined by the way the bosses, and everyone else in the unit, do their respective jobs. The reputation of the Naval Service, the unit, and the individuals in the unit depends on overall unit effectiveness.

Since the boss usually desires a reputation for being a capable officer, including being a capable leader, it is laudable in a subordinate to want to please the boss. There is certainly nothing wrong in pursuing that trait, unless pleasing the boss results in turning in a poor performance. It is usually not too difficult for the boss to recognize insincere support. Greasing seldom works in a classroom, and it succeeds almost as often in the fleet.

Each of us must make his own decisions about the meaning of integrity. I suggest that officers who want to be ready for the difficult decisions of life study the great military leaders of the world, their similarities and differences. Frankly, there is no shortcut to wisdom. Rules to cover all situations do not exist. All of us must find our own ways. Our ability to make the best decisions at the time will certainly be influenced by our knowledge of the past, our consultation with others, and our ability to "see" the future. At the moment of decision, we will have to use our best judgment on what we in turn will do about it. Good luck!

Appendix B

As with exercising the body through physical activity, it is generally considered useful to engage in discussion over ethical issues to sharpen the mind and help develop an approach to problem avoidance and solutions that will bring credit to the military services. The following cases have been provided for discussion by Dr. John Johns of the Industrial College of the Armed Forces.

Case 1: You are a student at the U. S. Army Command and General Staff College. While conducting research in the library you come across vital material for your paper from a U.S. Army War College Thesis. You are pleasantly surprised to discover that this thesis was written by Colonel Walkonwatter, who served as your brigade commander at your last assignment in Germany. From previous contact, you know that this officer is well-known and highly regarded. He is presently serving as chief of staff at a division less than 100 miles away. You are impressed by his research efforts, particularly because they reveal a side of his professional ability that you had not previously observed.

You also discover helpful data from a paper published by a large research corporation, the title of which is strikingly similar to the War College thesis. As you read this data you discover that major sections of the War College thesis are, word for word, the same as the report from the research corporation. At no point in the thesis is the report ever properly cited or even mentioned. You are left stunned by the realization that Colonel Walkonwatter plagiarized this War College thesis.

1. What is your responsibility in this case?
2. What are the ethical implications of this case?
3. As a CGSC student, what would you expect to be the outcome of such a report?
4. Would you take the same action if you didn't know Colonel Walkonwatter?

Case 2: Chief Warrant Officer Brees was very satisfied with his new job even though it required him to travel two to three times a month to distant installations. The traveling kept him away from home a lot, but he had found a way to make the government "pay" for the inconvenience. He discovered it one day when the airline he was planning to travel on had overbooked his flight. He was given a check for $250 for "denied boarding compensation." That was the good news. The bad news was that finance regulations required he turn it in to the transportation office.

The clerk at the transportation office informed him, however, that if he voluntarily gave up his seat on an overbooked flight, regulations permitted him to keep any compensation the airline might pay. The next time he was scheduled for TDY, CW4 Brees arranged his schedule to fly out on a particular flight that he knew from experience was often overbooked. He was right. As he sat in the crowded plane prior to take off, the pilot announced that the flight was overbooked and that some passengers with guaranteed seats were still not aboard. The pilot offered $200 and a ticket on the next flight out to anyone who voluntarily gave up his seat. CW4 Brees was up and out of the airplane like a shot. The finance officer did not question his voucher upon his return.

CW4 Brees was on a high roll. By carefully arranging this TDY schedule and picking certain times and certain airlines, he managed to get on overbooked flights two out of three times for the rest of the year. And he did it without incurring extended delays that would have to be charged to annual leave. His reimbursements totaled over $1,500 for the year. And it was all perfectly legal.

1. Is CW4 Brees's conduct questionable from a professional standpoint? Why or why not?

2. While it is true that CW4 Brees has not violated the letter of the law, do you think he has violated its spirit? Why or why not?

3. Army Regulations Number 600-50 cautions us to avoid even the appearance of misconduct. Could this case be interpreted as the appearance of misconduct? Do you, as CW4 Brees's supervisor, think he deserves to be counseled?

Case 3: You are stationed at a military base in Colorado. College tuition for state residents is considerably less than for nonresidents. For purposes of tuition, the state treats military persons, stationed on bases within the state, as residents. Once you transfer out of state, that status changes.

While stationed there, your children start college in a state university and complete two years before you transfer to another state. Your neighbors tell you that the custom is to list one of their addresses (your neighbor's) for your children so that they can continue receiving resident tuition rates.

You discuss this with your spouse, who makes the following observations. You are one of those military people who claim residency in a state that taxes military pay. You have paid taxes there for over 20 years without using your residency state's school system. Fairness and justice dictate that you take advantage of this situation, notwithstanding the technical letter of the law. The fact that it is common practice suggests that others view it in the same way. Laws are made to apply *in general,* not to impose injustice.

How do you respond to this situation?

Case 4: Major Promotable Smart is the division G2 (intelligence officer) at Camp Rock, Korea. In the three short months he has been on the job he has won the respect and admiration of the entire staff. He is conscientious, often returning to work after duty hours to continue his work. Major Smart has an outstanding military record, and was selected below the zone for 0-5.

Returning to work on Sunday to finish a few projects, he notices that a SECRET report has been left out in his office. Although a security violation has occurred, it is unlikely that the information has been compromised. His office is locked and has no windows. There is a specific policy requiring that all unsecured documents be immediately reported.

1. What ethical/moral principles are involved?

2. How does the concept of "personal responsibility" influence our action?

3. What should Major Smart do?

4. How differently would you act if the unsecured report had been CONFIDENTIAL or TOP SECRET?

These non-ICAF Fleet cases discuss pressures JOs must resist.

<u>Case 5</u>: On Monday of a Memorial day weekend, prior to an 0800 Tuesday departure, a JO had the watch with primary responsibility to flush a 3,200-gallon boiler with water, as required before lighting up after a sodium nitrite lay-up. As the hose connection on the boiler was broken the boiler technician had dumped the contaminated water into the bilge. The problem now was instead of putting 3200 gallons of contaminated water into a 5,000-gallon capacity HAZMAT truck, there were 15,000 gallons of contaminated bilge water to dispose of, and no ability to secure two more trucks on a holiday.

Since discharge within 50 miles of land was prohibited, the JO called the chief engineer at home, who said: "tell the captain whatever he wants to hear in order to pump those bilges." Since the JO wasn't going to lie to the CO and pollute the harbor, he told the CO the rules. The CO decided to wait until the next day for additional HAZMAT trucks, and steamed out at 1100, 3 hours late.

1. What were the pressures on the JO?
2. Why did the chief engineer say what he did?
3. Why didn't the captain waive the rules and sail on time?
4. How did this affect the chief engineer-JO relationship?
5. How could this incident affect the JO's sense of integrity?

<u>Case 6</u>: A berthed ship was receiving the following pier services: trash removal, CATV, potable water, steam, electrical power, and telephones. A well liked CPO had the 0000 to 0800 watch and signed the log indicating 0800 conduct of routine tests and inspections to be normal. A day later the CPO's JO discovered the log had been falsified and that the CPO left the ship during the night. When brought to the attention of the chief engineer, the JO was told to sign for the watch as if it had been executed. Instead the JO made a written statement and forwarded it through the chain-of-command to the CO. The chief engineer blew up at the JO and said he should be a team player, which was further echoed by the XO who dismissed the statement with a warning to the JO about being a team player; and the CO wasn't advised that the CPO had wandered off the ship without being relieved.

1. What message does this send to junior officers?
2. What message does it send to enlisted?
3. What are the rewards to the JO of his actions?
4. Did the JO make any mistakes in this matter?
5. Why did the chief engineer and XO say what they did?

Appendix C

Bedrock Standards of Conduct

To maintain the public's confidence in our institutional and individual integrity, personnel of the Armed Forces *shall:*

1. Avoid any action, whether or not specifically prohibited by the rules of conduct, which might result in or reasonably be expected to create an appearance of:

    a. using public office for private gain;
    b. giving preferential treatment to any person or entity;
    c. impeding government efficiency or economy;
    d. losing complete independence or impartiality;
    e. making a government decision outside official channels; or
    f. adversely affecting the confidence of the public in the integrity of the government.

2. Not engage in any activity or acquire or retain any financial or associational interest that conflicts or appears to conflict with the public interests of the United States related to their duties.

3. Not accept gratuities from Department of Defense contractors unless specifically authorized by law or regulation.

4. Not use their official positions to improperly influence any person to provide any private benefit.

5. Not use inside information to further a private gain.

6. Not wrongfully use rank, title, or position for commercial purposes.

7. Avoid outside employment or activities incompatible with their duties or which may discredit the Armed Forces.

8. Never take or use government property or services for other than officially approved purposes.

9.   Not give gifts to their seniors or accept them from their subordinates when it is not appropriate to do so.

10.   Not conduct official business with persons whose participation in the transaction would violate laws or regulations.

11.   Seek ways to promote efficiency and economy in government operations.

12.   Preserve the public's confidence in the Armed Forces and its personnel by exercising public office as a public trust.

13.   Put loyalty to the highest moral principles and to country above loyalty to persons, party, or government department.

14.   Uphold the Constitution, laws, and regulations of the United States and never be a party to their evasion.

15.   Give a full day's labor for a full day's pay, applying earnest effort to the performance of duties.

16.   Never discriminate unfairly by the dispensing of special favors or privileges to anyone, whether for remuneration or not, and never accept for himself or herself or for family members, favors or benefits under circumstances which might be construed by reasonable persons as influencing the performance of governmental duties.

17.   Make no private promises of any kind binding upon the duties of office.

18.   Not engage in business with the government, either directly or indirectly, inconsistent with the conscientious performance of governmental duties.

19.   Expose corruption wherever discovered.

(Derived from U.S.C. 2635.101 published in the Federal Register, Vol. 57, No. 153 on August 7, 1992 (Rules and Regulations).

Bibliography

1. Bach, Brian J. "Soldierly Ethics." *Marine Corps Gazette,* Sept. 1984, pp. 56-59.
2. Beran, Walter F. "How To Be Ethical in an Unethical World." *Vital Speeches,* June 1976, pp. 602-08.
3. Bloom, Allan. *Liberal Education and Its Enemies.* Colorado Springs: U.S. Air Force Academy, Nov. 14, 1991.
4. Bok, Sissela. *Lying: Moral Choice in Public and Private Life.* New York: Pantheon Books, 1978.
5. Brennan, J. G. *Foundations of Moral Obligation: The Stockdale Course.* Newport, RI: Naval War College, 1992.
6. Brown, J. and Collins, M. J. *Military Ethics and Professionalism.* Washington, DC: National Defense University Press, 1981.
7. Buckingham, C. T. "Ethics and the Senior Officer: Institutional Tensions." *Parameters: Journal of the Army War College,* Vol. xv, No. 3.
8. Carroll, Robert C. "Ethics of the Military Profession." *Air University Review,* November-December 1974, p. 39-43.
9. Carson, Frank L. "Teaching Military Ethics as a Science II," *Research Report.* Maxwell Air Force Base: U.S. Air University, Air War College, March 1989.
10. Chalker, Edsel O. *Ethics for the Air Force Officer.* Maxwell Air Force Base: U.S. Air University, Air War College, Air Force ROTC, 1973.
11. Corey, G.; Corey, M.; and Callanan, P. *Issues and Ethics in the Helping Professions.* Monterey, CA: Brooks/Cole, 1984.
12. Coutu, D. L. and Ungerheuer, F. "The Money Chase." *Time Magazine,* May 4, 1981, p. 58.
13. *Creating a Workable Company of Ethics.* Washington, DC: Ethics   Resource Center, 1990.
14. DeGeorge, Richard T. *When Integrity Is Not Enough: Responding to Unethical Adversaries in Business and the Military.* Colorado Springs: U.S. Air Force Academy, Nov. 10, 1991.
15. Denise, Theodore C. and Peterfreund, Sheldon P. *Great Traditions in Ethics,* 7th edition, Belmont, CA: Wadsworth Publishing Co., 1992.
16. Diamond, D. B. "Private Agony-Public Cause." *Ladies Home Journal,* June 1990, p. 125.

17. Diehl, William F. "Ethics and Leadership." *Military Review,* April 1985, pp. 35-43.

18. *Ethics: A Selected Bibliography,* 3rd revision. U.S. Army War College Library, Jan. 1993.

19. *Ethics in America. Part I: Military Combat & Part II: Under Arms, Under Fire.* Maryland Public Television, Oct. 31, 1987.

20. *Ethics Journal.* Washington, DC: Ethics Resource Center.

21. Facilities:
    a. *Hazardous Material Control and Management,* OPNAVINST 4110.2.
    b. *Environmental Protection and Natural Resources Program Plan,* OPNAVINST 5090.1A.
    c. *Boats and Small Craft Inventory and Accounting,* OPNAVINST 4780.6C.

22. Futernick, Allan J. "Avoiding an Ethical Armageddon." *Military Review,* Feb. 1979, p. 17-23.

23. Fotion, N. "Military Ethics: Looking toward the Future," Stanford, CA: Hoover Institution Press, 1990.

24. Fotion, N. and Elfstrom, G. "Military Ethics: Guidelines for Peace and War." Boston: Routledge & Kegan Paul, 1986.

25. Gabriel, R. A. *The Nature of Military Ethics.* Westport, CT: Greenwood Press, 1980.

26. Gabriel, R. A. *To Serve with Honor: A Treatise on Military Ethics and the Way of the Soldier.* Westport, CT: Greenwood Press, 1982.

27. Ginsburgh, Robert N. "Military Ethics in a Changing World." *Air University Review,* Jan.-Feb. 1976, pp. 2-10.

28. Greene, W. M. "What Is Right." *Marine Corps Gazette,* Jun. 1984.

29. Halloran, Richard. "Officers and Gentlemen and Situational Lying." *New York Times* (Washington Talk), Aug. 6, 1987.

30. Hamel, Raymond F. "Are Professionalism and Integrity Only a Myth?" *Air University Review,* May-June 1978, pp. 60-67.

31. Hauser, William L. "Careerism vs. Professionalism." *Armed Forces and Society,* Spring 1984, pp. 449-83.

32. Hill, Ivan. *Common Sense & Everyday Ethics.* Washington, DC: American Viewpoint, Inc., 1980.

33. Huxley, T. *Evolution and Ethics and Other Essays.* New York: AMS Press, 1970.

34. Integrity and Efficiency:
   a. *Standards of Conduct,* SECNAVINST, 5370.2J
   b. *Fraud, Waste, and Abuse,* SECNAVINST 5430.92A
   c. *Management Control Program,* SECNAVINST 5200.35C
   d. *Follow-up on Reports of Audits,* SECNAVINST 5200.34D
   e. *Contractor Support Services,* SECNAVINST 4200.31B
   f. *Efficiency Review,*SECNAVINST 5010.1A

35. Johnson, Kermit D. "Ethical Issues of Military Leadership." *Parameters: Journal of the Army War College,* No. 2, 1974, pp. 35-39.

36. Kilpatrick, William. *Why Johnny Can't Tell Right from Wrong: Moral Illiteracy and the Case for Character Education.* New York: Simon & Schuster, 1992.

37. Kreeft, Peter. *Back to Virtue: Traditional Moral Wisdom for Making Moral Confusion.* San Francisco: Igniting Press, 1992.

38. Matthews, Lloyd J. and Brown, Dale E. *The Parameters of Military Ethics,* Washington, DC: Pergamon-Brassey's International Defense Publishers, 1989.

39. *Military Ethics.* Washington, DC: National Defense University Press, 1987.

40. Montor, K. and Ciotti, A. *Fundamentals of Naval Leadership.* Annapolis, MD: Naval Institute Press, 1984.

41. Montor, K.; McNicholas, T.; Ciotti, A.; Hutchinson, T.; and Wehmueller, J. *Naval Leadership: Voices of Experience.* Annapolis, MD: Naval Institute Press, 1987.

42. Moore, G. E. *Principia Ethica.* London: Cambridge University Press, 1951.

43. O'Hara, Michael J. "The Challenge of Moral Leadership," *Proceedings,* Aug. 1977, pp. 58-62.

44. Personnel Readiness and Community Support:
   a. *Equal Opportunity,* OPNAVINST 5354.1C
   b. *Physical Readiness,* OPNAVINST 6110.1D
   c. *Tobacco Prevention,* SECNAVINST 5100.13A
   d. *Substance Abuse,* OPNAVINST 5350.4B
   e. *Sexual Harassment,* SECNAVINST 5300.26A
   f. *Navy Sponsor Program,* OPNAVINST 1740.3
   g. *Traffic Safety,* OPNAVINST 5100.12F
   h. *Pre-Separation Counseling,* OPNAVINST 1900.1C
   i. *Dependent Care Certification,* OPNAVINST 1740.4

45. Piper, Thomas R.; Goodpaster, Kenneth E.; and Gentile, Mary C. *Managerial Decision Making and Ethical Values.* Boston: Harvard Business School, 1989.

46. Potter, J. V. "War Games." *Journal of Professional Military Ethics—U.S. Air Force Academy,* Dec. 1982.

47. Purtilo, Ruth. "Ethicist Helps to Resolve Dilemmas in Patient Care." *Boston Massachusetts General Hospital News,* Vol. 47, No. 2, Mar. 1988.

48. Raspberry, William. "Ethics Without Virtue." *The Washington Post,* Dec. 16, 1991, p. A23.

49. Rescher, Nicholas. *In the Line of Duty: The Complexity of Military Obligation.* Colorado Springs: U.S. Air Force Academy, Nov. 15, 1990.

50. Security:
    a. *Physical Security,* OPNAVINST 5530.14B
    b. *Operations Security,* OPNAVINST 3070.1A
    c. *Information, Personnel, and ADP Security,* OPNAVINST 5510.1H

51. Shiner, John F. "The Need for Military Professionals." *Journal of Professional Military Ethics,* Vol. 2, No. 1, Sept. 1981.

52. Spinoza, B. *Ethics.* New York: E. P. Dutton, 1938.

53. Stockdale, James B. *A Vietnam Experience.* Stanford, CA: Hoover Institute Press, 1984.

54. Stockdale, James B. "The World of Epictetus: Reflections on Survival and Leadership." *The Atlantic,* Apr. 1978, pp. 98-106.

55. Stratton, R. A. "Where's our Code of Ethics?" *Proceedings,* Dec. 1986, p. 83.

56. Stromberg, P. L.; Waikin, M. M.; and Callahan, D. *The Teaching of Ethics in the Military.* Hastings-on-Hudson, NY: Institute of Society, Ethics and the Life Sciences, Hastings Center, 1982.

57. Taylor, Maxwell D. "A Professional Ethic for the Military?" *Army,* May 1978 pp. 18-21.

58. Toner, James. *The Cross and the Sword: Reflections on Conscience and Command,* New York: Praeger, 1992.

59. Turkelson, Donald R. "The Officer as a Model of Ethical Conduct." *Military Review,* July 1978, pp. 56-65.

60. *U.S. Air Force Academy Journal of Professional Military Ethics.*

61. Wakin, Malham M. *War, Morality, and the Military Professions.* Boulder, CO: Westview Press, 1986.

62. Walton, C. *The Ethics of Corporate Conduct.* Englewood Cliffs, NJ: Prentice-Hall, 1977.
63. Webb, Ernest L. "When Ethic Codes Clash: Absolute vs. Situational." *Army,* Mar. 1978, pp. 31-33.
64. Wenker, Kenneth H. *Ethics in the U.S. Air Force.* Maxwell Air Force Base: Air University Press, 1988.
65. Wiener, Philip O. *Dictionary of the History of Ideas.* New York: Charles Scribner's Sons, 1973. ("Right & Good," pp. 173-86 and "Moral Sense," pp. 230-34.)

"It is unethical not to be professional."
Anonymous

"One can learn a lot *about* morality without ever *being* moral. One can learn a lot *about* moral character without *developing* moral character."
Philosophy 313: Ethics - U.S. Air Force Academy

"Military officers must continually discuss ethics, responsibility, accountability, integrity, trust, and honor with their subordinates so that standards don't slip from one generation to the next, as they do in society in general."
Professor Karel Montor, U.S. Naval Academy

Index

Note: Index entries referring to items in issues will show the first page of the issue, regardless of which page(s) in which the item(s) appear(s).

A

Acceptance:
  of gratuities, 22, 39, 56, 58, 70, 148
  of voluntary services, 7
Adams, John, 141
Administrative discharge, counseling versus, 173
Administrative Discharge Board, 3, 171
Al-Ghazali, 44
Alcohol abuse, 40, 75, 133
  attitude of officers toward, 8
  performance of maintenance affected by, 28
Appearance(s):
  admonition of John Paul Jones regarding, 9, 48
  of inappropriate behavior,
    avoidance of, 7, 23, 48, 56, 67, 69, 70, 148
    reaction to, 82
  of misconduct, 282
  perception of wrongdoing and, 70, 85
  personal, maintaining proper standards of, 161
Assignment of personnel, 47, 80
Assumption of authority, improper, 172
Attention to detail, 52
Authority, assumption of, improper, 172
Aviation Career Incentive Pay program, 112

B

Base housing, waiting list for, 31
Bedrock Standards of Conduct. *See* Standards of Conduct
Behavior:
  aberrant, inquiring into cause of, 83
  ethical, rationale for, 1-9
  inappropriate, immediate action to correct, 156. *See also* Appearance(s) of inappropriate behavior
Bias, religious, racial, sexual, or ethnic, 8, 9, 45, 47, 60, 71, 80, 107, 112, 143, 157
Bill of Rights, 141
Bong, Richard, 146
Briefing, inattention to, 59
Brown, Gary E., 119-122
Bulkeley, John, 29, 127

Burke, Arleigh, 21, 71, 91, 114, 126
  treatise on integrity by, 271-280
  violation of procedural doctrine by, 1
Burke, Edmund, 28, 138

C

Cataldi, Richard, 75
Chain-of-command:
  inquiry via, versus hotline report, 23
  use of,
    to correct a wrong, 278
    to rectify a grievance, 8, 25, 33, 50, 71, 90, 107, 113, 118, 170
    to solve ethical dilemma, 92, 117, 123, 129, 138, 148, 151, 158, 284
Chaplain:
  marital counseling by, 132
  seeking advice from, 13, 95, 103, 118, 126, 158
Cheating:
  by contractor, 151
  in training competition, 102
Civilian attire, inappropriate, 153
Claim, false, 58, 100, 128, 133
Classified material, safeguarding of, 82, 116, 147
Climate, ethical. *See* Ethical climate
Coats, Dan, 119, 120
Combat readiness:
  pressure,
    to "go along" versus, 111
    to please senior versus, 15, 84, 105, 108
  self-interest versus, 15, 84
Commanding officer. *See also* Senior(s)
  approval of required for off-duty work of subordinate, 40
  inappropriate behavior by, 95
  responsibility of, for harmony within command, 93
Commissary, unauthorized use of, 7, 79
Communication(s):
  adequate, need for, 17, 93
  confidential, 158
Community, relationship of military base with, 29, 85
Competition, unfair, 102
Conduct unbecoming an officer, 17, 27, 37, 51, 58, 61, 76, 86, 95, 103, 104, 110, 117, 123, 135, 139, 168, 284

Confidence, breach of, 123
Confucius, 44
Conspiracy to falsify document, 91
Constitution:
    Bill of Rights introduced by first Congress,
        141
    officer's duty to, 44, 50, 64, 82, 91, 95, 13,
        123, 124
Contractor(s), relations with, 19, 39, 50, 56, 58,
    91, 148, 151
Conversion of government property for personal
    use, 133, 134, 139
Counseling of subordinate, 83, 103
    versus administrative discharge, 173
Courage, moral. See Moral courage
Criminal offenses, major, requirement of, to
    report, 17
Cumshaw, 125
Customs documents, falsification of, 106

D

Dalton, John, 10
Deception, straightforwardness versus, 51
Detail, attention to, 52
Disbursement, discrepancies in, 61
Discharge, administrative, counseling versus,
    173
Document(s). See also Record(s); Report(s)
    customs, falsification of, 106
    official,
        falsification of, 50, 53, 104, 149, 169,
            178
        forgery of, 13
        improper alteration of, 165
Double standards:
    perception of, 5-6
    preventing establishment of, 161
Drug abuse, 110, 133, 171
    attitude of officers toward, 8
    reporting of, self-interest versus, 126
    testing for, 37
Duty:
    to Constitution. See Constitution, officer's
        duty to
    failure to report for, 168
    inattention to, 59, 147
    unfitness for, failure to report, 59

E

Edney, Leon A., 141-145
Employment, off-duty. See Off-duty employment
Enforcement of rules, consistency in, 153, 204

Enlisted:
    family of, sympathy for, versus discipline of
        enlisted, 170, 171
    officer's improper financial dealing with, 136
Equal opportunity, 43-45, 47, 71, 80, 107, 157
Equipment, improperly operating, report of, 169
Error, reporting of, self-interest versus, 78
Espirit-de-corps, destruction of, 76
Ethical behavior, rationale for, 1-9
Ethical climate, 92, 105, 111
    of "look the other way," 94, 97
    study of, upon joining new unit, 6
Ethical leadership, trust as cornerstone of, 119-122
Ethical loyalty, 55
Ethics in military leadership, 141-145
Ethnic bias in military, 8, 9, 45, 143
Extra-marital relationship, 58

F

False claim, submission of, 58, 100, 128, 133
Falsification:
    of customs documents, 106
    of official documents, 50, 104, 149, 169, 178
    of official records, 104, 116
    of orders, 27
        travel, 13
    of personnel documents, 53
    of report, 21, 81, 84, 91, 105, 108, 115, 116,
        127, 134, 135
Family, enlisted, sympathy for, versus discipline of
    enlisted, 170, 171
Female officers, harassment of, 27, 60, 90, 113,
    143, 146, 156
Financial dealing, improper, with enlisted, 136
Fitness report system, manipulation of, 64
Flight jacket, obtaining by fraudulent means, 134
Fluckey, Eugene, 146
Forgery:
    of parking pass, 109
    of travel orders, 13
Form, official, improper alteration of, 53, 165
Fraternization, 54, 103, 135, 158
Fraud, 13, 23, 27, 31, 34, 36, 48, 53, 58, 66, 70,
    79, 85, 92, 97, 106, 112, 118, 128, 133,
    134, 138, 149, 151
Friend(s):
    counseling of, 109
    interest of, versus duty to unit, 89
    loyalty to,
        versus duty to unit, 110
        versus safety, 124

Fuel, budget for, versus usage of, 129
Fundraising, 29

G

Good order and discipline, prejudice to, 54, 204
Government facilities, unauthorized use of, 7, 34, 79
Government labor, use of, for personal benefit, 97
Government property:
    conversion of, for personal use, 133, 134, 139
    unauthorized disbursement of, 125
    use of,
        for personal business, 7,11, 48, 66, 67, 133
        unauthorized, 34, 66
Gratuities, acceptance of, 22, 39, 56, 58, 70, 148
Grievance, use of chain-of-command to rectify, 8, 25, 33, 50, 71, 90, 107, 113, 118, 170
Grievance hearing, support of XO versus CO in, 86
Group leadership discussions, 121
Gundecking, 115, 178

H

Hackett, Sir John Winthrop, 121
Hamilton, Alexander, 141
Harassment, 33
    sexual. *See* Sexual bias in military
Hayward, Tom, 156
Hotline(s), use of, 11, 22, 29, 31, 66, 69, 70, 79, 148
    chain-of-command inquiry versus, 23
    possible, as threat to cause ethical behavior, 174

I

IG. *See* Inspector General
Illegal order, obedience to, 21, 25, 81, 112
Impropriety, appearance of. *See* Appearance(s) of inappropriate behavior
Inattention to duty, 59, 147
Income, psychic, 53, 73, 108, 134, 173
Income tax return, fraudulent, submission of, 133
Influence, improper use of, 31
Injury, reporting of, versus self-interest, 179
Inspection, borrowing material for, 51
Inspector General (IG), investigations by, 56, 69, 100, 174
Integrity, 271-280
    components of, 21
    defined, 271
    nuclear officer and, 163-166
    personal, 91, 92, 99-101
Investigation(s):
    of contractor, 151
    by Inspector General, 56, 69, 100, 174

by subordinate, of senior's possible inappropriate behavior, 90
Issues:
    Accomplice, The, 131
    Air Show, 55
    Altitude, Briefed, 49
    Billet Assignments, 47
    Candidates, Selecting, 157
    Canteen Corks, The, 51
    Certification, 78
    Cheat, 133
    Civilian Attire, 153
    Combination, The, 82
    Communication, 93
    Communication, Inter-Aircraft, 52
    Competition, The, 102
    Complaint, The, 113
    Computer, The, 136
    Computers, 11
    Contractor, Working with a, 58
    Counseling, 173
    Courage, Lack of, 95
    Cover, The Car, 139
    Cowardice, 117
    Designation, 111
    Dinner, The, 148
    Discipline, 170
    Documents, Lost, 116
    Drinking Contest, 40
    Drug Test, The, 37
    Ejecting to Avoid Disaster, 32
    Emergency, Responding to an, 41
    Employment, Off-Duty, 85
    Equal Treatment, 60
    Equipment & Services, Government, 34
    Exam, The, 104
    "Experienced" Officer, The, 27
    Fail One's Self, To, 126
    Fall, The, 179
    Fitness Report, The, 64
    Flight, The, 67
    Flying a Scheduled Mission, 88
    Food for Friends, 79
    Fraternization, 54, 103
    Friend?, A, 124
    Friend, The, 132
    Fund Raising, 29
    Funds, Shortage of, 53
    Gift, The, 56
    Gift, The Christmas, 39
    Grievance Hearing, 86
    Haircut, The, 161

Happy, Keeping Everyone, 112
Harassment, Video, 107
Hotel, The, 70
Humor, 90
Information, Confidential, 123
Inspection, Passing, 178
Inventory, The Classified, 147
Inventory, Submarine, 25
Investigation, The, 135
Jacket, The Flight, 134
Labor & Equipment, Extra, 97
Letter from Home, 59
Liberty, The Bus to, 69
Lone Ranger, The, 108
Marijuana, 110
Missile Test Firing, 91
Missing Item, The, 125
Motivation Isn't Everything, 35
Munitions Case, The, 118
NATOPS Check Flight, 63
NATOPS Test, The, 149
Officer, The Disbursing, 61
Officer, The Junior, 94
Officer, The Legal, 158
Officers, Assignment of, 80
Orders, Travel, 13
Overpayment, 36
Papers, The Note, 174
Parts, Component, 23
Parts, Repair, 151
Party, The, 17
Pass, The Parking, 109
Pay, Locality, 138
Pay Day at Sea, 73
Performer, The, 83
Pictures, Submarine, 92
Prank, The, 154
Quarters Competition, 31
Readiness, Command, 15
Readiness Levels, Inflated, 105
Reporting Ready Status, 84
Rescue Mission, 21
Safety, 160
Sanitaries, 172
Software, 19
Souvenirs, 106
Speaking Up, 137
Specifications, 169
Standards, 71, 114
Stories, The, 156
Stress at the Bingo Point, 38
Supervision, Maintenance, 28

Supervision, Training, 24
Systems Acceptance, 50
Tailhook '91, 146
Take-Off Time, 81
Thief, The, 89
Training, 115, 127
Transfer, Request for, 33
Transportation, 66
Travel Claim, 128
Travel, Official, 48
Use, First Time, 171
Use It or Lose It, 129
Valve, The, 167
Vendor, Dealing with a, 22
Watch, Sleeping on, 176
Watch, Standing, 168
Weak Lieutenant, The, 76

J

JAG. *See* Judge Advocate General's Corps
Jefferson, Thomas, 141
Jethro, 276
Johns, John, 281
Jones, John Paul, admonition of, regarding
      appearances, 9, 48
Judge Advocate General's Corps (JAG):
      and attorney-client confidentiality, 158
      seeking advice from, 6-7, 11, 13, 23, 29,
            34, 39, 40, 54, 66, 85, 95, 103,
            118, 136, 148, 158, 167
Juniors. *See* Subordinate(s)

L

Large, Randy, 99-101
Leadership:
      ethical, trust as cornerstone of, 119-122
      military, ethics in, 141-145
Legal officer. *See* Judge Advocate General's Corps
Loyalty:
      conflicting, 158
      ethical, 55
      to law, versus to individual, 31, 204
      misplaced, 64, 76
      to peer, versus safety, 124
      of senior, to law, versus to subordinate, 31
      to senior, versus following standard orders, 172
      to subordinate, 64
Lying:
      versus admission of drug use during youth, 126
      on classified document destruction report, 116
      on customs form, 106
      by peer, 3-4
      by senior, 3-4, 277
      by subordinate, 3-4, 11, 51, 204

M

McBride, William P., 163-166
Madison, James, 141
Marital problems, counseling peer and his spouse with, 132
Merchants, town:
  relationship of military base with, 85
  solicitation of gifts from, 8
Military leadership, ethics in, 141-145
Misplaced loyalty, 64, 76
Misrepresentation of status, 13, 204
Mistake:
  owning up to, 61, 71, 78
  in pay, 7
    failure to correct in timely manner, 36
  pending, subordinate's responsibility to advise senior of, 55
Montor, Karel, 141, 271
Moral courage, 4, 25, 33, 50, 59, 71, 76, 78, 86, 88, 90, 92, 94, 107, 118, 120-121, 123, 126, 131, 137, 138, 146, 151, 156, 179, 204
Morale, destruction of, 76, 117, 123
Moses, 276
Moses, "Grandma," 274
Munro, Douglas, 146
Murphy, Audey, 146
Mutual respect, 120, 121-122

N

NATOPS. *See also* Regulations; Standard operating procedures
  consequences of failure to follow, 15, 32, 52, 55, 59, 63, 88, 137, 149
Naval Criminal Investigative Service, 17

O

Off-duty employment, 11, 40
  wearing of uniform during, 85
Officer's Code of Ethics, 8
Official documents, forgery of, 13, 109, 204
Operating procedures, standard. *See* Standard operating procedures
Order(s):
  falsification of, 27
  forgery of, 13
  illegal, obedience to, 21, 25, 81, 112, 149

P

Parking pass, forgery of, 109
Pay:
  improper, through fraud, 138
  increase in, through fraud, 53
  mistake in, 7
    failure to correct in timely manner, 36

Peer(s):
  acceptance of, versus ethically correct action, 146, 153, 168
  alcohol abuse by, 75
  counseling of, 109
  failure of, to report unfit condition of crew member, 59
  illegal behavior by, 110
  loyalty to, versus safety, 124
  lying by, 3-4
  with marital problems, counseling of, 132
  pressure from, to act unethically, 94
  request of, to sign false record, 116
  responsibility of, to intervene on behalf of officers being sexually harassed, 146
  suspicions regarding, 89
Perception. *See* Appearance(s)
Personal business:
  conduct of, while on duty, 59, 133
  use of government property for, 7, 11, 48, 66, 67, 133
Personal integrity, 91, 92, 99-101. *See also* Integrity
Personnel, assignment of, 47, 80
Physical exam, 179
Plagiarism, 281
Plato, 110
Pollard spy case, 82
Prank(s):
  participation in, to achieve peer acceptance, 154
  serious implications of, 109
  as sexual harassment, 60
Prejudice to good order and discipline, 54
Private business. *See* Personal business
Procedures, standard operating. *See* Standard operating procedures
Procurement, 22, 23
Professional services, subordinate's need for, 83, 103
Property, government. *See* Government property
Psychic income, 53, 73, 108, 134, 173
Psychological services, need for, 83
Purchasing, 22, 23

Q

Qualification, falsification of, 178
Quarters, waiting list for, 31

R

Racial bias in military, 8, 9, 45, 47, 71, 107, 112, 143, 157
Random drug testing, 37
Reading, while being briefed, 59

Record(s). *See also* Document(s); Report(s)
    need for completeness of, 24
    official, falsification of, 104, 116
Regulations. *See also* NATOPS; Standard operating
    procedures
    consistency in enforcement of, 153
    failure to follow, 15, 31, 32, 52, 59, 61, 63,
        82, 84, 88, 104, 124, 147, 168, 169,
        172
Reimbursement for false claim, 58, 128
Religious bias in military, 8, 9, 45
Report(s). *See also* Document(s); Record(s)
    falsification of, 21, 81, 84, 91, 105, 108,
        115, 116, 127, 134, 135
Resnicoff, Arnold E., 43-45
Respect, mutual, 120, 121-122
Ripley, John, 146
Rules. *See* Regulations

S

Safety:
    failure to follow procedures for, 160, 167
    loyalty to friend versus, 124
    pressure to "go along" versus, 111, 204
    pressure to please senior versus, 15
    self-interest versus, 15, 84, 179
SECNAVINST:
    1700.11C, 40
    5520.3A, 17
Security procedures, violation of, 82, 104, 116,
    147, 174, 283
Self-discipline, lack of, 49
Self-interest:
    versus combat readiness and safety, 15, 84,
        179
    versus duty to unit, 73, 86, 95, 108, 179
    failure to report improperly operating
        equipment versus, 169
    versus reporting,
        of error, 61, 78
        of injury, 179
        of personal infraction versus, 176
    violation of trust versus, 125
Senior(s). *See also* Commanding officer
    breach of confidence by, 123
    communication with, by subordinate, 17
    fallibility of, 35, 114
    falsification of subordinate's report by, 21,
        204
    inappropriate behavior of, 117
        possible, 34, 71, 90, 146
    intimidation of subordinate by, 25, 66, 81,
        138, 149, 204
    loyalty of, to law, versus to subordinate, 31

loyalty to, versus following standard orders, 172
lying by, 3-4, 277
pressure exerted upon subordinate by,
    to follow ethically inappropriate order, 50,
        114, 118, 139, 204
    to follow illegal order, 138, 149
    to submit false report, 135
pressure to please,
    versus combat readiness and safety, 15
    versus recommendation contrary to wishes
        of, 131
questionable order from, 88, 114
responsibility of,
    to face possibility of own fallibility, 35
    to inform subordinate of recommendations
        against subordinate, 33
    to know capabilities of subordinates, 24, 41
    to monitor results of subordinates' training,
        28
    to observe performance of subordinates, 28,
        147
    for relationship among subordinates, 93
    to seek advice from others, 35, 38
    for training of subordinates, 22, 27, 28, 41,
        55, 105, 108, 115
    testimony against, 86
    willingness of, to hurt feelings of subordinates,
        24, 38, 160
Sensory overload, 38
Sexual bias in military, 8, 9, 45, 60, 80, 143
    sexual harassment as, 27, 60, 90, 113, 143, 156
    and failure of peers to take action to stop,
        146
Sexual harassment. *See* Sexual bias in military
Sexual relations, improper, avoidance of, 132
Sexually suggestive comments, 9, 156
Signature:
    compromising of, 166
    meaning of, 50
Sleeping on watch, 176
Smith, Michael, 146
Solicitation of gifts from town merchants, 8
Special treatment, improper acceptance of, 70
Standard operating procedures. *See also*
    NATOPS; Regulations
    failure to follow, 15, 32, 52, 63, 82, 88, 124,
        147, 160, 167, 168, 169, 172
Standards, double, perception of, 5-6
Standards of Conduct, 3, 4, 8, 9, 11, 22, 29, 39,
    50, 56, 64, 73, 83, 85, 89, 93, 104, 109,
    115, 125, 127, 132, 136, 148, 153, 154,
    161, 167, 168, 169, 171, 172, 174, 176,
    178

annual review of, 7
Bedrock, *listed*, 285-286
violation of, for personal gain, 97
Standing orders, failure to follow, 172
Status, misrepresentation of, 13
Stockdale, James Bond, 19
Subordinate(s):
    communication with senior by, 17
    counseling of, 103
    discipline of, 170, 171
    disrespect for seniors by, 154
    failure of,
        to deal with inappropriate actions of
            CO, 95
        to follow standing orders, 172
        to properly inform senior, 172
        to report infraction to senior, 176
        to seek CO's approval of off-duty work,
            40
    intimidation of by senior, 25, 66, 81, 118,
        204
    loyalty to, 64
    lying by, 3-4, 11, 51
    off-duty employment of, 11, 40, 85
    poor performance of, 83
    questionable order from senior and, 88
    report of, falsified by senior, 21
    responsibility of,
        to advise senior of investigation of
            senior's behavior, 90
        to advise senior of pending mistake, 55,
            114, 137
        to confront senior regarding senior's
            inappropriate behavior, 34, 71,
            146
        to investigate possible inappropriate
            behavior of senior, 90
        to report possible inappropriate
            behavior of senior, 117
        to properly inform senior, 84
    training of, senior's responsibility for,
        22, 27, 28, 41, 55, 105, 108,
        115
    willingness of, to hurt feelings of seniors,
        55
Survey report, false, submission of, 134

T

Tailhook '91, 17, 146
Thefts within unit, appropriate course of action
    regarding, 89

Town merchants:
    relationship of military base with, 85
    solicitation of gifts from, 8
Training:
    competition during, cheating in, 102
    records of. *See* Training records
    senior's responsibility for. *See* Senior(s),
        responsibility of
Training records:
    falsification of, 105, 108, 111, 115, 127
    need for completeness of, 24
Travel claim. *See* Claim
Travel orders, forgery of, 13
Trust, as cornerstone of ethical leadership, 119-122

U

Unethical assistance, acceptance of, 114
Unfair competition, 102
Uniform, wearing of, during off-duty employment,
    85
Uniform Code of Military Justice, 7
United States Code, Section 1342 of Title 31 of, 7

V

Violation:
    discovery of, versus violation itself, 13
    of procedural doctrine, by Arleigh Burke, 1
    of security procedures, 82, 104, 116, 147, 174,
        283
    of Standards of Conduct, for personal gain, 97
    of trust, versus self-interest, 125
Voluntary disclosure of wrongdoing, 37
Voluntary services, officer prohibited from
    accepting, 7

W

Walker, Mary, 146
Walker spy case, 82
Washington, George, 141
Waste, 19, 69, 94, 97, 125, 129, 151, 173
Watch:
    failure to relieve on time, 168
    leaving early, 204
    sleeping on, 176
Whitewash, 135
Will, George, 119
Work, off-duty. *See* Off-duty employment
Wrongdoing:
    perception of, 70, 85
    voluntary disclosure of, 37

Z

Zero tolerance policy, 37, 171
Zumwalt, Elmo, 112

Note: Index entries referring to items in issues will show the first page of the issue, regardless of which page(s) in which the item(s) appear(s).

Key Words

(In accordance with page number on which the key word appears.)

accountable (accountability). . .2, 6, 25, 44, 61, 78, 143, 144, 201, 220, 226, 229, 236, 237, 245, 249, 254, 256, 269, 291

alcohol (drinking, intoxicated). . .8, 17, 40, 75, 95, 119, 135, 146, 164, 187, 188, 193, 235, 236, 243, 257

assignment(s). . .11, 27, 31, 32, 38, 47, 71, 80, 83, 101, 105-106, 108, 122-123, 131, 133, 148, 151, 157, 161, 181, 189, 194, 209, 216, 219, 235, 248, 251-254, 258, 281

authority. . .1, 5, 9, 22, 24, 43, 70, 72, 81, 88, 115, 121, 144, 149, 172, 176, 189, 191, 192, 197, 220, 224, 244, 260, 261, 264, 265, 280

careerist. . .2, 86, 278

chain-of-command. . .1, 5, 8, 13, 21, 33, 49, 54, 62, 75, 90, 93, 103, 113, 123,149, 153, 155, 160, 171, 182,183, 185, 186, 190, 216-218, 224, 225, 227, 230, 233, 238, 240, 241, 247, 255, 259, 262-264, 276-278

challenge. . .3, 72, 121, 123, 128, 143, 289

character. . .30, 119, 120, 122, 128, 175, 206, 267, 270, 273, 289, 291

command. . .1, 3, 5, 8-9, 11, 13, 15, 16, 18, 19, 21-23, 25, 27, 31, 33-34, 38, 41, 49, 53,54, 60, 62, 64, 67, 69, 71, 73, 75, 81-84, 90, 93-95, 103, 105, 108, 111-113, 115, 117, 123, 127, 130-131, 133, 135, 136, 141, 149, 151, 153-155, 157, 158, 160, 168, 171, 173, 174, 177, 181-183, 185-187, 190, 192-194, 198-200, 204, 208-211, 214, 216-222, 224-227, 229, 230, 233, 238-242, 244, 245, 247, 250, 251, 253, 254-256, 258, 259, 262-265, 270, 271, 276-278, 281, 290

Commanding Officer (CO). . . 3, 5, 11, 21, 24-26, 29, 32, 33-34, 38, 40, 60, 62, 64-65,73, 76, 86-88, 90, 92-97, 102, 107, 112, 114, 121, 125, 127, 131, 137, 139, 149-152, 154, 157,159,171-172, 176-177, 181, 184-186, 188, 190-192, 196-198, 200, 202, 204, 203, 206-208, 211, 214-220, 226, 228-233, 235, 239, 241, 242, 247-249, 252-254, 256, 258, 264-266, 268, 287, 290

commissary. . .7, 22, 79, 184, 208

commitment. . .45, 121, 141, 142, 144, 213, 264, 269

communication. . .6, 17, 18, 38, 93, 182, 197, 218, 219

competition. . .23, 31, 85, 102, 189, 221, 239

complaint. . .5, 11, 23, 27, 29, 33, 85, 113, 135, 184, 185, 188-190, 202, 205, 208, 209, 229, 230, 240

computer(s). . .11, 12, 19, 34, 48, 78, 136, 181, 182, 246,

Constitution. . .44, 50, 71, 75, 141, 164, 202, 217, 220, 225-229, 234-236, 254, 286

contract(s). . .19, 20, 22, 39, 51, 56-58, 151-152, 199

contractor(s). . .19-20, 22, 39, 50, 56-58, 148, 151-152, 182, 193, 196, 199, 200, 252, 254, 285, 289

coordination. . .16, 197, 198, 201, 246

counsel (counseling). . .39, 54, 83,103, 124, 158, 171, 173, 191, 193, 198, 212, 222, 226, 235-236, 238, 242, 252, 266, 289

courage. . .4, 30, 75, 78, 86, 88, 95, 96, 117, 120, 121, 183, 185, 186, 190, 200, 204, 208, 217, 219, 220, 242, 247, 249, 268

cover-up. . .196, 201, 265

deployment. . .25, 26, 76, 82, 95, 106, 131, 182, 191, 206-208, 219, 223, 224

dilemma(s). . .50, 85, 87, 116, 145, 157, 158, 175, 186, 204, 206, 263, 266, 290

discipline. . .16, 32, 40, 49, 54, 57, 59, 76, 94, 95, 143, 170, 195, 212, 219, 236, 255, 257, 263, 264

drug(s) (marijuana, pot). . .8, 37, 99, 110, 119, 126, 171, 191, 227, 237, 243, 264, 265 duty (duties). . .4, 8, 9, 11, 14, 25, 28, 33, 35-36, 40, 48, 53, 60, 66, 69, 75-77, 85, 103, 110-111, 115, 117, 119, 123, 129, 131, 133, 135, 138, 139, 141, 143, 144, 147, 158, 160, 165-168, 173-174, 176, 182, 188, 193, 198, 202, 206-207, 213, 224, 228-229, 234, 239 242, 245-246, 250-251, 255-256, 259, 261-265, 266, 268, 277, 278, 283, 285, 286, 290 equipment. . .11, 23, 29, 32, 34, 51, 58, 97, 125, 151, 160, 164, 169, 174, 189, 190, 199, 203, 204, 220, 232, 244, 246, 261, 263. 268, 269

ethic(s) (ethical, ethical dilemma, ethically). . .1-9, 11, 13, 16, 18, 20-22, 24, 32-35, 38, 41, 43, 49, 52-55, 57, 59, 63, 65, 67, 70, 77, 82, 87, 92-94, 97, 102, 105, 109, 116, 119-124, 128-129, 133, 138, 141-146, 149, 154-157, 163, 165, 178, 182-183, 186-191, 193-194, 198-200, 202, 204, 207, 212, 213, 217-219, 221, 225, 226, 229, 231-236, 238, 241-247, 243-254, 258-260, 263, 266-270, 276, 281, 283, 287-291

evaluation. . .3, 50, 61, 69, 75, 131, 241, 275

failure. . . 4, 13, 15, 16, 52, 55, 87, 95, 108, 113, 117, 125-126, 130, 138, 164-168, 173, 178, 181, 183, 185, 187-190, 192, 210-212, 215, 220-222, 229-231, 233, 236-238, 242, 246-248, 251, 253, 256, 261-263, 265-269

false. . .55, 100, 105, 122, 143, 183, 239

family. . .11, 30, 31, 33, 44, 69, 70, 79, 86, 89, 103, 113, 119, 132, 138, 170, 171, 181, 204, 205, 209, 221, 243, 249, 263, 264, 266, 272, 273, 286

fear. . .62, 65, 122, 130, 149, 169, 180, 181, 207, 247, 268, 276

fitness report. . .20, 64, 65, 69, 86, 149, 182, 186, 202, 214, 235

fraternization. . .54, 95, 103, 158, 159, 197, 198, 221, 222

gifts. . .8, 39, 56, 57, 106, 224, 286

harassment. . .27, 71, 107, 113, 143, 156, 170, 200, 224, 229, 230, 289

honor. . .2, 4, 29-30, 51, 84, 100, 102, 117, 154, 165, 166, 171, 200, 210, 214, 227, 239, 249-251, 256, 262, 264, 278, 279, 288, 291

illegal. . .7, 26, 27, 56, 57, 106, 110, 116, 118, 136, 138, 152, 183, 188, 198, 199, 202-205, 210, 217, 224, 227-229, 236, 238, 241, 245, 247-249, 253, 256

infraction(s). . .6, 54, 153, 197, 236, 271

inspections. . .6, 51, 62, 78, 164, 178, 263

integrity. . .2-4, 19, 21, 50, 54, 65, 71, 82, 94, 97, 99-101, 116, 126, 134, 142, 144, 163-166, 177, 183, 195, 198, 203, 207, 210, 213, 216-218, 223, 231, 232, 233, 237, 243, 244, 251, 254, 256, 262, 267, 269-277, 279, 280, 285, 287-289, 291

Iraq. . .118, 234

JAG. . .6, 7, 18, 23, 29, 40, 85, 181, 190, 198, 203

lead (leader(s)). . .5-7, 15, 22, 32, 43, 45, 51, 55, 68, 75, 85-86, 94, 96, 120-122, 139, 141-142, 144, 187-188, 198, 207, 211, 215, 219, 222, 227, 236, 243, 245-246, 251, 253, 266, 275, 280

leadership. . .5, 6, 9, 28, 29, 51, 60, 65, 76, 86, 90, 93, 97, 119-122, 141-145, 193, 196, 202, 214, 266, 267, 288-290

liberty. . .27, 44, 47, 69, 75, 113, 128, 141, 153, 161, 204, 255

loyalty. . .4, 19, 55, 65, 77, 86, 87, 95, 113, 154, 157, 172, 173, 183, 189, 196, 199, 202, 204, 207, 208, 229, 231, 233, 239, 256, 259, 260, 265, 278, 286

management. . .62, 82, 129, 130, 148, 240, 288, 289

Marines (USMC). . .51, 76-77, 119, 141, 157, 196, 207, 214, 249, 258, 271, 287-88

medal. . .29, 51, 145, 164, 249, 250, 254

Medal of Honor. . .29, 51, 249, 250

minority. . .43, 47, 71, 119, 194, 206, 258

mishap (mishap investigation, accident). . .15, 16, 32, 49, 52, 55, 82, 88, 114, 137, 163, 168, 181, 185, 187, 192, 194, 195, 197, 198, 200, 214, 215, 236, 242, 246, 247

mission. . .6, 15, 19, 21, 24, 49, 55, 59, 67, 78, 86, 88, 90, 108, 115, 125, 130, 143, 157, 161, 182-185, 208, 214-215, 220, 225, 231, 235, 237, 242, 245, 258, 263

mistake. . .2, 7, 23, 36, 55, 61, 89, 126, 133, 164-166, 175, 183, 199, 238, 260-262, 276 moral (morality). . .4, 30, 57, 77, 86, 88, 119-122, 142-145, 157, 165, 175, 188, 190, 200, 208, 218, 220, 242, 245, 251, 255, 267, 271-273, 283, 286, 287, 289-291

morale. . .9, 47, 54, 56, 57, 65-67, 69, 77, 80, 86, 95, 96, 111, 112, 117, 157, 177, 192, 197, 207, 212, 217, 224, 225, 228, 229, 233, 235, 243

nuclear (power, reactor, submarine). . .37, 126, 163-166, 176

oath. . .44, 71, 75, 142, 144, 202, 211, 217, 220, 225, 229, 234-236, 252, 256

orders. . .8, 13-15, 25-27, 33, 51, 70, 108, 118, 120, 134,142, 148, 150, 154, 161, 172, 181, 190, 210, 225, 260, 265, 266, 276

organization. . .6, 17, 51, 66, 90, 93, 112, 113, 133, 158, 181, 193, 199, 218, 219, 240, 258, 264, 272, 273, 275, 277, 279

pay. . .5, 7-8, 22, 36, 38, 48, 53, 56, 68, 73, 83, 92, 106-109, 112, 128, 134, 138, 147-149, 181, 197, 200, 204-206, 224, 234, 244-247, 253, 256, 267, 282-283, 286

policy. . .37, 54, 84, 107, 108, 129, 133, 158, 171, 177, 192, 198, 229, 259, 260, 264, 283

prank. . .109, 154, 155, 255, 256

priority. . .13, 36, 51, 73, 122, 163, 164, 166, 181, 191

problems. . .8, 32, 37, 38, 40, 75, 77, 83, 103, 113, 131, 132, 163, 164, 178, 196, 213, 222, 236, 242, 251, 261, 263, 269, 270

procedure(s). . .41, 61, 62, 82, 84, 143, 149, 160, 163-169, 174, 181, 197, 201, 210, 211, 225, 237, 259, 261, 264, 265

process. . .7, 25, 35, 39, 49, 65, 78, 92, 115, 141-143, 157, 167, 176, 178, 190, 201, 206, 217, 241, 246, 249, 265, 273

promotion. . .64, 65, 122, 133, 171, 174, 193, 202, 279

psychic income. . .53, 134, 207, 226, 266, 267

qualification(s). . .48, 108, 111, 133, 149, 174, 176, 179, 198, 225, 269

regulation(s). . .4, 6, 7, 16, 25, 28, 50, 54, 67, 82, 83, 94, 164, 184, 186, 188, 189, 200, 203, 204, 224, 228, 247, 255, 262, 270, 276, 282, 285-286

repair. . .21, 92, 151, 152, 169, 248, 254

reports. . .43, 64, 65, 76, 96, 115, 187, 201, 204, 206, 211, 242, 243, 251, 289

reputation. . .2, 5, 24, 77, 87, 94, 117, 152, 156, 169, 200, 201, 219, 221, 232, 240, 245, 250, 254, 262, 263, 277, 280

responsibilities. . .3, 6, 11, 12, 22, 25, 31, 45, 55, 60, 63, 86, 90, 112, 142, 144, 147, 192, 224, 232, 234, 235, 251, 262, 264, 265

responsible. . .5, 17, 18, 21, 28, 29, 32, 38, 59, 60, 82, 89, 92, 95, 101, 113, 125, 147, 151, 158, 169, 170, 181, 189, 194, 203, 220, 231, 253, 263, 272, 275

retirement. . .57, 100, 106, 126, 197

rule(s). . .1, 6-7, 11, 13, 16, 43-45, 49, 52, 63, 67, 82-84, 94, 97, 100, 110, 112-113, 124, 143-145, 148-149, 153, 163, 166, 170, 172, 179, 181-182, 192, 195, 197, 198, 201-203, 210, 213, 215, 217, 221, 223-225, 234-237, 243-244, 247, 251, 253-255, 260-262, 268, 272, 279-280, 285-286

safety. . .7, 15, 28, 37, 55, 103, 110, 111, 121, 124, 149, 160, 163-166, 169, 172, 195, 204, 247, 259, 261, 268, 289

schedule. . .25, 33, 59, 67, 79, 88, 92, 124, 173, 200, 204, 232, 268, 282

security. . .37, 82, 123, 141, 142, 146, 174, 175, 181, 211, 223, 233, 267, 283, 290

separation. . .31, 71, 171, 176, 206, 209, 212, 264, 289

service reputation. . .221, 232

shipmate(s). . .30, 43-45, 60, 113, 173, 201, 206-208, 226, 259, 270, 277-279

shipyard. . .167, 204

shortage(s). . .24, 53, 61, 62, 197, 201

software. . .19-20, 182

special trust and confidence. . .188

spouse. . .31, 38, 69, 73, 79, 103, 128, 131-133, 144, 158, 170, 206, 216, 239-243, 283

staff. . .121, 154, 199, 205, 210, 248, 271, 281, 283

standards (standards of conduct). . .4-9, 11, 22, 29, 39, 44, 54, 71, 72, 95, 97, 104, 105, 111, 114, 119, 120, 122, 131, 133, 136, 142, 143, 148, 154, 160, 161, 174, 184, 186, 187, 188, 193, 205, 206, 213, 218, 220, 228, 230, 245, 246, 251-253, 259, 260, 267, 272-275, 278, 279, 285, 289, 291

stealing. . .134, 164, 165, 226, 237, 279

stress. . .35, 37, 38, 75, 178, 192

submarine. . .25, 26, 37, 92, 126, 160, 167, 172, 176, 186, 217, 250, 268

subordinate(s). . .1-5, 7, 9, 17-18, 22, 24, 28, 38, 50, 65, 67, 75-77, 85, 93, 97, 117, 120-122, 125, 149, 157, 181-182, 184, 187-189, 194, 202-205, 208, 211, 215, 218, 220, 224, 229, 234-235, 237, 241-242, 248, 251, 255, 258, 260, 261, 264-266, 268, 272, 280, 286, 291

team(s). . .59, 75, 76, 93, 99, 114-115, 120, 143, 147, 160, 207, 217, 220, 221, 251, 252, 258

testing. . .50, 167, 176, 179, 208, 268

tradition. . .45, 132, 146

training. . .1, 8, 15, 16, 24, 32, 35, 41, 49, 75, 76, 82, 84, 93, 102, 105, 111, 114, 115, 118, 122, 127, 131, 143, 149, 154, 157, 179, 184, 185, 188, 190, 191, 192, 198, 211, 213-215, 218-221, 223, 228, 231, 232, 238, 239, 247, 258, 261, 266, 269, 274, 277

traits. . .120, 122, 142, 144

transportation. . .66, 128, 181, 202-204, 282

trust(ed). . .2, 86, 119, 122, 134, 147, 164, 165, 197, 203, 207, 217, 242, 250, 251, 261, 262

unethical (unethically). . .1-2, 4-9, 56-57, 71, 76, 86, 99, 102, 106, 117, 136, 149, 152, 155, 156, 178, 181, 182, 190, 199-201, 204, 205, 212, 221, 224, 226, 228, 231, 233-234, 237, 239, 241, 244, 245, 248-250, 256, 267, 287, 291

Naval Academy (USNA). . .117, 141, 179, 191, 250-251, 278, 287, 290-291

value(s). . .1, 22, 44, 45, 61, 77, 119-122, 142-145, 164, 181, 183, 187, 203, 204, 259, 271, 272, 290

violation. . .9, 11-13, 29, 54, 59, 67, 82, 124, 158, 184, 188, 222, 228, 265, 283

winning. . .94, 102, 143, 221, 233

wrongdoing. . .1, 9, 85, 90, 184, 188, 203, 240, 247, 277